More Than a Ticket

More Than a Ticket

Memoirs Flying with American Airlines

from Props to Jets

Former American Airlines Stewardess
Argie Ella Hoskins

© 2014 by Argie Ella Hoskins
All rights reserved. Published 2014.
Printed in the United States of America

Cover images: Flagship California Boeing 707 © Boeing, with permission to use; Argie in uniform. All photos come from Argie's personal collection unless otherwise notated. Photos in the contributor pieces come from the contributors themselves unless otherwise notated. The celebrity photos in chapters 8 and 11 were found in the public domain.

Cover design © 2014 Daniel Reneer

Interior design by Lauren Bangerter Wilde

More Than a Ticket was written for educational purposes as it documents selective aspects of commercial flying on props and jets during the golden age of air travel.

Dedicated with love and respect to my flying friends. This book is an expression of appreciation for the community of American Airlines.

Somewhere in the clouds of time,
we met, embraced, and parted.
Moments remembered from here to eternity.

—*Argie*

Table of Contents

Acknowledgments	ix
Preface	xi
Part One: My Life as a Stewardess	1
1: A Young Girl from Animas Valley	3
2: Following My Restless Spirit	11
3: Stewardess School	17
4: Grooming for Graduation	29
5: First Flights	43
6: A Visit Home	55
7: Based in and Flying from Los Angeles	59
8: VIP Passengers before Jet Travel	89
9: The First Jet Flight	101
10: Four Friends for the Jets	129
11: VIP Passengers after Jet Travel	151
12: Final Flights	169
Part Two: On Wings of Time	193
Willis Heath Proctor: PILOT AND TRAINER, 1927–1957	195
Roy G. Jacobson: MECHANIC AND FLIGHT ENGINEER, 1941–1984	203
MaryLou Parkes Whipple: SECRETARY AND STEWARDESS, 1955–1959	207
Audrey Radziwon McGinty: STEWARDESS, 1957–1967, 1972–1976	229
Gerry McMasters Lockhart: STEWARDESS, 1957–1959	237
Polly Harlan Viertel: STEWARDESS, 1957–1958	245
Joan Scofield Sheldon: STEWARDESS, 1959–1961	261
Margaret Bassetti: PASSENGER, JANUARY 25, 1959	265
Robert Cawley: PASSENGER	273
Diane Miller Engelskirger: STEWARDESS, 1961–1966	277
Judi Stilwell Martino: STEWARDESS, 1963–1968	283
Tony Vallillo: CAPTAIN, 1977–2008	289
Contributors	301
Argie's Challenges for Success	303

Acknowledgments

Heartfelt thanks to many friends and family who shared their advice, support, and patience during the process of making my blog look like a book. My heart is grateful to:

My son Daniel Reneer who first encouraged me to write down my stewardess experiences on a blog and gave me creative suggestions.

My other sons and their families for their suggestions and support: Chris and Annie Reneer, Brad and Marné Reneer, Randy and Julie Reneer, and Blair and Angie Shumway.

Lauren Bangerter Wilde, my editor, for reading my mind and heart.

The contributors whose stories and photos are contained herein, for allowing me to share.

The photographers who created pictures worth a thousand words.

Gene Shumway, my husband, for the untiring support with many tasks of life and for reading and rereading my words.

To all, hugs and more hugs!

Preface

The journey of this book began as a few posts on a blog. The more I wrote and shared the more I found to say, and it laid the foundation for this book.

I was blessed to serve as a stewardess during the golden age of flying for one of the best airlines out there, American Airlines. Our slogan was, "American Airlines, doing what we do best," and I hope I have shared an adequate glimpse of the honor and privilege it was to fly with them during this time. I have written from scraps of paper that hold my heart in a way that will not be forgotten. They retain the taste of moments in time which passed too quickly but which are impressed on my soul forever.

In the 1950s, to serve the traveling public, American Airlines trained young ladies to be the world's finest stewardesses. I first flew on the DC-6, the DC-7, and the Convair 240. These aircraft were all propeller (or prop) driven. These flagships continued to bring comfort and service even after American Airlines introduced the country's first jet service on January 25, 1959, with the Boeing 707. I was honored to be one of the few stewardesses chosen to serve on that first commercial jet flight across the United States.

Although our training was superb and the aircraft we flew on was breathtaking, it was the connections and friendships I made with people that really influenced me. We connected in a professional but friendly manner, with both warmth and a mutual sense of appreciation for the wonders of flight. These relationships and opportunities to serve are what touched my heart. They are what changed my life, created instant friendships, and made my experience more than a ticket.

As you read these words just know that they represent memories. I encourage you to write down your own journey, to document history that is fast fleeing. They will be of interest to generations to come, and they will prove that life itself is more than a ticket.

Welcome aboard! Thank you for flying with me today.

Part One
My Life as a Stewardess

Clockwise from top left: Feeding chickens in the front yard; me, C. L., Mama, and Daddy; cattle on the range with cottonwood trees and white desert poppies; C. L. and I in the fields with Daddy (he never missed an opportunity to teach us—we studied this fence and this grass); the family on a trip (my hair was not quite ready; I was preparing for the museums we were to visit). Our parents would say, "Let's stop." We were not allowed to whine or object. Yes, sir. I am grateful.

Chapter One
A Young Girl from Animas Valley

I grew up on a ranch in Animas Valley in southern New Mexico with my brother, Charles Leslie, or C. L. for short. I was born in 1935 in Deming, New Mexico, in the midst of the Great Depression, the same year that Franklin Delano Roosevelt signed off on the Social Security Act. We were poor of means, but I didn't know it at the time, and I don't remember ever going hungry. We had little, but that was how things were for everyone we knew. My wise parents, Al and Edna, instilled in me the values of honesty and hard work. They taught me the importance of staying clean, keeping out of debt, being a good citizen, respecting the flag, appreciating America, and minding manners, including "please," "thank you," "yes ma'am," "no sir," and "how can I help you?"—phrases that flow naturally from me now.

My parents descended from immigrant ancestors who had sacrificed and worked hard to become part of our great United States of America. They were self-reliant, responsible, and principled. And they had faith in God. I grew up feeling the love and depth of belonging to a good Christian family. I made the choice to follow those teachings.

Most often Mama and Daddy taught us by example. My Daddy taught me to keep things in order to accomplish a task. Tasks were done with strict discipline, a legacy Daddy inherited from his mother. She was a German lady who understood the nature of success. So in our home, obedience to the task was demanded and expected. C. L. knew the way out to the smelly barn to shovel manure, and I knew where the ironing board was waiting. I would iron

Daddy's and C. L.'s shirts way into the night with an amiable attitude, listening to western music. We weren't given the option to be lazy, and I have since learned that those who do not learn to internalize discipline cannot focus and accomplish goals.

Mama had an intuitive soul and good judgment. She taught me to think outside the box. I can still hear her voice echo in my memory, "Sister, if you cannot do it one way, you can do it another," "Think before you act," "Think of others before yourself," and "Do your best!" Mama wasn't perfect, but she hung in there and kept trying until something worked. It was hard work, but it was worth it.

From November 1951 to August 1966, Daddy worked as a windmiller for the Victoria Land and Cattle Company's Diamond A Ranch in Animas Valley. He took his job very seriously. It could be a dangerous venture, climbing up

Daddy showing his windmill helpers what needed to be done, and they knew Daddy expected it to be done with precision.

a windmill tower to repair whatever was needed. One of Daddy's cowboy friends said of Daddy, "Al would tell me what he wanted to get done. He would than tell me what he was going to do, tell me what I was going to do, and then say, 'Now be careful!'" When I look at pictures of Daddy I like to look at his large hands; a former windmill helper told me that Daddy had to cut the tops of gloves to fit his hands.

When a windmill needed to be fixed, Daddy was in charge of seeing that done. It was too far from town to get new parts, so Daddy would design and weld a new part, which often worked better than a new one would have. Once a mechanical engineer, having watched Daddy at work, said that he was outstanding and clever with his mind and hands. Sometimes Daddy would even invent what he needed if there wasn't a tool available on the market.

Before he was a windmiller, Daddy worked from April 1939 to November 1951 as a machinist in the Kennecott open pit copper mine in Santa Rita, New Mexico. He welded in overalls which he always managed to keep clean. He was a machinist by day and a mechanic by night, working on cars at home. While Daddy worked and welded, Mama sewed gowns for the wives of the Big Bosses.

Mama was a professional seamstress. She taught herself to sew and earned a degree via mail from The Woman's Institute of Domestic Arts and Sciences, a division of the International Correspondence Schools, in Scranton, Pennsylvania. My memories of our kitchen table are of it covered with her coursework for dress making and designing. Mama taught me to sew as well. I remember the hours I spent on the sewing machine—and the hours more ripping out the wrong stitches. But my Mother's tutelage paid off. After we got electricity, I made the most lovely of lovely prom dresses in my room. I still have two of Mama's textbooks which I display on my dresser, *Sewing for Profit* and *Decorative Stitches and Trimmings*.

Our home had six rooms. Two of the bedrooms were made out of adobe bricks. One of them was mine, and I had painted it yellow. These rooms were very old and unique, with very thick walls which provided adequate insula-

When I see my Animas Valley home as it sits today, I am flooded with memories, but I also feel a sense of emptiness. Gone is the friendly porch, the mowed lawn, the fruit trees, garden, and flowers. Gone are the cats and dogs and chickens. Gone are Daddy's and C. L.'s cowboy boots on the front porch. And gone are Daddy and Mama's energy that busied the humble home.

tion. This form of building had been used by the Indians and Mexicans for hundreds of years.

Because the walls were so thick, the window sills were deep enough for various potted plants to sit on, and they gave a colorful touch to my yellow room. Through the walls, my brother and I would always say good night to each other and our parents; our bedrooms were so close we didn't need to lift our voices to more than a mere whisper. How I loved my small, charming old adobe bedroom. I loved our whole home! There was no telephone or electricity, but we had the warmth of a gas heater to keep us warm. We drank raw milk and lived off the land, the "Land of Enchantment," where the power of nature is amazingly stated and graced with beauty both on the land and in the sky, my home!

C. L. and I had a wonderful childhood, and as we came of age we attended New Mexico A&M in Las Cruces, now known as New Mexico State Univer-

Whenever I looked out my bedroom window I saw this view and felt the silent strength of Animas Peak in southwestern New Mexico.

sity. I have some great memories of that time, including yelling my lungs out while the Aggies played ball on the basketball court. One of those Aggies was C. L. who was there on a basketball scholarship. I also loved western dancing. When we'd go to the dances, C. L. and I would show off our dance routines that we originated in the kitchen back at the ranch. The kids at college thought I was going to the dances with two guys; my date would dance with other girls while I was "kicking up a step" with my brother. We danced the hours away in our stylish clothes—western shirts for C. L. and skirts, blouses, and dresses for me—which had been sewn for untold hours by Mother for us so we could look our best at college. Some of those skirts were made out of chicken feed sacks. Back in those days it was really good material, and I felt like a beauty queen.

Around this time I learned about and joined The Church of Jesus Christ of Latter-day Saints. I was drawn to this church because it embraced and taught the values with which I had been reared, and my heart was touched by the emphasis placed on families, family history, and compassionate service. It was a change, but in some ways it was no change at all. I credit my parents for the solid foundation of faith upon which my life has been built.

I'm so grateful for the environment in which I grew up. Each morning, as Daddy would light my bedroom heater, he would encourage me with the greeting, "Sis, get up and amount to something!" This was the standard of my day, my year, and my life. He taught me the lessons of obedience, industry, and independence. I listened to his words of common sense—how to perceive, understand, and judge things are emblazoned on my spirit.

One of the highlights of my childhood and growing up years was the summertime. Every year, my parents worked hard and saved money so we could go on a road trip highlighted with National Parks. We would jump waves, get stung by jelly fish, have sand fights, race on beaches, talk to people, make up games, and argue about who saw the ocean first. We would visit family and get to know distant cousins during Fourth of July celebrations where we'd nearly burn each other with our sparklers. We visited museum after museum—sometimes boring and sometimes exciting. And we'd admire the many glaciers, mountains, rivers, and streams that cover our nation. I learned to love an adventure. My heart was always looking for another way to see the world, and sometimes I would wonder, "Where will I find my path of adventure and independence?"

Left to right: Daddy on a horse—he sure loved his horses; Daddy on his horse, Sugar; Daddy and Mama in front of our home around 1958.

Clockwise from top left: Our family in front of our car on one of our yearly road trips, I'm holding my doll with her handmade look-alike dress; C. L., Mama, and me at the famous Yosemite Falls; a bear at Yellowstone—you could feed the bears from your car; C. L., Mama, and me at Mount Rushmore; C. L. and me by our car on a drive through the Redwoods.

C. L. and me in 1957 right before we left home. We were visiting family in El Paso and ran across the line into Juárez, Mexico, to get this picture taken.

From left to right, Aunt Boo, Uncle Bill, and my cousins Freddie and Effie.

Chapter Two

Following My Restless Spirit

While we loved our home, C. L. and I both had restless spirits that yearned for adventure, and leaving our small ranch home for the first time was just such an adventure for C. L. and me. Our journey took us away from rattlesnakes, horned toads, and Mama's home cooking, with its steaks from range-fed cattle, cakes made from scratch, and ice cream cranked by hand. We picked up our suitcases and went our separate ways into an unknown world. We were both transitioning into an adult world of college and work. C. L. made his way to California and became an actor in Westerns on television, and I, step by step, made my way to the big city, Chicago.

For a graduation present I had received some durable, new Samsonite luggage from my mother's sister, Aunt Boo. I had a burning desire to pack it up and hit the road—now I had two sets of luggage waiting in the closet for that graveled road. One was saddle tan, and the other green. Soon they were packed and all set for travel. I was ready to go somewhere!

My first step was to El Paso, Texas, to live with Aunt Boo, who was like a sister to me. Her real name was Beulah, but I couldn't say that as a child, so I called her Boo, and the name stuck. Uncle Bill and Aunt Boo, along with cousins Effie and Freddie, supported me while I worked for El Paso Natural Gas Company. One day, a friend with whom I was working suggested that I would be a likely candidate to become a stewardess.

Become a stewardess? Now, that was a novel idea. I was afraid of flying and, what's more, afraid of heights. As a child, after running or other rigorous activities, I would faint on the playground. Having had this dizziness challenge, the dream of flying was "pie in the sky," as my mother would say. My dad said that my itchy feet had sprouted wings. The closest that I had ever gotten to big planes was watching them fly overhead while visiting my grandparents in El Paso. As a small child, while playing on the patches of lawn with my dolls, I would hear and watch the Warbirds from Fort Bliss fly over the yard. The sound droned across the sky. Those planes seemed so remote to me.

Left to right: My cousin Dub, C. L., and me in our grandma's yard in El Paso.

And now this new idea presented itself: me? Become a stewardess?

I knew that being a stewardess and serving in a fashionable manner was a desirable goal for a young lady of my time; however, the job market was very competitive. I had heard of her poise and charm. Filmmakers and novelists had encouraged the wanderlust and want for glamour in the American girl. Stewardesses acted as hostesses on the planes just as a lady would be a hostess in her home. I had seen a stewardess advertisement that read, "Think of her as your mother." I have always been a caretaker, so the thought of being a stewardess appealed to me.

And it was a chance to see the world while meeting all kinds of interesting people, including passengers who could afford to be pampered. In turn, the stewardess would be rewarded with the attention of a celebrity. I had seen this all depicted in American Airlines' advertisements. I had been trained by my mother and grandmother to be a lady, and I figured that in the sky would be a good place to be one. It appealed to my femininity. Sounded good to me. I applied.

Some of the requirements for being a stewardess at that time included being between the ages of 20 and 27, being between five feet two inches and five

AMERICAN AIRLINES LEARNING CENTER
AMERICAN AIRLINES PLAZA • FORT WORTH, TEXAS 76125

FLIGHT ATTENDANT APPLICANT

The following information is to acquaint you with our Flight Attendant selection procedures. Please review the basic requirements carefully: AGE - RELOCATION - VISION AVAILABILITY - CITIZENSHIP - EDUCATION - HEIGHT AND WEIGHT CHART. We will not be able to arrange for a personal interview if you do not meet these requirements.

If an interview has been arranged, our representative will forward your application and an interview report to the Flight Service Recruitment Office. Applicants selected for final interview will be advised within 14 days from the date of interview. If you have received no word within 14 days, you must assume that you were not selected for final interview.

Interviews are conducted by our representative in major cities throughout the United States when sufficient vacancies warrant new training classes.

HEIGHT/WEIGHT

Weight must be in proportion to height. A chart giving maximum (not necessarily the most desirable) weights for specific heights follows.
Applicants whose proportions exceed the maximum will not be selected for training.

FEMALE WEIGHT CHART

HEIGHT	MAXIMUM WEIGHT
5'2"	118
5'3"	121
5'4"	125
5'5"	129
5'6"	133
5'7"	137
5'8"	141
5'9"	145
5'10"	149
5'11"	153
6'0"	157

MALE WEIGHT CHART

HEIGHT	MAXIMUM WEIGHT
5'2"	130
5'3"	135
5'4"	140
5'5"	145
5'6"	150
5'7"	155
5'8"	160
5'9"	165
5'10"	170
5'11"	175
6'0"	180

HEIGHT 5'2" - 6'

Height is measured in stocking feet, with hair pressed down on the top of the head. The applicant who is a fraction under 62" or over 72" will not qualify. Sorry, no waivers are granted to this or any of the other basic requirements.

AGE - AT LEAST 20 YEARS

Interviews and consideration for selection are limited to applicants whose age is at least 20 years.

VISION - 20/50 WITHOUT GLASSES

Vision must be at least 20/50 in each eye separately. If vision is not this good, correction must be used to attain at least the 20/50 standard. Eyeglasses or contact lenses are acceptable for correction. Contact lense wearers must be able to tolerate lenses without signs of eye irritation for at least 10 hours per day.

AVAILABILITY

Please do not submit an application or request an interview unless you are available for training within the next six months.

CITIZENSHIP

Must be a U.S. Citizen or registered alien.

List of requirements to become a stewardess.

feet seven inches tall, weighing not more than 130 pounds, having a university degree or adequate business experience, and being physically fit and attractive. American Airlines also looked for the qualities in character, personality, and the desire to be helpful to people.

The interview with American Airlines was draining. Afterward, I remember sitting in the terminal at Amon Carter Field in Fort Worth, Texas, waiting for my flight and thinking that I had failed the interview. A wave of sadness washed over me. I prayed that whatever happened would be for the best, and I was comforted in thinking, "Well, at least, when I looked in the mirror, I did look sorta cute in the cap the interviewer had me try on, and I really do like to visit with people." My acceptance telegram beat me back to El Paso.

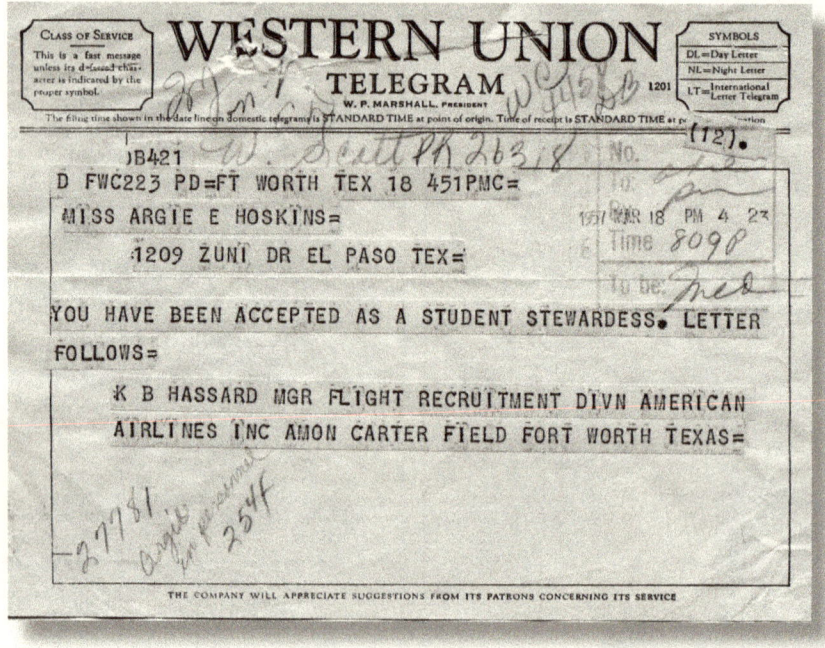

The telegram telling me I had been accepted to stewardess school.

My hands still tremble with excitement when I see this telegram! Some would say it is old age, but as I ponder this telegram I know the tears of joy are anything but old age. That moment changed my life. My family was so excited when they picked me up at the El Paso Airport! Little did I know that this would be the airport into which I would most frequently fly, either as a destination or a stop along the way. I didn't know that in the future, I would be thrilled by glorious southwest sunsets and powerful thunderstorms that would rock the plane this way and that as the route took us through huge puffy clouds. And little did I know on that evening that I was about to embark on a journey that would challenge me intellectually and emotionally while helping me learn a lot about myself.

The DC–6 was the first American Airlines plane that I flew on; it took me to my American Airlines interview. It came to mean a lot to me: I flew it over and to El Paso, it was the plane which saw my checkrides, it was the baby that flew over the ranch and wagged her wings at my mother. Yes, it is an important plane to me. Note the curtains on the windows. I remember straightening the curtains so they looked just right for passengers to have a nice look outside the plane. Every little act of caring was important. As I remember, the curtains had tie backs. They could be dropped or the ties could be dropped so the curtains could close the view for better sleeping. Each seat had a head cloth that we could change. We always changed the pillow cases after a use. No head lice on our planes. The DC-6 was a response to a military requirement during World War II. It became Douglas' most successful four engined piston aircraft. This photo was taken by Bob Proctor, © Jon Proctor.

The Sixth American Airlines Stewardess Class of 1957 (Class 57–6). These pretty faces were faces of tired, enthusiastic, and very smart young ladies who were pushed and pushed again to learn all that was required to be the "best of the best" as American Airline stewardesses. What a privilege! Back row left to right: Chris Debraggio; 9th Dixie Dodd; 10th Maureen Comensky; end, Gail Bunn (behind Connie Rutkowski). Fourth row from bottom: flowered dress, Marian Wachovo; 3rd from right, Joanne Pinkerton; end, Connie Rutkowski. Third row from bottom: me wearing a necklace, Polly Harlan, Marilyn DeHaan. Second row from bottom: 3rd from left, Mabel Harrison. Front row right to left: Carol Blessington; Jane Grubb; Polly Sterle; seated with birthday cake, Audrey Radziwon.

Left: the hangar where the stewardess school was located. Right: the Midway Airport terminal. Photos courtesy of Pat Bukiri.

Chapter Three

Stewardess School

I was in American Airline Stewardess Class 57-6; that is, I was in the sixth class in the year 1957. When I attended school in April and May of 1957, the Stewardess College was housed in American Airlines' hangar at Midway Airport. American Airlines originally conducted pilot and stewardess training in an old Air Force base in Ardmore, Oklahoma, but that school closed and they opened a stewardess training school at the Midway Airport in Chicago on April 15, 1949. We were housed in dormitories that were built into American Airlines' hangar at the airport. They had even set up a section of a DC-6 flagship cabin and equipped it to simulate flight in turbulent air. It gave us the opportunity to practice balancing coffee cups and food trays in rough weather while in flight.

The hangar we were housed in was 620 feet long and 240 feet wide. There was enough room for 36 students (six students in six dormitories), three instructors, and a housemother. Although we were housed in an airport hangar, the atmosphere at the college was along the lines of a select women's college. I was in one of the last classes to be trained in that hangar because later that same year American Airlines built the world's first facility for flight attendant training, the American Airlines Stewardess College, in Dallas/Fort Worth, Texas.

Newspaper clipping announcing the opening of the stewardess school in Chicago.

My memories of this hangar are so vivid that I can still taste the smells of the takeoffs and landings. I can still remember the smell of the rain on the tarmac. While coming and going from the hangar with rain pouring on my head I learned what the phrase *inclement weather* meant. And I still feel a thrill whenever I see an airplane take off or land. What an astonishing engineering feat! Thousands of pounds of metal flying like a bird! I am so glad that I attended class in that humble hangar and that I wasn't in a later class at the fancy college.

The stewardess school for American Airlines was located in the hangar at Midway Airport in Chicago. Photo courtesy of Pat Bukiri.

The Chicago Municipal Airport had been renamed Midway Airport in 1949 to honor the brave heroes of the Battle of Midway, which occurred June of 1942 and was one of the most important naval battles of World War II. When I was in training, Midway was the busiest airport in the world. It is located on the city's southwest side, eight miles from Chicago's Loop. It is in the area of 55th Street and Cicero Avenue. This was the setting for Alfred Hitchcock's movie *North by Northwest* starring Cary Grant. Incidentally, both of these gentlemen would later fly on flights with me.

More views of the Midway hangars at different periods of time. Above: Taken by Bob Proctor © John Proctor. Two middle pictures courtesy of Pat Bukiri. His amazing photo gallery spans the nearly 88-year history of Midway Airport. He is a member of the group who grew up so close to the end of Runway '31 Left' that he could see the pilots' faces from the top of his house. Bottom: The hangar, which is now Southwest's hangar, as it looks today. Photo © Jon Proctor

More DC–6s courtesy of Pat Bukiri. Pat was once reported to have said that when the planes came over they "would wag their wings and land.... Now today you couldn't imagine a 707 or a 747 at O'Hare wagging its wings at some kids, but they did it all the time."

Becoming a stewardess was not an easy experience for me. Although I had finished two years of college, I never had experienced the rigors of education such as I encountered in that hangar. Our unwritten mantra seemed to be "Learn it fast, learn it now, and don't forget it!"

The Stewardess Manual covered a wide range of material and learning it all—making it become second nature to me—was hard. Our subjects covered everything from administrative procedures, basic procedures, and restrictions and irregularities, to familiarizing ourselves with the different aircraft and the procedures associated with each: the Convair 240, DC-6, and DC-7. Along with all this, there were sections on special procedures, emergency procedures, oxygen, illness and injuries, forms and reports, and of course, the reference material.

My experiences in studying for each of these topics, and the added pressure of learning it well and fast and how to apply them in a professional manner, could fill a book. I had to, and I mean *had to*, study, memorize, and role play everything I learned and be tested on the same. All this was done in fighter pilot mode, full throttle ahead, while the fear of washing out and going back home with egg on my face and an ocean of tears in my heart weighed heavily on my being and lingered in the back of my mind. My challenge in that hangar at Midway Airport was to overcome my fear of failure with my excitement of becoming who I desired and expected to be. There was so much to learn, but I'll give just a brief overview of my training on one of our topics and how it changed me, namely, emergency procedures.

For the successful handling of any emergency, it was important to know the tasks that needed to be done and how to do them on an automatic level, so much so that you could depend on your knowledge and skill with no guess work. Wow! I needed to learn so much. But as I looked at what was required I remember what my Daddy would say, "*This* is the task that needs to be done, *this* is what I am going to do, *this* is what you are going to do. Now be careful," and it gave me courage to start. "*Besides*," I reasoned, "good old American Airlines picked me, Argie Hoskins, because they knew I could do it!" I did my best to suppress my self-doubts and have only confidence inside of me.

My first emergency training was focused on the different areas of the different aircraft: DC-6, DC-6B, DC-6 Coach; DC-7, DC-7 Coach, DC-7 Dual Service; and the Convair 240. For each, I needed to know (1) where the exits were and how to open the window exits from inside, and in some cases, the outside of the aircraft; (2) where the ropes were located in the exit windows and doors of certain aircraft; (3) where the fire extinguishers were located in various locations on the several aircraft; (4) where the oxygen cylinder, outlets, and walk-around bottles were strategically placed and how to use them; (5) where the flashlights were on some aircraft as well as the emergency lights that replaced flashlights on all aircraft; and (6) how to use the fire axe that was located on the forward side of the cockpit door on all aircraft. We received training on fire detectors, extinguishing equipment, and flotation seat cushions. Additionally, we always checked the service kit which contained first aid equipment. We were trained to remember to take the service kit with us if we evacuated. And we learned where the evacuation slides were stored on the cabin doors and how to use them.

It was intimidating to practice while overcoming fear. When it was my turn to practice on the evacuation slide, I was nervous. I get dizzy when I ride an escalator going down, and I thought, "How can I, with all my learning challenges, be successful at these things that are difficult for me?" I looked at the girls around me. These gals were courageous. They set aside their fears and forged on through their tears. I found control of my heart and my mind and jumped! And I did it! The slide moved in a floating way. I remember that thrill as if it were this very day. Sometimes I dream of the excitement.

We were taught that "aviation is not unsafe, but like the sea it is terribly unforgiving of any carelessness or neglect." We were trained to be prepared for any situation. It was also impressed upon us to "waste not, want not." Part of a training booklet we received reads:

> Little wastes repeated throughout the system amount to staggering loss throughout the year. American does not pinch pennies on essential expenses, but waste is unnecessary and should not be allowed.
>
> For example, lights left burning needlessly cost money that could otherwise be spent to advantage. Save paperclips instead of throwing them into the waste basket. These are little things, true, but if we are constantly careful about them we can wipe out a mighty amount of waste. Use company material as though you had purchased it for your own needs.

I thought this was wise counsel.

Depending on where we were assigned to work on the plane, we had different responsibilities if an emergency occurred. We differentiated between these responsibilities with the titles First Stewardess and Second Stewardess. If the specific location of the First Stewardess made it difficult or time-consuming to accomplish her duties as outlined, then good judgment dictated that she carry out the Second Stewardess' duties and vice-versa. The Second Stewardess under such conditions should take her cue from the First Stewardess.

One challenge for me in this regard was to know what responsibilities were assigned to both the First Stewardess and Second Stewardess and to focus only on what I was assigned depending on which one I was. I felt that I could do both at the same time. That seems to always have been my challenge; I think that I can do it all, but I can't! I must be in charge of my stewardship, and others must be committed to their stewardship. In case of an emergency, I must know what I can do and do it, and not expect someone else to solve the problems that I must handle.

Not only did I learn and know the procedures, but I learned good judgment. My American Airlines manual states:

> The successful handling of any emergency aboard an aircraft depends to a large degree on you and your knowledge. There is never an emergency in which there isn't something you can do to help. Safe procedures require a

cool head. The ability to think straight and operate calmly requires knowledge of what to do.

There is no substitute for good judgment. That's something you can't learn from a book. Always have in mind Plan A and a Plan B for survival. Later, as a school teacher, I had workshops on "thinking outside the box." I realized that thanks to my stewardess training I had been thinking outside the box for years and years.

The thoroughness of our training comforted me and gave me confidence that American Airlines was the best in their concern and training for emergency procedures. Their philosophy boiled down to three points:

1. Know your procedures.

2. Use good judgment.

3. Keep cool.

The kind of emergency situations that I was trained for back in the 1950s were varied. A belly landing occurred when the wheels of the airplane would not come down prior to landing. This was not very different from a normal landing, but there was the possibility of a harder shock, depending on whether the nose or the tail hit first. The captain would announce which landing configuration to expect. If the captain's announcement was "nose wheel up, main gear down," then the final position of the aircraft would be with its nose down and tail up! Learning this position business of landing was hard for me because of the sequencing challenge in my brain. "Up, down, down, up!" I repeated over and over to myself. I had to over-learn these concepts!

Our job as stewardesses in such situations was to be prepared for any eventuality. In case of such a landing I remember the advice from stewardess school was to inform the passengers to relieve their bladders so that on impact the bladder would not burst. I never found that in the manual, but thought it was a good idea. Along with that idea, we encouraged passengers to use pillows and the position of their bodies to lessen the impact from the landing.

I remember when I learned the difference between *knowing* something and actually *doing* it. I knew what I needed to do to open an exit window, but doing it was a different matter! I found the rope in the exit window then pulled it on to the wing and down to the ground with me hanging on to the rope. I did it!

While in training, I was told by an instructress that I was shy and didn't talk much. She concluded by reassuring me that I was going to make it, but I was always afraid that I was going to wash out, which meant getting my walking papers and being sent home. But I knew that I was driven to graduate from that school on the south side of Chicago, so day after day, night after night, I groomed myself for that eventful day of graduation. Miraculously, along the way something really great happened. I found in me a new me. Just as a caterpillar evolves step by step, I experienced an amazing metamorphic change from caterpillar to butterfly.

Close-up of an American Airlines' sign with their slogan, "Doing what we do best."

The terminal at Midway Airport.
Photo courtesy of Pat Bukiri.

Four photos of the old American Airlines Midway stewardess school which is now in Southwest Airlines' area. The three photos on the left are courtesy of Jim Wissemes. The black and white photo of the hangar is courtesy of Pat Bukiri.

Air Line Operates Glamor School

Girls Are Taught How to Become Stewardesses

(Pictures on page 1)

BY EDWARD SPELLMAN

Lured by the prospects of travel, adventure, and a touch of glamor, eight pert and pretty young women from Chicago and suburbs recently left jobs as teachers, secretaries, and clerks for the life of an air line stewardess.

They now attend a 5½ week course at American Airlines stewardess training school at Midway airport. The girls, all college trained, say life at the air line school is "just like being back on the campus."

They are earning silver wings as stewardesses by attending daily classes from 9 a. m. to 5 p. m. in a three story building adjoining a hangar at 5301 55th st. They receive instruction in 65 subjects related to commercial air line travel and must maintain an average of 85 to continue their training.

While attending the course, prospective stewardesses live at the school in 18 dormitories and keep hours similar to those required at colleges. The girls must check in by 11 p. m. on week days and 1 a. m. on week-ends. The eight from this area are allowed to go home week-ends.

The 5½ week course is conducted on an accelerated basis by eight instructors, former stewardesses. Subjects include theory of flight, emergency and safety procedures, first aid, radio, personal grooming, and many others.

Tests Twice Weekly

Tests are given twice weekly. Night problems also are included in the course. Students must familiarize themselves with all types of aircraft and be able to identify all parts, inside and out. Short observation flights to nearby cities, such as Washington, Cleveland, and Detroit, are provided for each student so that she may watch an experienced stewardess during actual flight.

The school was set up in 1949. The only stewardess school in Chicago, it is operated by Mildred Jackson, Fort Worth, Tex., and Ellie Roman, Cleveland.

The Chicago area girls are among 77 young hopefuls recruited this year from all parts of the country. The school trains approximately 700 girls each year. Miss Roman said one of about every 50 girls to apply for a stewardess position is accepted.

Teacher Takes Course

Helen Parkes, 25, daughter of Mrs. Raymond W. Parkes, La Grange, a first grade teacher at the Spring av. school in La Grange for three years, said she is taking the course because she "wants to see the country and meet lots of people."

"It's a good chance to see America and other parts of the world," according to Josephine Pacioni, 25, daughter of Mr. and Mrs. Vito Pacioni, Melrose Park, a onetime secretary in an advertising agency. "Besides, I enjoy travel," she said.

Joan Groth, 21, daughter of Mr. and Mrs. Charles J. Groth, Mount Prospect, said she wants to become a stewardess because "I've always admired them and I want to see the country."

Studies at U. of I.

Miss Groth, a former teacher at Lincoln school in Mount Prospect, is a graduate of Arlington Heights High school and the University of Illinois.

Joan Cassidy, 24, daughter of Mr. and Mrs. John B. Cassidy, 425 Roscoe st., a reservation clerk at American Airlines for the last year, said she enjoys flying and wants to meet people.

Margie Wojtas, 20, daughter of Mr. and Mrs. Gust Wojtas, 1450 Edgewater av., a former secretary, said she wants the chance to fly, meet people and at the same time earn a living.

Georgia Ann Schuller, 21, daughter of Mrs. Ann Schuller, 4111 N. Narragansett av., also a onetime secretary, said she wants the chance to commute to and from Mexico City, where her family will take up residence soon.

Wants to Travel

She is a graduate of Steinmetz High school and attended Wright Junior college, where she studied languages. Miss Schuller said she also wants to travel and see the country.

A friend who became a stewardess inspired Mary Walton, 20, daughter of Mr. and Mrs. Harry E. Walton, 838 Marion st., Oak Park, to make the switch from clerk to stewardess.

"It rubbed off on me while I was working as a reservation clerk for American," said Rosanne Radcliffe, 21, daughter of Mrs. J. L. Radcliffe, 2542 Summerdale av. "I watched other stewardesses and just decided to be one myself," she added.

Requirements for American Airlines stewardesses are stiff. A girl must be between 21 and 28 years old; between 5 feet 2 and 5 feet 7 inches tall; weigh not more than 130 pounds; have 20-50 vision or better because glasses cannot be worn on the job; a high school graduate with college or equivalent business training preferred; have good physical health; be "fairly attractive"; single; be well groomed, have a pleasing personality, and have "good character," according to Miss Roman.

Uniforms Issued

Girls are given wings and diplomas and are issued uniforms—tan for summer and blue for the three other seasons—at graduation ceremonies usually held in the Shoreland hotel and attended by company officials.

Stewardesses are paid a starting salary of $255 per month and given full travel privileges while working and half fares for other air travel. From the Chicago center, they are sent to one of 13 American Airlines bases thruout the country.

If a stewardess becomes married while on the job, she will be transferred to another department in the company, Miss Roman said, because it is a general practice of most commercial air lines to hire only single women.

Miss Roman discounted the myth of romance for young stewardesses. She said the average stewardess "marries the boy back home."

This news article was published right before I went to stewardess school. It gave me a good idea of what was coming for me.

Stewardess Argie Ella Hoskins

A pair of my wings.

Chapter Four

Grooming for Graduation

Coming from the rural area of southern New Mexico, I well remember the first time I walked down the streets of Chicago. Surreal! Where on earth were the open spaces of Animas Valley and Cotton City? Every outing, from going to church to riding the subway and the elevated rail, was an awesome awakening. I saw laundry hanging outside the apartment "flats" as we flew by on the elevated train, or 'L' as it was called. I will never forget the face of a child looking at me out a window. For one brief moment our eyes met, never to meet again. There were many emotions contained in that one moment—gratitude for having grown up in southwestern New Mexico, gratitude to my parents for a life of "don't fence me in."

One Sunday, riding back to the hangar from church, I made it from the 'L' to the bus just fine, but then I got so distracted looking out the window of the bus that I missed my exit. The first I knew of it was when the driver announced, "End of line. Everyone off." It was dark and I had no idea where I was. It was so scary! The driver was helpful enough to direct me to a bar around the corner for a phone, but the bar man told me to use the phone outside. That didn't really matter, though, since I had no idea who to call, where to go, or what to do, and I had very little money. All I knew was that I was on the south side of Chicago and that my parents would be very worried if they knew anything about me being there alone at night! On a very low level of awareness I knew of gangs. And to make things worse, it had been a cold April day, and it brought a night that was even more biting, to which one of my new friends at the hangar had responded by insisting that I borrow her fur, or at least fur-looking, full-length coat.

So here I stood. Alone in the cold night in front of a bar. No transportation to the airport hangar, no money for a taxi, young and pretty, and wearing a fur coat. I did the only thing I could do. I prayed. After my fervent prayer, a car stopped with several people in it. I couldn't tell, but it looked somewhat like a family. They took me to the airport and dropped me off without engaging in much conversation. I was so grateful!

Eventually, I became familiar with the transportation system of Chicago. My first apartment once I graduated and no longer lived in the hangar was on Wrightwood Avenue, north of the Loop. From Wrightwood Avenue I took a trolley car to the Midway Airport to catch my planes. I would board the trolley in front of a Chinese laundry, where interesting, foreign-looking people gathered to have conversations. As I observed them my curiosity of a new world was spiked with questions. My eyes and my heart opened as I reached across cultures and learned to understand different people.

I made many friends during my time in Chicago. One of the students in that hangar with me was Polly. We became friends forever and ever. We both understood what it was like in that hangar on both the sunny and rainy days. The rigors we went through with determination paid off as we journeyed to build character that would sustain us through the growing experiences of life.

Polly (right) and me (left). Friends liked to take photos in those fast, small "walk in and out" booths in shopping places. Personal cameras were not as plentiful then as now.

Often, when I was confronted with new challenges, I would think back on lessons I learned at the ranch in Animas: commitment, loyalty, and focusing on the task at hand. Even if it's cold, the cows won't wait to be milked, the chickens won't wait to be fed, the eggs won't wait to be gathered. Doing what needed to be done when it needed doing was a valuable lesson from home that I took with me into stewardess training. The word *lazy* wasn't used in our home, and staying in bed wasn't an option. When I was discouraged I would go forward and remember Daddy's words, "Sis, get up and amount to something!"

One new experience came when I had to learn to mix drinks. I'd never had a mixed drink before, but I seemed to catch on faster than most. Figure that! I never indulged because it didn't make sense to me, but I still remember that Martinis have an olive and Manhattans have a cherry.

I did not spend every minute training in the hangar. When I wasn't exploring Chicago and learning the intricacies of big city life, I had to do certain things to look as attractive as possible. One assignment relating to my appearance was to find the person who would fit my uniform to me. It was a nightmare for me to figure out how to get to the tailor for uniform fittings, and learning how to get from the hangar to Washington Street and back again was quite a challenge for my sequencing deficit. That was not easy. But I will never forget that gentle man, Mr. Colangelo, hired by American Airlines, who

---

PHONE RAN. 3106

Colangelo

Ladies' Tailoring ∴ Furriers

PITTSFIELD BLDG, SUITE 741

55 EAST WASHINGTON STREET   CHICAGO 2, ILL.

Mr. Colangelo's business card. Life was more simple then. Just take a look at the phone number.

helped guide me to his store when he heard my pitiful, "I'm lost," over the phone. That was back when phone numbers were easy for me to remember.

Mr. Colangelo was a kind man and very talented as a tailor. I say talented because he designed my American Airline uniform to make me, Argie Hoskins, really look like a stewardess. In computer terms, he knew where to "cut and paste."

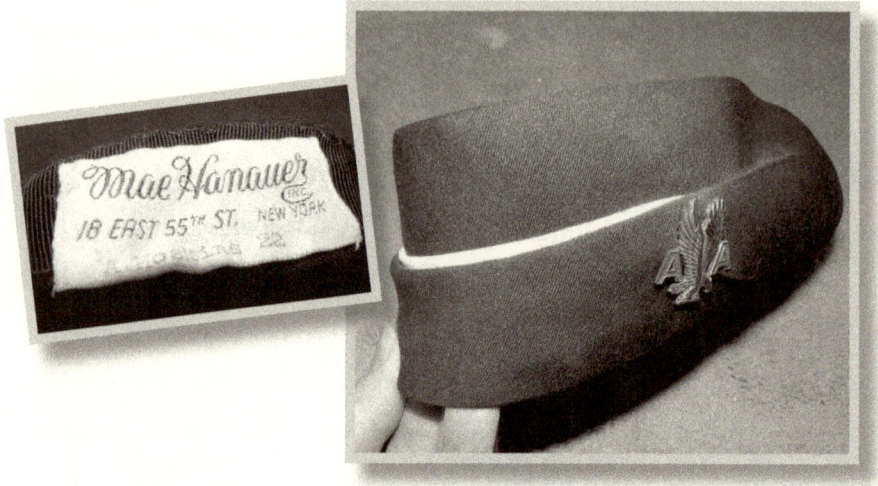

My stewardess cap. It was designed by Mae Hanauer of New York.

Another day a hair stylist came to the school to fix us up with a new hairdo. Wow! I could not believe what happened to my long, beautiful hair. It was very hard to keep the tears from bursting forth. I had had thick, lovely locks and then, suddenly, no hair. After the hairdo, the photographer took our pictures to send home to the local newspapers announcing our training success. I did my best to smile.

My hair may not have been what I liked, but oh, that brown uniform was grand. I loved our spectator pumps, because I liked the two-toned look. Looking at my uniform I thought back to how I had learned about style and dress design from a mother in a mining camp, and I knew that the American Airlines uniform was one I'd be proud to wear.

The president of American Airlines at the time was Cyrus Rowlett (C. R.) Smith. In the business of life, C. R. Smith's informal, but no-nonsense, approach to leadership created trust that formed close relationships with both executives and employees. Convair president Jack Naish noted once that "you can close a $100 million deal on [C. R. Smith's] word alone." It is said that he generally communicated through personally typed one-page memos and that he knew every American employee by name until the end of his first term as CEO.

American Airlines gave each employee a booklet entitled "Welcome to American" with this note from C. R. Smith inside:

> You are joining the organization of American Airlines, Inc. First, that is a tribute to you, for American Airlines has always sought and has been able to secure the interest, work, and loyalty of men and women of superior worth and competence. We believe that you have those excellent qualities, otherwise you would not have been employed. You, by your work, will demonstrate the soundness of our judgment of you. In return, we offer you the right of reasonable opportunity; to engage in an interesting business in an important field of public service; to enjoy continued association with serious, agreeable, able people; and to receive promotion and additional income, when merited by your record, in accordance with growth and availability of better jobs.
>
> You will find that the men and women holding positions of responsibility in American are there for the reason that they have demonstrated their capability. They are not there for the reason that they attended or graduated from some specific college, or any college; or that their families aided them in securing promotion; or that they or their friends owned stock in the company. This is a company in which reward is based on merit. It is a company in which ambitious, able people will want to work.
>
> American Airlines is a great organization, certainly one of the most able and respected in the industry. It has reached its position of leadership by the combined ability of the many thousands of men and women associated

together in the enterprise. You will have the opportunity to contribute to the further advancement of American Airlines; we expect you to do that.

Signed, C. R. Smith, President

I felt honored to belong to such a team. C. R. Smith surrounded himself with businessmen, scientists, and engineers that supported his no-nonsense and straight forward approach toward the serious purposes at hand. He had a clear understanding of the contributions that each of these professions could make to the growth of American Airlines. In World War II, C. R. Smith became a Colonel and eventually a Major General due to his experience, vision, administrative style, tenacity, and capable leadership. He played a major role in the creation and effective functioning of our military's Air Transport Command. After the war, he and his team dusted themselves off and plunged full force into making American Airlines the best it could be. He made sure his employees knew our creed—passengers are people. About that he wrote, "Tell [passengers] the truth in an understandable, friendly non-technical manner. They will understand and appreciate your consideration and the information you give them." I think every person employed by American at this time felt that they were part of something great. C. R. Smith sure had confidence in them. In that same booklet we received, it also says,

Unknown, President C. R. Smith, Mildred Jackson, and unknown.
Photo courtesy of Martha Mason, Mildred's niece.

You will find that the supervisory men and women of American have a broad knowledge of the whole company, and that they are good judges of human nature as well. If you feel that you would do better work in some other department or location; if something has gone wrong at home; or if there is sickness or you have financial difficulties that are interfering with your work, tell them your story. They will help you all they can.

If at any time you have a personal problem and would like advice or help, see your supervisor.

The first supervisor I really had contact with was Mildred Jackson, or Millie. Millie was the Director of Stewardesses and Customer Services while I was in school. This meant that she was over the whole stewardess operation for American Airlines. She was a key person in the organization. She had a vision of what being an American Airlines stewardess was and taught that it should be at the heart of airline travel. Millie taught us that *we* were American Airlines because our passengers interacted with us more than anyone. When I stood there with a satisfied or an irate passenger, I was the "main person." I took this face of American Airlines very seriously. What a huge responsibility!

Millie was also responsible for the training of the instructresses. They were the ones who trained the student stewardesses. Millie never married, I think, because she was, in a way, married to American Airlines. We were trained to be loyal to American Airlines, and believe you me, Millie was loyal to the end. I know that is one reason why I loved American Airlines, because they taught us to be loyal and obedient to the task. No slackers!

Millie's collection of wings.
Photo courtesy of Martha Mason.

The Pittsburgh Post-Gazette printed an interview with Mildred on December 17, 1957, about stewardesses and their lifestyle. I remember her telling us what she told them, "It's not all glamour. You have crazy hours, sometimes up at 4:00 a.m., and you work Sundays, Christmas, and New Year's unless you can trip trade. After walking from coast to coast, your feet hurt."

Left: My three instructresses, Ellie Roman, Connie Rutkowski, and Chris Debraggio. They started out as stewardesses and were then trained as instructresses. Right: Mildred Jackson, Director of Stewardesses and Customer Services.

She also told them that stewardesses make practically perfect wives since they learn to take care of people, including irate passengers. She even said that a survey had shown that stewardesses have the lowest divorce rate among former working girls. It was reassuring the day she told us that, though I know some of us ended up being exceptions to the rule. Mildred also pointed out that, while stewardesses may make perfect wives, "they all do not wed rich passengers or handsome pilots. I don't know how you can tell a wealthy passenger." She mentioned this because that is what the general public sometimes thought of us. They stereotyped us into pretty girls looking for the rich, famous, or handsome men to live or sleep with. But that is not who we were! My friends, roommates, and classmates were the nicest girls with solid

Clockwise from left: Mildred and Jack Benny; Class of 1953 in AA formation; kids flocking around Gene Autry at an AA function with Mildred in the top left corner; Roy Rogers and Mildred at an AA function; Mildred pinning the Class of 1951; Mildred and Milton Berle with a group of stewardesses at an AA function; a group of stewardesses with C. R. Smith and Mildred front row left.
Photos courtesy of Martha Mason.

values and good morals, some of the strongest individuals it has been my privilege to know.

Under Millie's tutelage, the exhilarating day of graduation drew near, the company's needs were analyzed as to where stewardesses were needed, and our base assignments were announced. I remember some girls being disappointed. There were great big tears in their eyes because the placement assignments did not meet their expectations, while other girls were elated! Some didn't really care. I remember one girl, crying, yelling, and trying everything she knew to persuade the system to change its mind and have her reassigned. But it didn't work. That was part of the deal when we signed up—you go where you are needed. Didn't she know that when she signed on the dotted line?

I ended up being pleased with my assignment. It wasn't what I had wanted—I wanted to be based in Los Angeles because one of my old sweethearts was living there, and I really wanted to see him—but I was assigned to Chicago, and that didn't seem too bad to me. I was immersed in the view of the world that I was experiencing, so Chicago was just fine. It felt good to know where I would be after graduation.

The day of graduation came, and I earned my wings on Tuesday, May 21, 1957. Graduation was held at Fourth and Halstead at the historical Stock Yard Inn in the Four Seasons room at 1:00 p.m. That was an event! Millie pinned our wings on us, and we received our diplomas. It was an honor to have my wings pinned on my uniform by the one and only Mildred Jackson. That brief, quiet, simple moment—filled with excited heart beats—defined my life. It gave me a vision of my potential; a vision that I had not had before stewardess school. It felt so good to hold my diploma in my hand. That important paper said "successfully completed" and was signed by both Millie and C. R. Smith. Hallelujah! Hallelujah!

Above:
Close-up of my wings.

Left: After all was said and done this newspaper article appeared in the local paper. It reads:

Miss Argie Hoskins Gets Wings as American Airline Stewardess

Miss Argie Hoskins, daughter of Mr. and Mrs. Allen E. Hoskins of Howe Ranch, Animas, has won her wings as an American Airlines stewardess, after completing her course of training at the airline's stewardess school in Chicago.

She has been assigned to flight crew duty on American Airlines flagships, operating out of the Chicago area.

Miss Hoskins, a green-eyed, brown-haired beauty, is a native of Deming. She attended high school at Animas and Lordsburg. She also attended New Mexico Western College and New Mexico A&M.

In high school, she was cheerleader for two years and Homecoming Queen at Lordsburg High in 1954. In college, she was 1955 Sun Princess at New Mexico A&M, 1956 Military Ball Queen, 1956 Spring Carnival First Beauty, Engineering Ball Princess, and 1956 Maid of Cotton Princess.

Before joining American Airlines, she was employed by El Paso Natural Gas Co. in El Paso.

Miss Hoskins pointed out that Americans' current expansion program will require at least 750 new stewardesses during the next 12 months, and any girl interested in a flying career should write to her in care of the stewardess department of American Airlines at Chicago's Midway Airport.

Basic qualifications include a high school education or better, 20 to 27 years old, and five feet two to five feet seven inches tall.

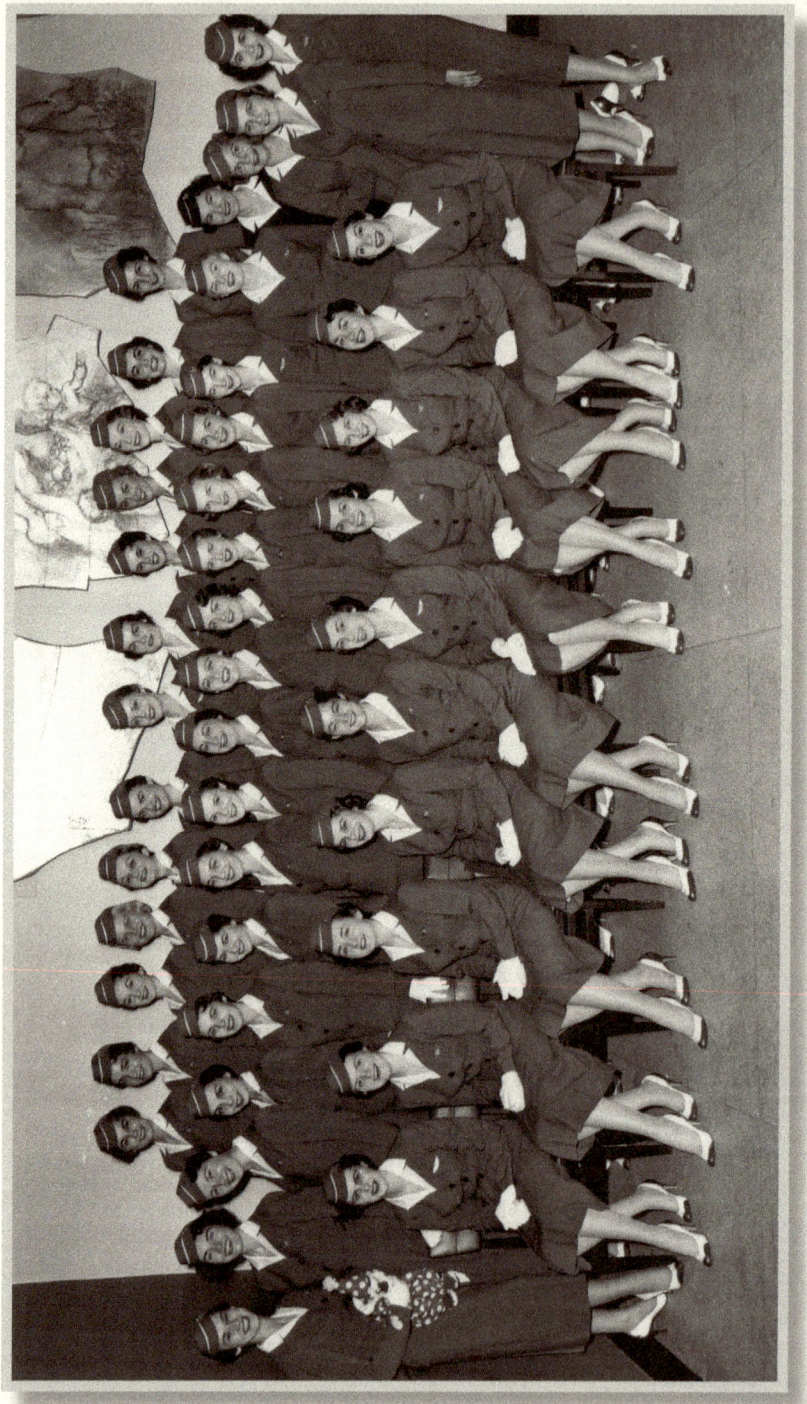

American Airlines Class 57–6: I am in the second row, sixth from the right.

FLIGHT STEWARDESS CORPS

This is to certify that

Argie Ella Hoskins

having been accepted in the Stewardess Corps of

AMERICAN AIRLINES

on the __21st__ day of __May__ A D 1957 and having successfully completed the Flight Stewardess Training Course,

Class of 57-6 1957

is on this day awarded her flight wings insignia in recognition of her competency to perform flight duties assigned her, and her worthiness to uphold the fine principles of the Flight Stewardess Corps.

[signature]
President, American Airlines, Inc.

Attest:

Mildred E. Jackson
Instructor

Ellie Roman
Chris Debraggio
Connie Rutkowski

My diploma signed by Mildred E. Jackson, C. R. Smith, Ellie Roman, Chris Debraggio, and Connie Rutkowski.

Pictures of Convair 240s at the Chicago Airport. These were small planes that only required one stewardess. Photos courtesy of Midway Historian Pat Bukiri.

Chapter Five

First Flights

My first month of flying presented a whole new learning curve. One experience almost promised that it would be a very short career! I boarded a Convair 240 headed from Chicago to Indianapolis. I had never seen the captain or copilot before, and I was scared to death. Convairs only required one stewardess, so I was alone, without anyone to help or cue me into the right timetable and procedures.

Squaring my shoulders, I walked onto the plane in a ladylike, dignified manner. I checked all the necessary things and made mental notes as to where things were: the service kit, magazines, the coat closet, pillows, and blankets. I also had to check to see that the meals were all accounted for before takeoff, to make sure that we wouldn't be a meal short (our meals were provided by Sky Chef—a wholly owned airline catering service that American Airlines created). I wanted to make sure that any plane where I was serving as stewardess was a place someone would like to come back to over and over again. But knowing that I would need to memorize the names of 40 passengers in about an hour and serve them all a meal was daunting. My, oh my. This was an absolute test in sequencing, multitasking, and time management.

Well, I got the names down, but the plane started to descend, and I had not served the meal. Back then we routinely served nice meals—not like the packaged meals they sometimes serve on planes today. The meals were served on lovely china plates with designer flatware, cloth napkins, and logoed glasses. Most of the time the meals were served hot, and they helped create the homey atmosphere that was central to a passenger's positive experience. And now I, having just graduated, would miss this meal and single-handedly ruin this flight. Nervously running into the cockpit, I said, "I haven't started to serve the meal yet!"

"We are landing," came the voice from the Captain. I felt like jumping out the door. All I could hear was his encouraging, "Get started." In a few minutes, our good-humored captain came back and helped me serve the food! He had put the plane in a holding pattern to give us time. I made sure to never let that happen again. Lesson learned!

After we landed, the pilots got off for a 45 minute layover, and I sat on the plane knitting and crying. When the crew came back, the captain brought me a candy bar, smiled, and announced that new passengers were coming. Never had I received such a needed gift, dear man, and I don't even remember his name. American Airlines hired amazing people!

I have the utmost respect for the pilots with whom I flew. Never were my values compromised or offended with remarks of disrespect. My memory tells me that most of these men had earned their wings as military pilots. They were caring men with good senses of humor and sound personalities. They appreciated a delectable meal with good conversation and had adventurous spirits. I completely trusted their cockpit skills and was never afraid.

I continued to be on reserve, or on call, and was called to work the Convair again and again and again and again. I couldn't help but wonder, "Are they trying to wash me out with all these one gal flights?" There was so much to do on those flights. The meals we served are a great example. Our plane made many stops on our way to our final destination—there could be several stops between Chicago and Dallas or Chicago and New York. After we got in the air, we would serve passengers their meals. Then the plane would stop, and more passengers would get on, Sky Chefs would load more meals, and we would keep track of who had eaten and who hadn't eaten and then serve the new passengers their meal. Then we'd prepare for the next stop to do the same

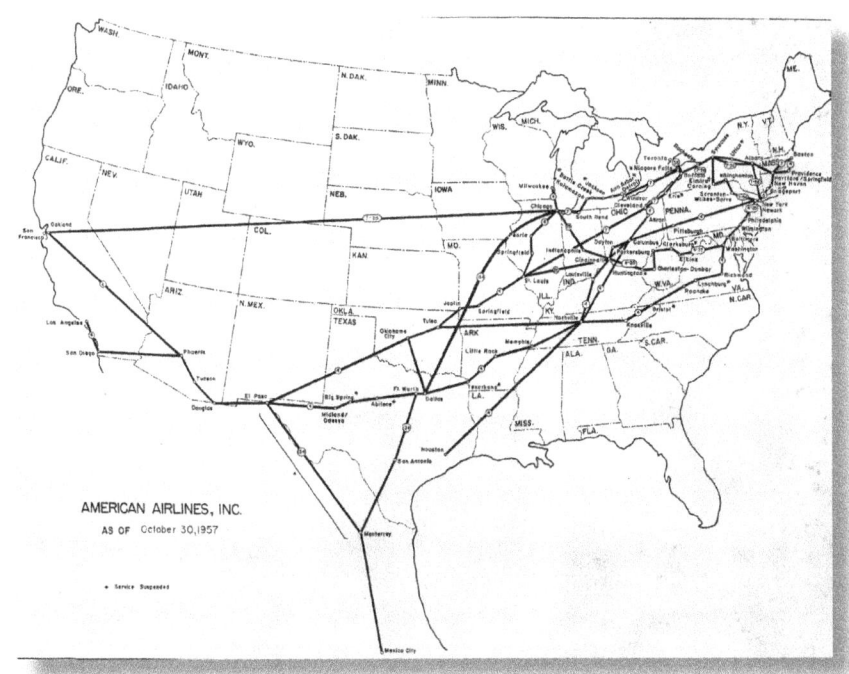

Flight paths for American Airlines planes, October 30, 1957.

thing over and over. We even had special meals for special needs—we never served pork because we had a Jewish population that flew.

Just as Millie had promised, it was not all glamour. Sometimes the stresses of the schedule caught up with me. I remember a startling wake-up call one early morning in the country suburbs of Louisville, Kentucky. The evening before I had fallen into bed at that small motel, completely exhausted, and I had forgotten to set my alarm. I had made sure to hang my uniform on a dresser drawer, shower, and curl my hair, but I had forgotten that one crucial step of setting the alarm clock. I was awakened by loud banging and the call through the door, "Our cab is here!"

I jumped out of bed, threw on my uniform, and flew out the door with curlers in my hair. I hadn't brushed my teeth or put on makeup, and as I hurried out the door and into the cab my face was red with embarrassment. I will never, and I mean *never*, forget Louisville, Kentucky. The crew got a good laugh over that one! Looking back, I'm glad to have brought them some laughter, but at the time I thought, "Am I really cut out for this job?" That was yet another lesson learned.

After graduation we were assigned to stewardess supervisors to whom we were accountable. They were like an all-seeing eye of a concerned parent guiding the child to perfection, watching over us, checking on us, and reprimanding us when needed. If we were not doing our job, we had to "straighten up

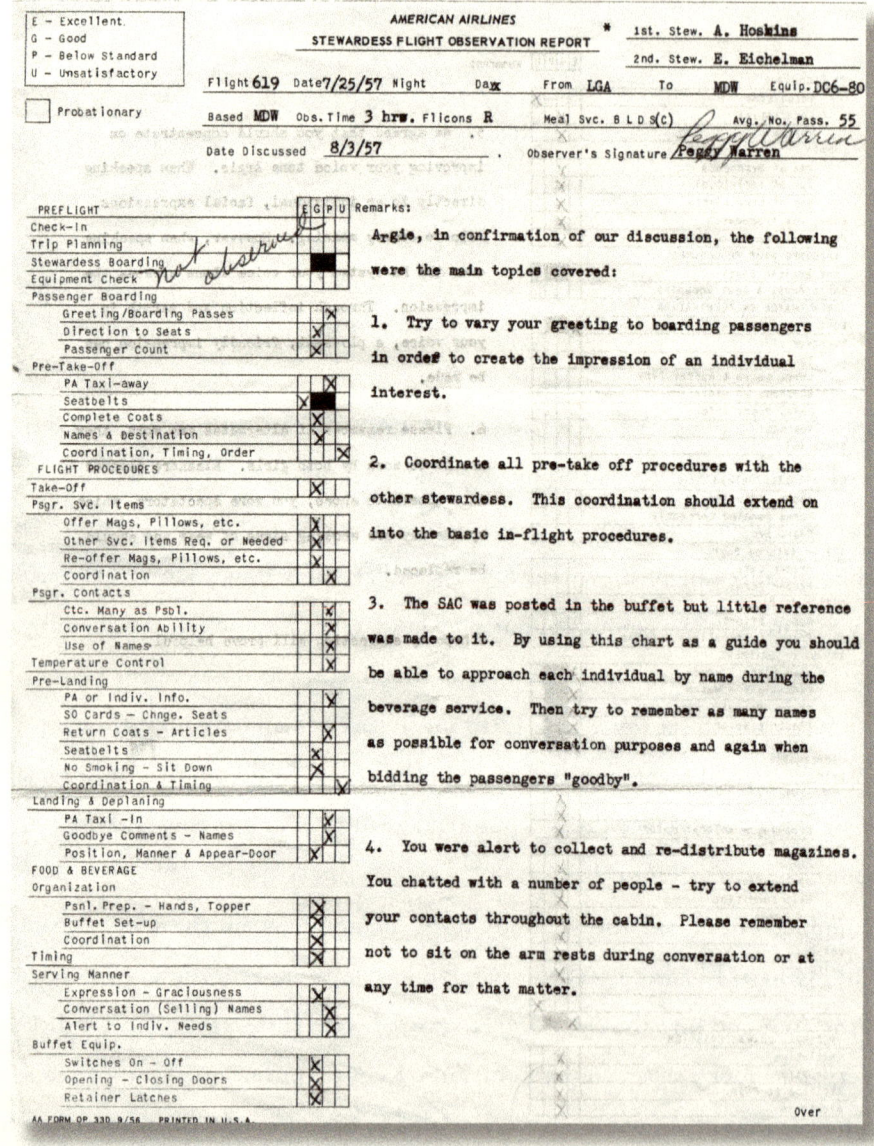

and fly right" or out the plane we went. It was a highly disciplined organization from top to bottom.

It soon came time for my first checkride, where a supervisor would board the plane and ride as a passenger. With clipboard in hand, and eyes in the front and back of her head, she watched, wrote down, and evaluated everything I did.

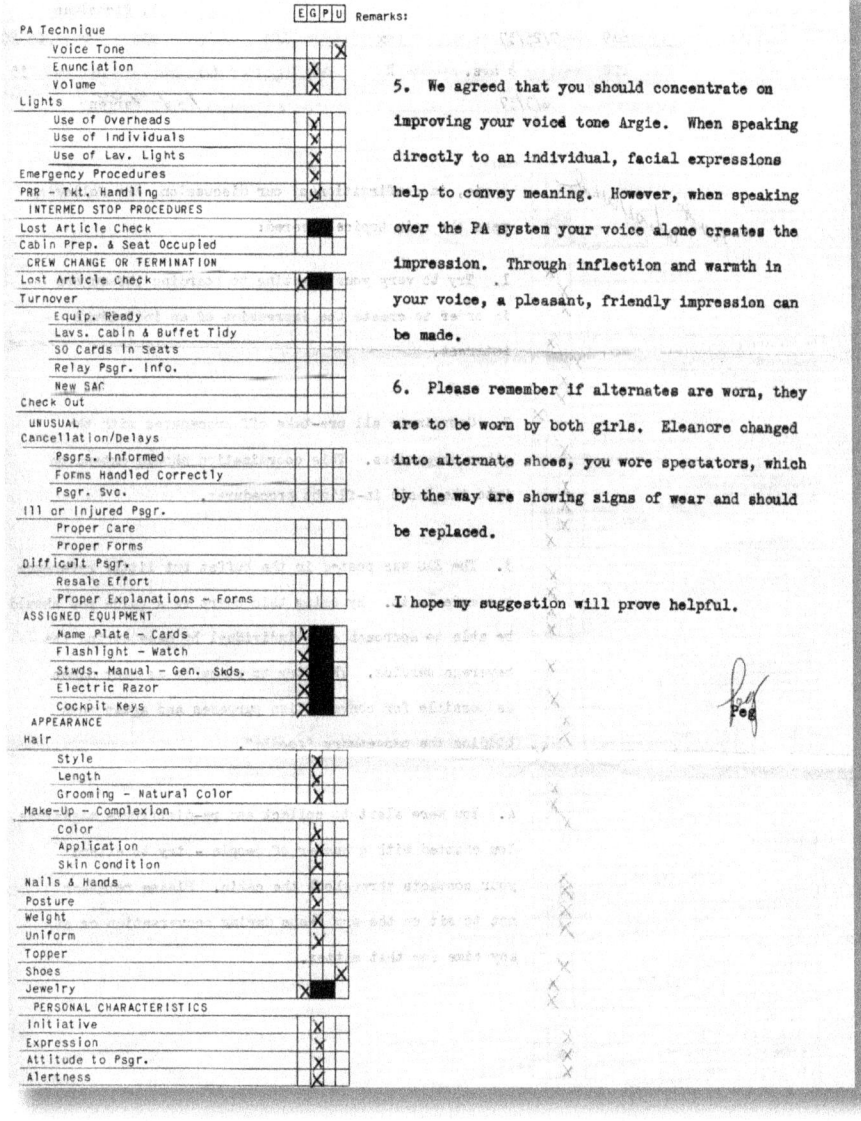

The front and back of my first checkride evaluation.

The first thing I noticed when I received my evaluation was the absence of *excellent* check marks. That came later! As the saying goes, "Anything worth having is worth working for." I was terrified of the supervisors until I had been flying for a while. They even started telling me that I would be a really fine supervisor. Ummmmm, perhaps!

Bettye Harris was the first supervisor who gave me the idea that I could become a supervisor. She was an inspiration for me. When I heard her words of encouragement something clicked in my head, and I started to view myself as being made out of the "stuff" that would take me there. I learned the truth of the statement, "As a man thinketh, so is he."

Our supervisors worked in the details. One time, I remember walking into the stewardess office and being told that the supervising staff needed to "take a look."

"Wrong color of nail polish!" I was told. I quickly took it off and put on the right color—I called it American Airlines Red.

Another time, being a few pounds overweight, they asked "Argie, do you have a girdle on?"

"Yes, ma'am, Playtex."

"Well, you need to lose a few pounds." I wish I had some of that same supervision now! We looked sharp and served with enthusiasm and poise. We were proud to be stewardesses for American Airlines.

I could hardly wait to dress in that neat, tailored uniform with the cap on my head. I would put on my best smile and strive to be of service to the air traveling population. Knowing that passengers would dress up in their Sunday best and put *their* best foot forward to receive first class service, whether it be in the front or rear of the plane, spurred me to meet their expectations.

I met a variety of colorful personalities. I feel I was privileged to have been serving the public in such a special way during this period of history. We were trained to learn our passengers' names and engage them in conversation. Sometimes my own name started it! Before we flew on jets, we would display our name plates in metal holders located in both the forward and aft cabins. The stewardess who worked the forward cabin placed hers in the forward holder, and the stewardess who worked the aft cabin placed hers in the aft holder. For a small period of time our wings also had our names on them. I really appreciated when my wings had my name on them. But mostly, it was the name plates that told our passengers who was serving them. If it was not a dual service flight, then only one name plate was displayed. Many times the question was asked of me, "What does the A stand for?"

"Argie."

MISS A. HOSKINS

We provided many services for our passengers. We hung up coats, helped place things in the overhead rack, memorized the passengers' names, passed out magazines, and offered a pillow and blanket. For emergencies we carried small oxygen tanks. For babies we had jars of baby food and sometimes Girl Scout Cookies, and we always had wings or rings for the older children.

On board we had the greatest Girl Scout Cookies to serve our passengers. I would put the Gerber apple sauce jars in the ice to get nice and chilled. When we needed a snack we'd eat the Girl Scout Cookies and the chilled apple sauce.

Right: A junior stewardess ring that we would give to young girls.

Left: My friend Claire giving some children an American Airlines balloon and wings.

My, oh my, it was tasty! For the idle traveler, we could hand them a deck of playing cards to play their favorite game, or they could join us in the lounge at the rear of the plane for some nice conversation. It was wonderful! We weren't just servers, but generous, interesting hostesses. Imagine how our passengers must have felt when they left our home in the sky. They had enjoyed one brief moment with comfort and attention.

Among the many niceties that we provided were American Airlines stationery and envelopes. The passengers were able to do any corresponding they needed done on the plane and give the finished letter to us. We then gave the written, unstamped items to the agent for mailing—true airmail! Additionally, every passenger had access to some American Airlines stationery that had this direction on top:

> American Airlines has often been described as the leader in air transportation. I hope we merit that distinction and will continue to merit it. To do that we must continue to please you, the customer. Never entirely satisfied with our service, each day we endeavor to make it better.
>
> If you have suggestions to improve the service, please give us the benefit of them. If your journey has been pleasant, tell us about it; it will encourage us. If any individual rendered outstanding service, give me the name and we will commend him or her for you. We are glad to have you aboard; I hope that you will travel often with American.

It was always so rewarding and encouraging when the letters were directed toward me. They validated me as a contributor. Growing up I had been taught that "it's not what you get, but what you give that makes you happy." I learned first-hand that that is true. One of the most valuable lessons I learned was to look outward for joy, not inward to be satisfied.

The first passenger letter I received was from a dear, elderly woman named Clara M. Herring who was nervous about flying for the first time. As the only stewardess on the flight, I was as tense as Clara was nervous. I felt like I had this constant inner dialogue playing through my mind, "Am I doing

My first passenger letter. This was from Clara M. Herring on July 16, 1957, flight number 561 from Cincinnati to Indianapolis. It reads:

I enjoyed my flight service, wonderful. Your hostess was efficient.
    I came up on Delta airline from Miami, Florida on 74 flight. My trip all way was wonderful. I will return on the same Rt. back to Miami.
    Signed, Mrs. Clara M. Herring

everything that I should be doing? Am I so concerned about what I'm doing and how I look that I'm forgetting others' needs?" How generous of her to write a note expressing her thanks for the service she enjoyed, because what she didn't know was that I was as nervous as she was on that flight and that I needed some reassurance. I kept her letter because I remember Clara Herring, and she warms my heart.

We often had military recruits on our flights. They seemed to be lonely before they even started their training, and I felt like me being friendly was always appreciated. Larry Westrater was one such passenger, and he wrote me a touching letter. Often these recruits reminded me of my brother, C. L., and my heart would go out to them even more.

I gave out my address with regularity. Looking back, I am not sure that it was a wise decision and certainly would not be now, but the world was a safer place back then. I felt that I could discern the intent of the heart. I realized that both the good and the bad in us needs to be understood, and I made it a personal mission of mine to encourage others to climb up, while not letting them pull me down. Sometimes we all really need a friendly hand to lift us up.

The more I flew the more I learned to put myself aside at the gate and then walk across the tarmac and climb the portable stairway to enter the plane. This walk could have been on a happy, sunny day or a cold, windswept, rainy, snowy night, and sometimes it was hot and humid, but they were all brief, very real moments. This trip was not about me, Argie. It was about our passengers, as our crew served, protected, and cared about them.

Letter from passenger Larry Westrater, August 18, 1957. It reads:

Hi Argie,

    I know you don't remember me, but you gave me your address when I was flying out to San Diego to take up recruit training at the marine base here. This is the first time I have really had time to sit down and write to you.

    I've told the boys here about you and they really carried on about you. I know I would like a picture of you if you can spare one.

    If at any time you could find time, would you please drop me a line and tell me how things are on the outside world.

    It's been a long time since I have seen the outside but in a few days we will [go] out, and I want you to send me if you would, the flights you're on from Diego to Chicago so I can get on your flight again. Well Argie, since I don't know you I can't think of any things else to say right now. So I'll sign off until next time. P. S. Write if possible.

    Yours Truly, Larry

Me in my uniform with Daddy in El Paso at the airport.

Chapter Six

A Visit Home

Chicago had been exciting for me, but I felt the need for a change. Time to go West! I put in for a transfer to Los Angeles, and it came through. A few mornings before I was to leave, I got up to go grocery shopping only to find that Autumn Leaves, my Chevy convertible, a 1954 Bel Air beauty, was not in the place I had parked. I looked and looked again. No car. As I was walking back into the apartment I noticed, way down the alley, was my car. It was unlocked and had no gas, but I was so pleased that after a little "joy ride" Autumn Leaves had been returned.

I motored from Chicago to St. Louis. After having a flat tire, and with no money to buy another one, I decided that I needed to stop for the night. Next morning, I left with no spare tire for the next leg on my journey—driving from St. Louis to Las Cruces, New Mexico. C. L. and his wife, Joan, lived there. I arrived there late, thankful that I had a great car to speed me through the roads of the Midwest down to the Southwest. Did I really know what I was doing? Probably not, but I made it.

After some good conversation, a lot of hugs, and a good night's rest, I was determined to check my estimated time of departure and head my wheels on west. It was on to Animas Valley to see Mom and Dad. I had a new appreciation for their simple, honest lives. They were amazed that their little girl had been to the big city and had made her way home, all by herself. Was that ever so nice!

I could not believe that in my heart and mind, I had moved from thinking I could not make it as a stewardess to thinking that I was one of the best. It took a lot of hard work to overcome having negative thoughts about myself. But the one thing that I had going for me was the hard work ethic which had been instilled in me while growing up in the mining camp and on the cattle ranch. I dug in my heels, knocked off the manure, made myself "cowboy up" (as the cowboys would say), and viewed myself as the person I wanted to be. After a while, I became the person who I am. My journey with American Airlines had challenged me to be me.

Coming back home after accomplishing so much caused me to reflect on what I had learned, and it was rewarding. I learned that talent is more than dancing, singing, acting, and looking pretty. I learned that I had talent for understanding people and their feelings, for knowing their hearts and expecting nothing of them, for making them feel welcomed. I learned from my instructress Chris Debraggio not to ask if someone wants a pillow, but to have the pillow in hand to give them. What a powerful lesson! Don't make people ask for your love; give love without asking for it back.

I took my time to relax while I was home. I uttered frequent sighs of contentment as I thoughtfully strolled along the old rutted country road beside the dry river bed lined with cottonwood trees, keeping my eyes open for rattlesnakes. I looked up through the leaves of the trees, sat on the old dead tree stumps, and reflected back on the long walks that my brother and I used to take here. As we walked along we often talked of what life was going to be like when we grew up—we dreamed of having a ranch, and together we would run it and give money to the poor.

I continued my reflective stroll on up the road to the windmill where the cups hung on the side of the tank. I tasted the refreshing well water. Waiting for me stood the dogs, wagging their tails, ready to play.

It soothed my soul to be back with these familiar sights. Not to mention the wonderful smells that continually came from the kitchen. It felt so special to be pampered by Mama and by Daddy, too, in his unique, silent way. In his billfold, Daddy carried a treasured picture of me in my uniform. Thinking of that sweet gesture of his always brings tears to my heart.

That next week I left Animas again. I wasn't alone this time. As I left that unobtrusive home on the range, my friend, my teacher, my mother climbed in Autumn Leaves with me, and we headed to California. Along the way, Mother silently listened to story after story of how life had been for me. She soaked up the stories like a canvas does paint—in her mind's eye she painted the pictures of my life as a stewardess, only to pause with wonderment because she had never experienced what I shared. There were moments where I was saddened by her excitement for me because the experiences had not been hers; I would have liked for my journey to have also been her journey. But she did not envy me—she found joy in my accomplishments. I was so grateful to finally share my sunset of beauty with her. What a sweet trip that was.

Me and Mama

My roommates and me (left to right: Claire Bullock, me, Barbara Whaley, and Gerry McMasters) posing in our flight toppers which covered our uniforms and which we wore when we served meals. This photo was taken on one of our trips from
Los Angeles to New York on the Boeing 707, flight number 2.

Chapter Seven

Based in and Flying from Los Angeles

In Los Angeles I lived with three very good stewardess friends: Claire Bullock, Barbara Whaley, and Gerry McMasters. These ladies were my friends and flying companions with whom I shared rent, utilities, and food that looked a lot like peanut butter. We prayed and played together, laughed and cried together. We most regularly worked the flights from Los Angeles to New York and back. On many mornings before we boarded our flight to New York, we would play on the Santa Monica Beach. Then in the evening we would walk with our sunburns in the snow on the streets of New York City to see the Perry Como or Andy Williams shows. We enjoyed our sixteen hour layovers. It was such a privilege to work with these wonderful ladies.

On one evening flight Gerry and I had closed the curtain of the buffet to eat. A passenger opened the curtain and announced with surprise, "You *eat?*" Our passengers thought we were glamorous superwomen without appetites. And then the passenger looked down, and our shoes were off! We hoped that we wouldn't get a passenger letter about that flaw in our service performance. I think that was the worst thing I ever did in the buffet area. It was embarrassing at the time, but oh, how we laughed about it later!

Whew! The days flew by, and the flights and memories run together. I worked hard and enjoyed it. I couldn't pinpoint the actual moment when I felt that I had mastered the tasks that had so stretched me before. Nevertheless, I think my growth and ability came as I diligently applied myself to the task, day in and day out, flight after flight. Eventually, some of the things that had been so hard became second nature to me. And the passenger letters kept coming as well! They were a constant reminder to me that a little kindness goes a long way. These little bits of paper paint a history of what it meant to be a stewardess during my time with American Airlines.

Checkride on October 4, 1957, from LAX to PHX on a DC–6 80. My observer was Willie Collier.
[Page 1] Argie, you checked in and boarded your flight on time, made a thorough equip. check, assisted passengers in the forward cabin in a friendly, gracious manner. Checked belts and took names before take-off. #1. No pillows ever offered out of SAN. Always make use of all service items

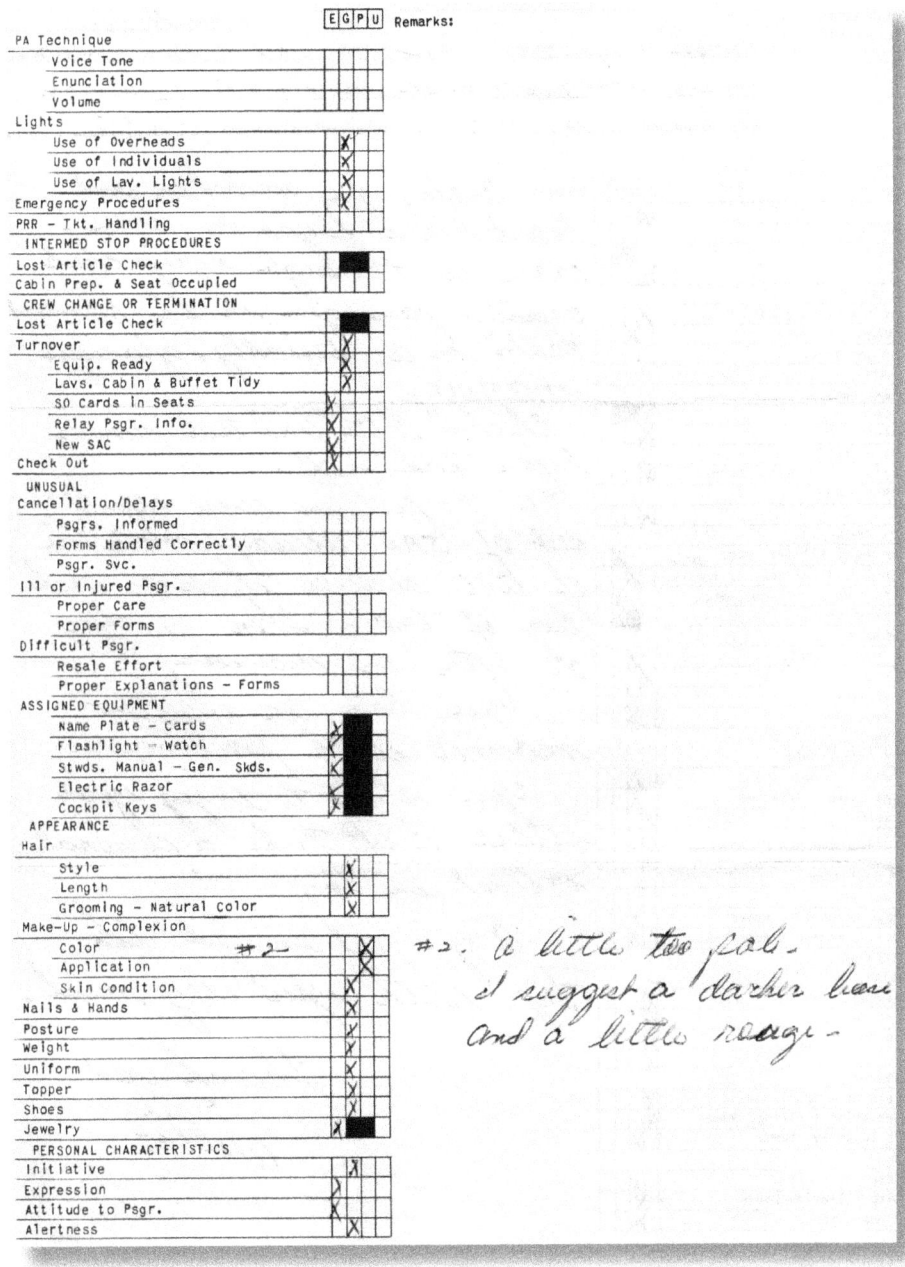

	E	G	P	U	Remarks:
PA Technique					
Voice Tone					
Enunciation					
Volume					
Lights					
Use of Overheads	X				
Use of Individuals	X				
Use of Lav. Lights	X				
Emergency Procedures	X				
PRR – Tkt. Handling					
INTERMED STOP PROCEDURES					
Lost Article Check					
Cabin Prep. & Seat Occupied					
CREW CHANGE OR TERMINATION					
Lost Article Check					
Turnover	X				
Equip. Ready	X				
Lavs. Cabin & Buffet Tidy	X				
SO Cards In Seats	X				
Relay Psgr. Info.	X				
New SAC	X				
Check Out	X				
UNUSUAL					
Cancellation/Delays					
Psgrs. Informed					
Forms Handled Correctly					
Psgr. Svc.					
Ill or Injured Psgr.					
Proper Care					
Proper Forms					
Difficult Psgr.					
Resale Effort					
Proper Explanations - Forms					
ASSIGNED EQUIPMENT					
Name Plate – Cards	X				
Flashlight – Watch	X				
Stwds. Manual – Gen. Skds.	X				
Electric Razor					
Cockpit Keys	X				
APPEARANCE					
Hair					
Style	X				
Length	X				
Grooming - Natural Color	X				
Make-Up - Complexion					
Color #2			X		
Application			X		
Skin Condition	X				
Nails & Hands	X				
Posture	X				
Weight	X				
Uniform	X				
Topper	X				
Shoes	X				
Jewelry	X				
PERSONAL CHARACTERISTICS					
Initiative		X			
Expression	X				
Attitude to Psgr.	X				
Alertness	X				

#2. A little too pale. I suggest a darker base and a little rouge.

on each leg of trip. Then re-offer as often as necessary. You have an excellent manner with passengers. You seem to enjoy your work and take a personal interest in it. Argie, I enjoyed the trip with you very much. Thank you, Willie

    [Page 2] #2. A little too pale. I suggest a darker base and a little rouge.

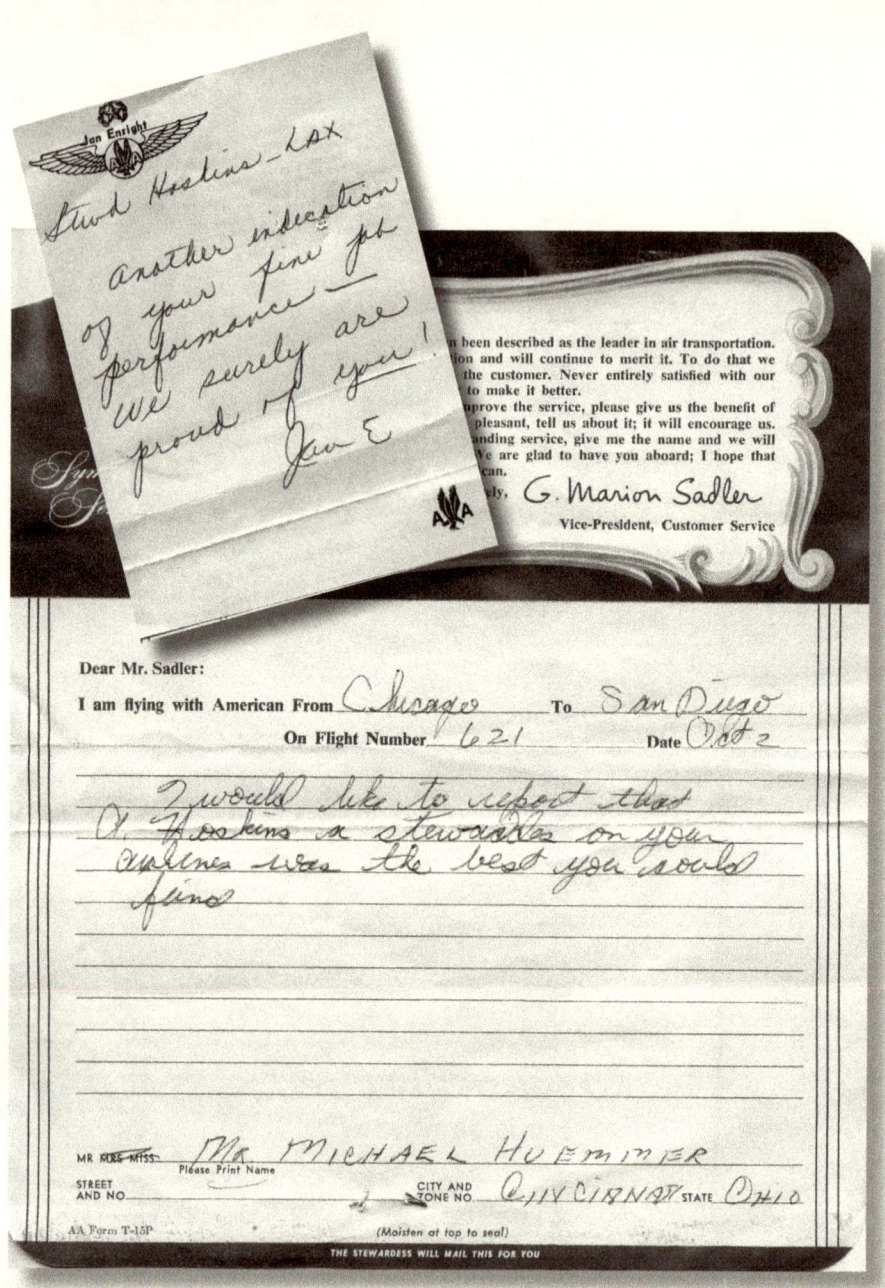

Passenger letter from flight number 621 from Chicago to San Diego on October 2, 1957. It reads:

I would like to report that A. Hoskins a stewardess on your airlines was the best you could find.
    Signed, Mr. Michael Huemmer from Cincinnati, Ohio
The attached note from my supervisor, Jan Enright, says, "Stwd. Hoskins—LAX. Another indication of your fine job performance—we surely are proud of you! Jan E."

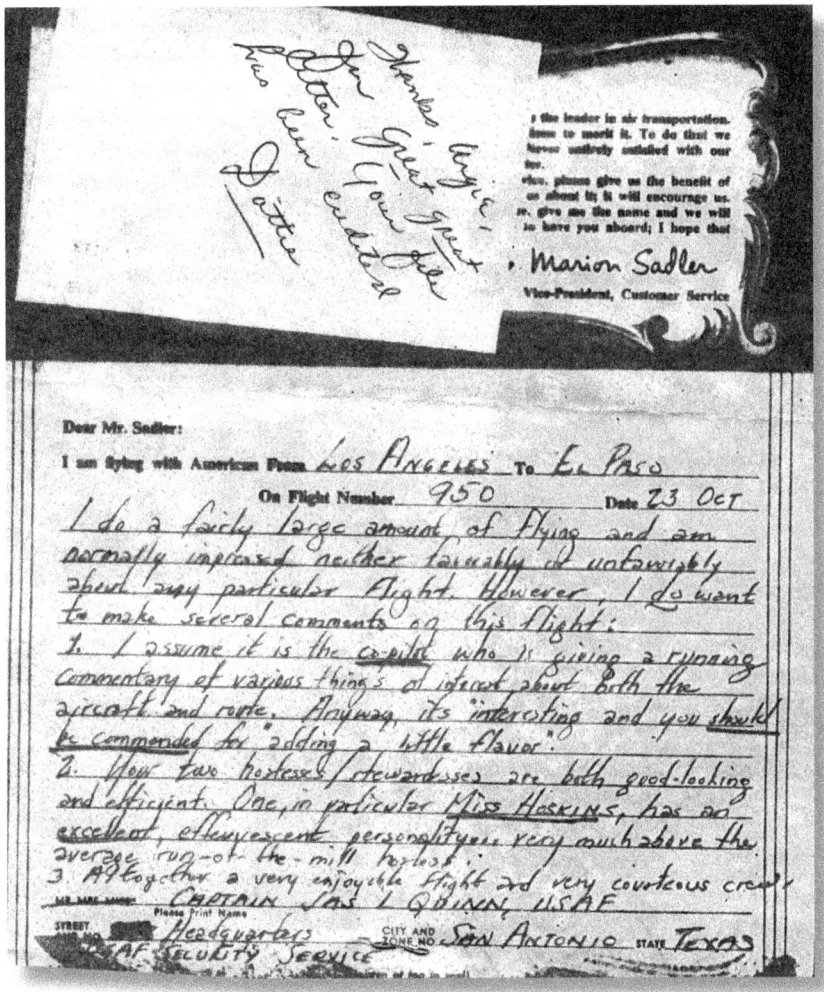

Passenger letter from flight number 950 from Los Angeles to El Paso on October 23, 1957. It reads:

I do a fairly large amount of flying and am normally impressed neither favorably or unfavorably about any particular flight. However, I do want to make several comments on this flight:

    1. I assume it is the copilot who is giving a running commentary of various things of interest about both the aircraft and route. Anyway, it's interesting and you should be commended for "adding a little flavor."

    2. How two hostesses/stewardesses are both good-looking and efficient. One, in particular Miss Hoskins, has an excellent effervescent personality . . . very much above the average run-of-the-mill hostess. 3. Altogether a very enjoyable flight and very courteous crew.

    Signed, Captain James L. Quinn, USAF

    Headquarters USAF Security Service, San Antonio, Texas

The attached note from my supervisor, Dottie, says, "Thanks, Argie, Fun, great, great letter. Your file has been credited. Dottie."

Letter dated October 30, 1957, from passenger Harry Fried. He was a member of the Christian Business Men's Committee. I remember the energy with which this dear man explained this Christian organization to me. The letter reads:

Dear Miss Hoskins—

You may recall that I promised to send you some literature regarding the Christian Business Men's Committee. You will find some enclosed along with some other reading material which I hope you will study. Also, as I mentioned, I have asked Mrs. Loren Griset to get in touch with you as early as she can, which she has promised to do. Many thanks for your excellent service. May God bless you as you go along day by day and have fellowship with His Son, our Lord Jesus Christ.
   Sincerely,
   Harry Fried

Passenger letter from flight number 950 from Los Angeles to San Antonio on April 3, 1958. It reads:

I'd like to commend our stewardess Miss Hoskins on her commendable service. Throughout the entire flight she wore a smile and was so exceedingly polite. It was a pleasure to fly American. If all the stewardesses are of her caliber your instruction course is to be highly commended.
   Signed, Mr. Robert Donin

Passenger letter from flight number 950 from Los Angeles to San Antonio on April 15, 1958. It reads:

I wish to commend the wonderful abilities of your stewardesses, especially Miss Hoskins. I've never before been treated so well. Thank you,
   Signed, Mr. Richard A. Ryles
The note underneath from my supervisor, Jean Johnson, says, "Good for you Argie! J. Johnson."

Letter dated May 4, 1958, from passenger Major General Willard Wadsworth Irvine, U. S. Army, retired. It reads:

Dear Miss Hoskins:

My sincere appreciation of your letter giving me correctly the dates on the MOWW card. Congratulations on being the first and I will make good of my promise of a "gift or present" as soon as I get back to my home at La Jolla the last of this month.

My "American" ticket takes me to New York tomorrow. Then I go to my home state of Georgia for a week, then to Texas, Colorado, etc.

Both of my daughters once worked for the airlines: one was with Eastern at Statler Hotel Washington. The other at Delta in Forth Worth, Texas.

Cordially, Willard Irvine

WILLARD W. IRVINE

Major General Willard Wadsworth Irvine, U.S. Army, ret., a member of the La Jolla chapter was elected Junior Vice CinC at Miami Beach. He formerly was Commander Region 14.

A native of Warrenton, Georgia, General Irvine graduated from Emory University, Atlanta, Georgia, with a BS degree in 1913. He was elected to membership in ATO and the honorary fraternity Phi Beta Kappa.

Enlisting as a private in the Georgia National Guard he became a captain and entered Federal Service. In 1917 he accepted a commission as 2nd Lieutenant Regular Army and was advanced to the rank of captain the same year. He attained the rank of Major in 1918 and was made a Battalion Commander.

Between World Wars I and II, and after, General Irvine attended many army schools. In 1922 he graduated from the Artillery School, took the advanced course in 1927 and served three years as an instructor from 1932 to 1935. He graduated from the Command and General Staff College in 1928. In 1938 he returned there as an instructor. He graduated from the Army War College and the National War College in 1936. Upon the advent of nuclear weapons General Irvine took the Defense Department Special Weapons Course at Sandia, New Mexico in 1952.

When World War II broke he was assigned to the War Department General Staff, 1941-1942. He then became Brigade commander and a Division commander from 1942-1943, and was Deputy Assistant Chief of Staff, U.S. Army in 1944. From 1945 to 1947 he commanded, Western Pacific Command, Iwo Jima to Admiralty Islands, under General MacArthur.

During his service in the Korean War he was commander, Army Anti-Aircraft Command, under the Joint Chiefs of Staff, from 1950 to 1952. From 1952 to 1956 he was a special student at the University of California.

General Irvine is married to the former Lilian Scott, who was born in Griffin, Georgia. They have two daughters, Mrs. Diana I. Weir, Colorado Springs, and Mrs. Virginia Quirey, of Stuttgart, Germany.

Long an active Churchman, General Irvine became chairman of the official board and Trustees, Methodist Church, La Jolla, California, where he resides. He also is associate lay leader, San Diego District, and lay member of California and Nevada Conference. In 1955 he became a member of the National Commission of Chaplains, at Washington, D.C. He has a business interest, and serves as Director of Pacific Homes, of California.

While serving as Regional Commander he stimulated membership growth in the region. Among other means he employed a series of Bulletins to assist state and chapter officers in activities to foster the aims of the Preamble.

As Junior Vice CinC he is coordinator of several committees among which are Chapter Activities, Membership, Massing of the Colors, the Scholarship Fund, and a committee to study ways and means for development of greater interest in the study of American History in schools and homes. He serves as chairman of the committee on chapter activities, and is a member of the committee on the NATIONAL BULLETIN.

VIGILANT CITIZENSHIP

R. Admiral Reginald R. Belknap, past CinC, was prevented from attending the mid-year staff meeting. He had been ill, but sent greetings.

His letter contained a reminder that the rights of citizenship involve a moral obligation, and in this time of stress and international uncertainty, the Companions of the Order enjoy an unusual opportunity to show the quality of their dedication to the American Ideal. The BULLETIN was requested to reprint a resolution which Admiral Belknap presented at the annual convention.

Resolved that the convention urge all Chapters as bodies and all members as individual citizens

1. To be vigilant and attentive to information from the press and other reliable sources affecting the honor, integrity and independence of the United States of America,
2. To be active in civic affairs for promotion and safeguard of the interest and welfare of the people,
3. Keep their respective senators and representatives informed of their interest and pay attention to the attitude and actions of their representatives on issues pending,
4. To be persistent in following up the said communications;
5. To express commendation or other form of approval, with a view to establishing a growing sense of mutual confidence and achieve serious consideration of the views of the people.

CINCINNATI HONORS A FOUNDER OF THE ORDER

A new Ohio National Guard Armory in Cincinnati named in honor of General P. Lincoln Mitchell, was dedicated 23 November. The Cincinnati chapter presented a dedicatory plaque. Lt. Comdr Joseph B. Andrews, chapter commander officiated.

General Mitchell attended the first meeting of the Order at Detroit in 1920, and presided at this organization meeting. Returning to Cincinnati he organized the chapter and was named first commander. Annually he is re-elected Honorary Chapter Commander.

As he began his eightieth year during the past month he became a Perpetual Member

CHAPTER N[...]

We have received [...]
Companions are not [...]
TIONAL BULLETI[...]
manders are request [...]
membership to dete[...]
ceives the Bulleti[...]
advise Headquart[...]

NATIONAL BULLETIN
1706 Eye Street, N.W.
Washington 6, D.C.

Entered as second-class mail matter March 21, 1923, at the post office at Washington, D.C., under the Act of March 3, 1879.

EDUCATION FOR NATIONAL SECURITY
Patriotism—History—Arts—Sciences—Research

Newspaper clippings of Willard W. Irvine. It was always so fun to read about people in print whom I had served in person! MOWW (Military Order of the World Wars) is a patriotic Veterans Service Organization (VSO) founded in 1919 by officers who had served under General of the Armies John J. "Black Jack" Pershing. The purpose of the Order, then and now, is to promote patriotism, civic responsibility, and leadership.

Passenger letter from flight number 953 from Houston to San Diego on May 1, 1958. It reads:

Miss Argie Hoskins, one of the hostesses on this flight, has played an essential part in making my and my companions trip a complete success. We all join in complimenting Miss Hoskins and wishing we will have the honor of seeing her on our next flight.
    Signed, Mr. Loren Richard Hodge
The note from my supervisor, Jean Johnson, underneath says, "A wonderful recommendation Argie. Thank you! Jean."

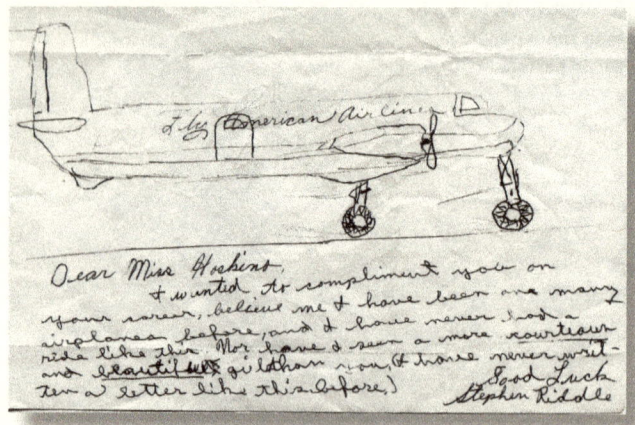

A passenger drew me this picture and wrote this note underneath:

Dear Miss Hoskins,
    I wanted to compliment you on your service. Believe me I have been on many airplanes before, and I have never had a ride like this. Nor have I seen a more courteous and beautiful girl than you. (I have never written a letter like this before.) Good Luck,
    Stephen Riddle

Passenger letter from flight number 663 from Houston to San Diego on September 3, 1958. It reads:

I have enjoyed my flight very well. And also your stewardesses are very alert and nice to the passengers and babies. Thank you,
    Signed, Mr. Frankie Jones
Note from my supervisor, Dottie, underneath says, "Argie— this is yours. Your file is credited. Thanks for being so pleasant and helpful. Dottie."

One passenger I vividly remember is Dr. George M. Lamsa, a native Assyrian. He and many other Eastern Christians feel that the Aramaic Bible is the only Bible. He worked on translating the Aramaic Peshitta into English, resulting in the Lamsa Bible. He was also the technical advisor on the film *The Big Fisherman*. After he asked about my beliefs, he told me that as he studied the Book of Mormon he felt it to be a legitimate writing from an interesting point of view. We had a nice talk with each other on the plane. Afterward he sent me this letter with a small book containing Psalm 23.

The note and package I received from Dr. George M. Lamsa. The note reads:

Dear Miss Hoskins,
    Just a few lines to tell you how happy I was to talk to you and how much I enjoyed my trip on the plane. I am sending you a copy of a small book by me. I am sure you will enjoy reading it. I have written about 12 books and translated the Bible. You were so good to remember my name. Hope to have the pleasure of seeing you again.
    God's blessing be upon you,
    Sincerely yours,
    Signed, Geo. M. Lamsa

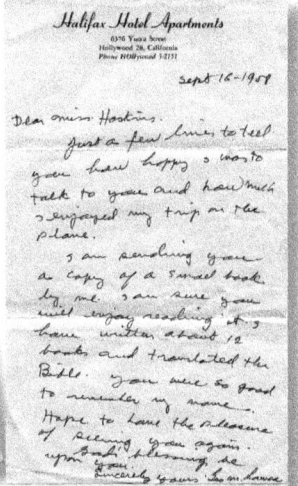

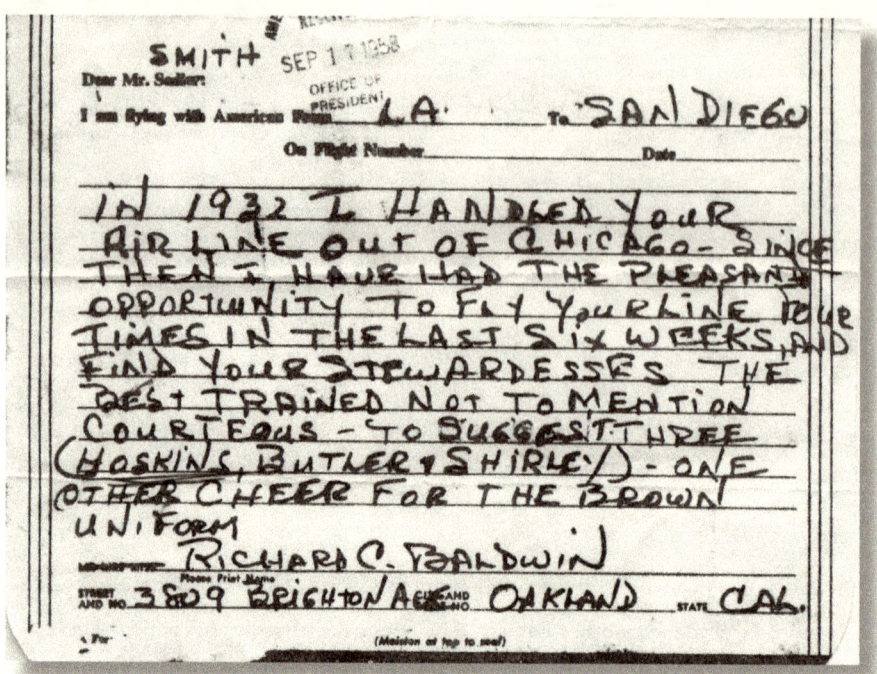

Passenger letter addressed to American Airlines' president, C. R. Smith, on a flight from Los Angeles to San Diego on September 17, 1958. It reads:

In 1932 I handled your airline out of Chicago. Since then I have had the pleasant opportunity to fly your line four times in the last six weeks, and find your stewardesses the best trained not to mention courteous. To suggest three (Hoskins, Butler, and Shirley) One other cheer for the brown uniform.
    Signed, Mr. Richard C. Baldwin

Right: C. R. Smith replied on September 18, 1958. His note reads:

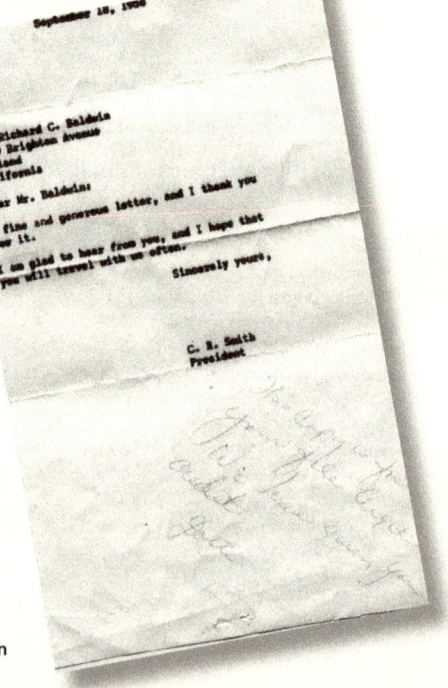

Dear Mr. Baldwin:
    A fine and generous letter, and I thank you for it. I am so glad to hear from you, and I hope that you will travel with us often.
    Sincerely yours,
    C. R. Smith, President

The note written below by my supervisor, Dottie, reads, "This copy is for your file Argie. We have given you credit. Dottie."

A passenger letter from flight number 663 from Houston to Los Angeles on September 26, 1958. It reads:

My husband and I have flown the Atlantic seven times and all through the U. S. We came from Trinidad, by the way, and we have enjoyed this flight more than any other. Stewardess Miss Hoskins was terrible sweet and most kind to us. I would like for you to tell her so for us.
Signed, Mrs. Gwen Plummer

The Plummers were so dear and generous. I enjoyed being their stewardess. Memories of passengers like this couple fill me with both regret and joy. Joy at the new friendships that were created on a flight, but regret that I only saw them for a moment in time. It is interesting to me how I was able to connect so closely to some people after such a short acquaintance. I can't help but feeling that somewhere, sometime, I will have the privilege of continuing the friendships I made in the sky.

Picture drawn for me by Nancy Ver Burg. Nancy and her family were delightful. Nancy spent her time on the plane productively—drawing this picture for me. That day I learned a lesson that when you give children tools for productivity, they are delighted.

Passenger letter from flight number 950 from Los Angeles to El Paso on October 23, 1958. It reads:

We particularly liked the comments by the pilot on the points of interest in flight, and the references to mechanical changes. Also your "Welcome Aboard" booklet had been enlarged since I last saw one, and I think the technical information about the plane, "hold," procedures, etc., is very interesting. The stewardesses were most courteous and attractive.
 Signed, (Mr. and) Mrs. Don C. McNamara.
The note below written by my supervisor, Dottie, reads, "Argie, Thanks again for your wonderful traits—Dottie. Another credit in file."

Passenger letter from flight number 961 from San Antonio to San Diego on December 10, 1958. It reads:

I certainly did enjoy the trip. I arrived so refreshed and especially enjoying our stewardess service so much. They were really nice.
 Signed, Mrs. Flora Henderson

Passenger letter from flight number 961 from El Paso to Los Angeles on December 14, 1958. It reads:

I think everything is just beautiful. It's my second time on a plane. Everything is going so nicely. The stewardesses are very cute and kind.
 Signed, Mrs. Edith Geress

The note along the side from my supervisor reads, "Miss A— these are A-plus and so are you. Many many thanks. Betty."

UNITED STATES AIR FORCE Oct. 24, 1958

Dear Argy,

You brought me here, you come and get me. I don't like it here.

I doubt if you'll remember me, but I'm one of the guys that was on flight 660, from L.A. to San Antonio, on the night of Oct 14th. And I'm also the guy who was dressed in the light blue suit. I'm from San Jose, Calif. Roger, Major, & I sat back in the lounge playing poker.

We never got to San Antonio on that flight, because of weather conditions. We by-passed San Antonio to Huston, then back to San Antonio. Gee, by the time we got there I was pretty sleepy. I'd had 1 hours sleep in 40 hours.

I imagine you put up with a lot of stuff that you had to put up with me, and I'm sorry, because I think you're a pretty nice kid. I just wish you were a little younger or me a little older. The reason I'm say this is because I don't really expect to hear from you or see you.

THE AIR FORCE WRITES VIA AIR MAIL

(over)

The front and back of a letter from a passenger named Jonesy written on October 24, 1958. It reads:

Dear Argy,

You brought me here, you come and get me. I don't like it here.

I doubt if you'll remember me, but I'm one of the guys that was on flight 660 from L. A. to San Antonio, on the night of Oct. 14th. And I'm also the guy who was dressed in the light blue suit. I'm from San Jose, Calif. Roger, Major, and I sat back in the lounge playing poker.

We never got to San Antonio on that flight, because of weather conditions. We by passed San Antonio to Houston, then back to San Antonio. Gee, by the time we got there I was pretty sleepy. I'd had 1 hours sleep in 40 hours.

I imagine you put up with a lot of stuff that you had to put up with me, and I'm sorry, because I think you're a pretty nice kid. I just wish you were a little younger or me a little older. The reason I'm say this is because I don't really expect to hear from you or see you. (over)

I wrote this letter for 2 reasons. I felt like writing and I wanted to apologize for the way I acted on the plane.

I'll say one other thing before I close, you were the nicest stewardess we had on all our flights, and you're the first person that treated me like I wasn't dirt, thanks and I'm sorry for my punkish actions.

Yours Truly,
Jonesy

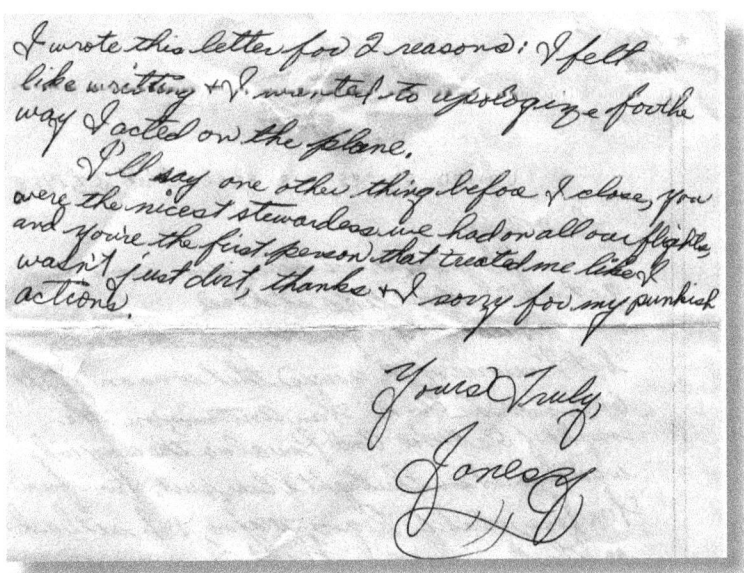

I do not naturally have a talent for patience. But when I read this letter from Jonesy I felt that perhaps I was improving in that area. I firmly believe that weaknesses, which we all have, can become strengths. As I look back on my life I've seen how this has been accomplished. The lessons in patience I learned while flying not only helped in situations like Jonesy described but also brought me through the years of rearing four sons and teaching special education.

In addition to the letters from passengers, I once received a letter from the White House! No, we didn't have the President on our flight. E. R. Quesada, the Special Assistant to the President, wrote me in response to a letter I had sent regarding air safety. One day en route between Tucson and Los Angeles, a military jet invaded our commercial space. The crew was concerned, as were many of the passengers, so I wrote to the White House about it. This is the letter I received back. I considered it a responsible and informative reply.

THE WHITE HOUSE
WASHINGTON

June 9, 1958

Miss A. E. Hoskins
5904 South Wooster
Los Angeles 56, California

Dear Miss Hoskins:

    The President has asked me to reply to your recent letter, and to thank you for your interest and support in our efforts towards solving the many air safety problems we now face.

    I am sure you are aware of the fact that the rules under which military and civil aircraft operate in the United States are identical. However, in the past the military has imposed even more severe restrictions on their aircraft than are generally applied to civil aircraft. Many people have the impression that the military operate outside of the rules established by the civilian control agencies.

    In recent weeks, both the civil and military branches of both Government and private aviation have taken a series of interim steps to increase safety in the air, until a more permanent and lasting solution is available.

    As of May 23, the military has voluntarily submitted their jet aircraft which plan to operate under 20,000 feet to the positive control procedures of the Civil Aeronautics Administration. As of May 28, the military has forbidden their jet aircraft from operating into and out of civil airports, unless specifically authorized by the airport management and the appropriate military commands.

    The airline industry has voluntarily agreed to place all flights operating above 10,000 feet under the positive control of the Civil Aeronautics Administration.

    The Civil Aeronautics Administration and the Civil Aeronautics Board have expedited action to create, as of June 15, high-altitude transcontinental airways between 17,000 and 22,000 feet, in which all civil and military aircraft will be under the positive control of the Civil Aeronautics Administration.

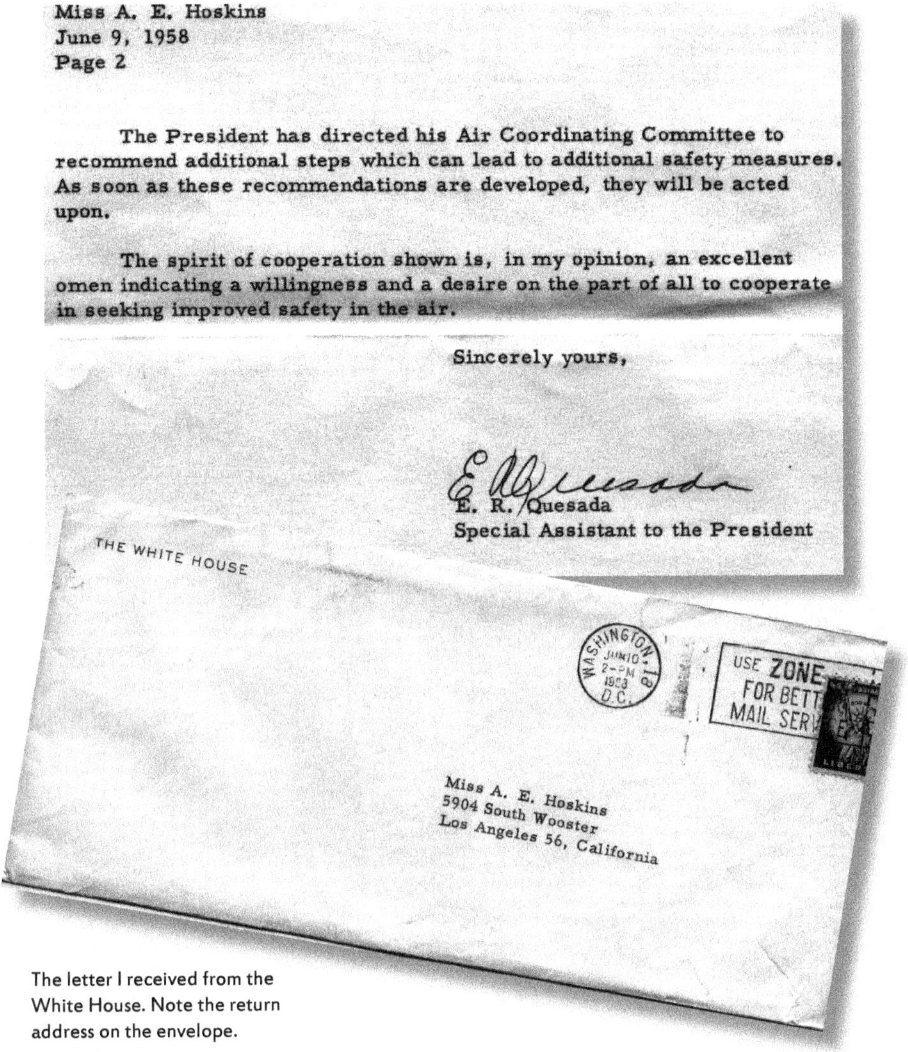

Miss A. E. Hoskins
June 9, 1958
Page 2

The President has directed his Air Coordinating Committee to recommend additional steps which can lead to additional safety measures. As soon as these recommendations are developed, they will be acted upon.

The spirit of cooperation shown is, in my opinion, an excellent omen indicating a willingness and a desire on the part of all to cooperate in seeking improved safety in the air.

Sincerely yours,

E. R. Quesada
Special Assistant to the President

THE WHITE HOUSE

Miss A. E. Hoskins
5904 South Wooster
Los Angeles 56, California

The letter I received from the White House. Note the return address on the envelope.

One of my favorite parts about layovers was staying in fancy hotels, little homes away from home. For an Animas girl, staying in a hotel was a real treat. I thrilled whenever I walked into one and thought, "Oh, my! People really stay in these places!" When we went on vacation as a child, we wouldn't dare look in the doors of these beautiful old gracious homes of hospitality. As a stewardess, I well remember staying at the Dallas, Phoenix, New York, and Detroit hotels. I also vividly remember my hotel in Boston. It was within walking distance of the Boston Commons and the Old North Church.

The Adams Hotel in Phoenix, Arizona

The Sheraton-Cadillac Hotel in Detroit, Michigan

The Adolfphus Hotel in Dallas, Texas

The Coronado Hotel in St. Louis, Missouri

Left: The Belmont Plaza Hotel in New York City, New York

Right: The Morrison Hotel in Chicago, Illinois

My busy life was grounded in my faith. On Sundays, I often found myself in many different cities. If time permitted I would rush to church to give thanks. I am grateful for the wonderful experiences that I was privileged to have as I met thought-provoking people who added a depth to my understanding of the world and the diverse population of our culture. I appreciated enriching my view of my brothers and sisters as they expressed their beliefs far beyond the boundaries of what I thought that life was all about. The weekly meetings both here and there helped me forge the strength to be me. I found that caring for people of different cultures and backgrounds has influenced my whole life.

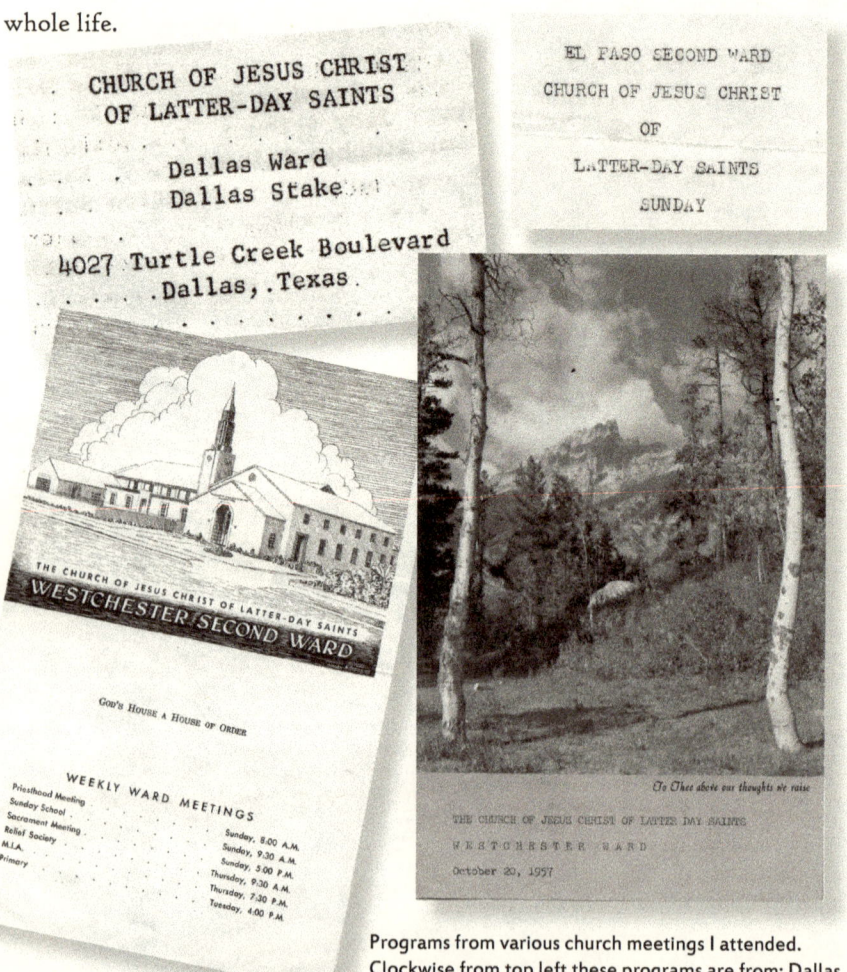

Programs from various church meetings I attended. Clockwise from top left these programs are from: Dallas, Texas; El Paso, Texas; and Westchester in L. A., California.

WESTWOOD SECOND WARD
Bishop Pat H. Luke, Presiding
October 4, 1959

SUNDAY SCHOOL - 11:30 A.M.
TESTIMONY AND FAST DAY SERVICE
Bishop Pat H. Luke, Conducting

Organ Prelude ..... Marjorie Edgel (A)
                   Shauna Scanlon (B)
"Lord, Accept Our True Devotion" ..... No. 101

Invocation

Blessings and Confirmations
Sacrament Hymn ..... No. 217
"While of These Emblems We Partake"

Sacrament Gem ..... Stephen Jensen (A)
                   Jerolyn Bleak (B)
"Adam fell that men might be, and men
are that they might have joy."

Sacrament Service ..... Aaronic Priesthood
To Membership of the Church

Inspirational Talk ..... Rita Renfro (A)
Concert Recitation ..... Course #15
    Carol Nilsen - Teacher
Inspirational Talk ..... Janice Jensen (B)
Concert Recitation ..... Course #7
    Tomiko Shiroto - Teacher

Inspirational Talks ..... Mavis Geismar (A)
                         Frank Edgel

Closing Hymn
    "When Upon Life's Bill...

Benediction

Reassembly for Testimony Mee...

M.I.A. SUNDAY EVENING SERVICE

Organ Prelude ..... Janet Thomson
Opening Hymn ..... Congregation
    "Sweet Is the Work, My God, My King"
Invocation ..... Howard Winn
Introduction ..... Arthur Wallace, MIA Superintendent

"THAT THERE MIGHT BE PEACE" (PSALMS)
"The Lord Is My Shepherd" ..... Choir
    23rd Psalm by Felix Mendelssohn
    Patricia M. Haglund - Director
Marjorie Cheney, Pianist - Janet Thomson, Organist

Reader 1 ..... Mary Lu Millardson
Jan Worley, "Blessed is the man whose delight is the
    law of the Lord."
Reader 2 ..... Clifford DeGraw
Reader 3 ..... Judy Madsen
Janet Cartwright - "God is our refuge and strength."
Reader 4 ..... Oscar Larson

"The Lord is a Mighty God" ..... Choir
    95th Psalm by Albert Hay Malttee
Reader 5 ..... Rita Renfro
Eldon Lloyd - "The righteous shall inherit the
    earth and dwell therein forever."
Reader 6 ..... William Treu
Reader 7 ..... Lynn Tanner
Sandra Taylor - "The mouth of the righteous speaketh
    wisdom."
Reader 8 ..... Jens Madsen
Reader 9 ..... Louise Rolapp

CHURCH OF JESUS CHRIST OF LATTER-DAY SAINTS
MANHATTAN WARD, NEW YORK CITY
SUNDAY, APRIL 12, 1959

SUNDAY SCHOOL 10:30 A.M.

PRELUDE ..... Joyce Gibson
GREETING ..... A. Lee Petersen
HYMN 135 O Holy Word of Truth and Love
INVOCATION
SONG PRACTICE ..... conducted by Dick Oldroyd
TWO AND ONE-HALF MINUTE TALKS ..... Clara Neilsen
                                     Morten Neilsen
SACRAMENTAL HYMN 271 O Lord of Hosts
SACRAMENTAL GEM ..... Toni Petersen
    "And Jesus said unto them, I am the bread of
    life: he that cometh to me shall never hun-
    ger; and he that believeth on me shall never
    thirst." (John 6:35.)
SACRAMENT OF THE LORD'S SUPPER

SEPARATION FOR CLASSES
Gospel Doctrine ..... Chapel ..... Albert Woodbury
Gospel Message ..... Rec. Hall ..... Martin Mals
Gospel Essentials ..... Ward Library ..... Robert Am...
Genealogy ..... R.S. Room ..... Neil Thomp...
Course 11 (11-14) ..... Balcony ..... Maria Voj...
Course 7 (8-10) ..... Old Library ..... Clyde Hei...
                                         Bishop
ANNOUNCEMENTS
HYMN 3 A Mighty Fortress
BENEDICTION
POSTLUDE ..... Joyce Gi...

The top program is from Westwood in L. A., California. Below is the front and back of a program from Phoenix, Arizona.

Along with flying to New York often, I flew into El Paso a lot. The agents were friendly there, and they would ask me about Bertha (Bertie) Candelaria. She was a stewardess I loved to fly with and was an El Paso hometown girl. Sometime after I quit flying Bertie became a stewardess supervisor in Los Angeles. She was a no nonsense gal with a heart of gold. I viewed her as an American Airlines social worker. There wasn't such a role, but she embodied the values which pushed her into social issues. She was a solid supporter of principles. She eventually married a man who was similarly minded, Fernando Oaxaca. He was a man of passion for his country and maintained a strong conviction to his principles. They both had unmatched dedication, loyalty, and patriotic fervor and devoted their lives to their love of America.

During my layovers in El Paso my Aunt Boo would come to pick me up, no matter what hour I touched down, and take me to the airport again in the early morning hours before dawn. In between, she took me home, doted over me, and gave me lots of hugs. It was good ole' southern hospitality all around, even down to the big bowl of fruit on the dining room table. She would get upset if I didn't bid a flight to El Paso. My favorite cousin, Effie, and her brother, Freddie Scott, were little and felt like younger siblings, and oh, how I loved them. Effie would call her bed "Argie's bed" when I was there. In every way, Effie was my little sister and I her big sister.

Aunt Boo and I had always been close, and she couldn't have been more excited to have me flying for American Airlines. While I enjoyed a nice home-cooked meal, the rest of the crew stayed at the Hilton Hotel downtown near the Mexican border.

The ranch where my folks lived was located between El Paso and Douglas, Arizona. From El Paso to Douglas, American Airlines' flight path took us right over the ranch. Mother knew the times when I'd be working the flight that flew over the ranch house, and she would take her apron out and wave to the plane as we flew over. Our plane would be descending into the area of Douglas at an altitude which made Mama visible though the plane's window,

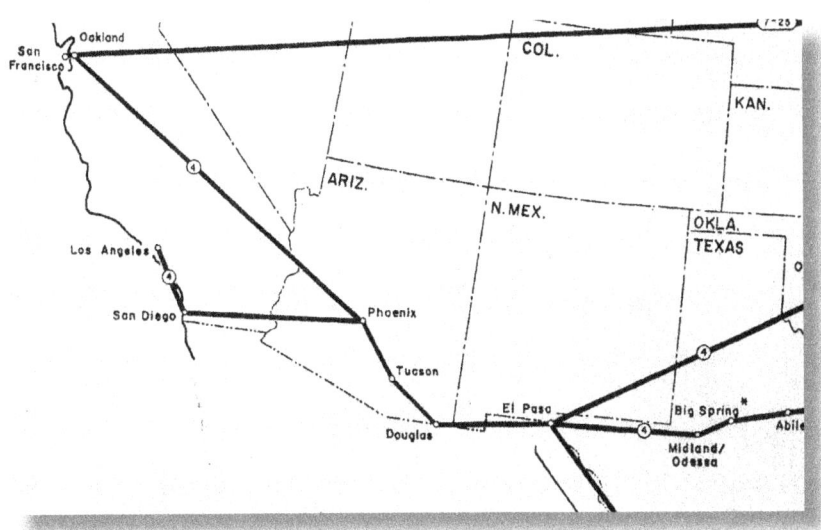

The route of my flights from Los Angeles to El Paso where I'd fly over Mama.

and I would hurry to the window to see her. One day a passenger asked me what I was looking at outside the window. She laughed when I said, "My mother!"

On another occasion, as we flew over the ranch, the pilot banked the plane to the right and then to the left as a salute to Mama. I looked out. Yes, there was Mama, waving a rather large white dish towel, or cup towel, as we called it.

"What's happening?" voiced a passenger.

"Well, we just aim to please," I replied. Little did anyone know that the person we were pleasing was that little lady on the ground waving to her daughter. If I were working a night flight I knew that mother, with her sleepy head, would be thinking of me as I worked my flight thinking of her.

It always did my soul good to get that glimpse of home. As the plane flew on I'd picture all the activities Mama could be doing in that small house, making it inviting with her homemade bread and pickled peaches, washing clothes in the wringer washing machine, gathering and candling eggs to be taken to the market in Lordsburg, wringing off a chicken's head for dinner, or hurrying out to the garden to dig up some carrots. I smiled as I thought of this life I knew so well before I started on my journey away from Animas Valley.

Mother was pleased that my heart had wrapped itself around this dream and had still retained my love of home and being an Animas Valley girl.

And then I would think of Daddy and how he would hold the soil of Animas Valley in his huge hands or skillfully and artistically repair the windmills among the puzzle of dust devils, cockleburs, thistles, devil's claws, and tumbleweeds. The rain, snow, or dirt would be blowing in his face, or the sun would be beating down. He worked hard. I never heard him complain. Not once. I could picture him standing with his arms resting on the old wooden gate next to the barbed wire fence and see the lines of time both in the wood and on his face. I often wondered what was in those lines that kept him from enjoying the invitation to "come fly with me." Even now it is such a vivid memory, seeing him standing there with a distant look in his eyes. I wondered what joy came to him as he stood looking at Animas Peak in the far distance. Daddy what were you thinking? Daddy never did fly on an airplane, but he was proud of me and liked hearing about all my adventures.

Can you even imagine the threads of emotion I felt flying over this land below me? How I wished that I could tell my passengers about my life down there. Life that captured the colors of history, the landscape, and the feelings of the wide open spaces—the very thought of which filled my heart with the tears and laughter of nostalgia. It epitomized the words of Daddy's favorite song, "Don't Fence Me In." I rejoiced that I grew up in the southern area of the "Land of Enchantment."

On May 6, 1958, I received my letter stating that my probationary period was completed and that I was now a full-fledged stewardess!

And on July 14, 1958, I had another checkride. My supervisor this time was Jean Johnson who became my very good friend. Here, finally, were the *excellents* for which I had been striving.

INTEROFFICE CORRESPONDENCE
AAL FORM C-177F—10-56—175M—©—PRINTED IN U.S.A.

AMERICAN AIRLINES

DATE 5/6/58

TO Stwds. A. Hoskins - LAX

ATTENTION

FROM Supervisor of Stewardesses - LAX

SUBJECT Probationary Letter

REFERENCE

Congratulations, Argie, on the successful completion of your probationary period. As of November 4, you became eligible for seniority privileges and as of December 4, entitled to the following company benefits, paid vacation, sick leave, 1500 miles of non-revenue transportation, unlimited half fare mileage and an increase in salary.

During the past months, your records have shown a steady improvement in procedural technique. You have been most cooperative in your attitude and have accepted constructive suggestions well. You have received several passenger commendation letters, which indicate the fine job you are doing in the contact and passenger service phase of your work.

Argie, it is a great personal satisfaction to welcome you as a full fledged stewardess to the "AA Family". I'm sure you will continue to strive to uphold the high standards of American Airlines and its Stewardess Department.

Sally Robinson

The letter stating that my probationary period was completed.

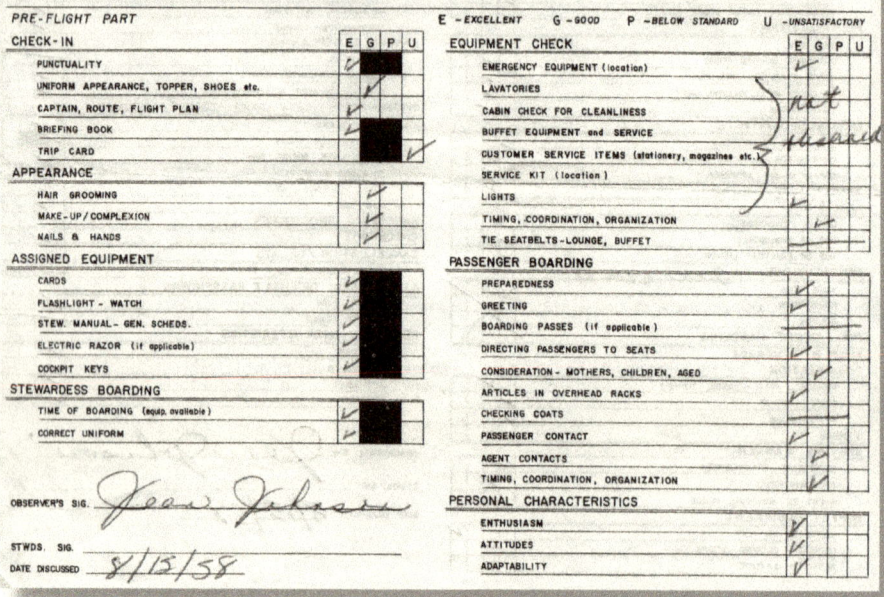

July 14, 1958 checkride with Jean Johnson and lots of *excellent*s!

Remarks:

Together" cards on every flight, except those where seats are reserved or where airport seat selection is available. These were not distributed on this flight.

4) As we discussed, it is a courtesy to the men who remove the jugs at the buffet on termination that you turn off the switches at least twenty minutes prior to landing.

Thanks for a nice trip!

Jean

IN-FLIGHT PART	E	G	P	U
PRE-TAKE-OFF				
PA TAXI-AWAY		✓		
SEATBELTS				
COMPLETE COATS				
NAMES & DESTINATION	✓			
COORDINATION, TIMING, ORDER	✓			
FLT- PROCEDURES				
TAKE-OFF	✓			
CUSTOMER SERVICE ITEMS		✓		
OFFER. MAGS., PILLOWS etc.		✓		
RE-OFFER MAGS., PILLOWS etc.		✓		
COORDINATION	✓			
PASSENGER CONTACTS				
CTC. MANY AS POSSIBLE		✓		
CONVERSATION ABILITY and MANNER OF SPEECH		✓		
USE OF NAMES - APPROACH		✓		
TEMPERATURE CONTROL				
LIGHTS				
USE OF OVERHEADS	✓			
USE OF INDIVIDUALS		✓		
USE OF LAVATORY LIGHTS	✓			
PA TECHNIQUE *2nd stwd*				
VOICE TONE			X	
ENUNCIATION			X	
VOLUME			X	
PRR - TICKET HANDLING				
FOOD & BEVERAGE				
ORGANIZATION				
PERSONAL PREP. - HANDS, TOPPER		✓		
BUFFET - SET-UP	✓			
COORDINATION	✓			
TIMING	✓			
SERVING MANNER				
EXPRESSION - GRACIOUSNESS	✓			
PRESENTATION		✓		
ALERT TO INDIVIDUAL NEEDS	✓			
BUFFET EQUIPMENT				
SWITCHES ON - OFF			✓	✓
OPENING - CLOSING DOORS		✓		
RETAINER LATCHES	✓			

E - EXCELLENT   G - GOOD   P - BELOW STANDARD   U - UNSATISFACTORY

	E	G	P	U
PRE-LANDING				
PA & INDIVIDUAL INFO.		✓		
SO CARDS - CHANGE SEATS				
RETURN COATS - ARTICLES				
SEATBELTS	✓			
NO SMOKING - SIT DOWN	✓			
COORDINATION - TIMING	✓			
LANDING & DEPLANING				
PA TAXI-IN	✓			
GOODBYE COMMENTS - NAMES		✓		
POSITION, MANNER & APPEAR DOOR	✓			
INTERM. STOPS - CREW CHNGE - TERM. PROCEDURES				
EQUIP. READY				
LOST ARTICLE CHECK				
CABIN, LAVS, BUFFET TIDY	✓			
SO CARDS IN SEATS	✓			
RELAY PASSENGER INFO	✓			
NEW SAC				
EMERGENCY PROCEDURES	✓			
CHECK OUT	✓			
CANCELLATION / DELAYS				
PSGRS. INFORMED / CARED FOR				
ILL, INJURED, DIFFICULT PASSENGERS				
PROPER CARE		✓		
PROPER FORMS				
PERSONAL CHARACTERISTICS				
INITIATIVE	✓			
EXPRESSION	✓			
ATTITUDES	✓			
INTEREST	✓			

OBSERVER'S SIG. *Jean Johnson*

STWDS. SIG. _____

DATE DISCUSSED 8/15/58

Above: Me in my borrowed dress, as Gary Crosby and I dance the Christmas evening away at the Palladium Ballroom on Sunset Boulevard.

Left: A flyer about the Bonaires that they signed for me. The notes on the bottom read, "Argie! Hope you like our new record 'Rock N' Roll Olara' Best wishes, Tom Powers" and "Argie! Hope we see you again sometime. Its so rough I can't hold this pen!
 Our very best wishes. Happy Landings, Pat Dougherty, 8/6/58."

Chapter Eight
VIP Passengers before Jet Travel

Before each flight, we received a VIP list that told us which Very Important Persons would be flying with us that day. This was very helpful for me because I didn't always know who was VIP and who wasn't—which was a good thing for me because I was so nervous at first!

After we read through the list and other briefing materials, we would look in the lavatories for stowaways. I never found one, but we took this precaution so we would not chance blowing up the plane while it was being fueled. Although passengers could smoke on the plane after the seat belt went off, they couldn't before, and a few would sneak into the lavatory to get a smoke. That could blow up the plane, but some people didn't understand why they could smoke in the air but not on the ground. Once, I smelled some cigar smoke and we delayed takeoff until we could verify that everyone was in their seat.

Before takeoff, we went with clipboard in hand to each seated passenger and asked for their name and destination. Along the way there could be many stops with passengers getting on and off the flight, and we needed to know who was going where so we could wake the sleeping ones if they needed to get off. If there was time for passengers to get off the plane and back on before the next leg of the trip, we would need to place a reserve sign in their seat.

I got to meet some famous people up there in the sky! I didn't just meet them though—I served them meals, helped them get comfortable, and had fun and insightful conversations with them. Here is a list of some of the VIP passengers with whom I flew before jet travel.

STEPHEN BOYD

Stephen Boyd

Stephen Boyd was a young actor when he boarded American Airlines. He was one of the first actors I had on board. He seemed shy to me. I will always remember him because I felt like I wanted to know him as a person. When I was flying we made sure to take down the names of our passengers. We did our best to memorize their names and then figure out ways to engage them in conversation. If or when we had them on another flight, we then had something to talk about for an opener. I didn't get an invitation to visit with the strong, handsome Stephen Boyd, but I did get a sideward smile as the seat belt sign went on for the landing.

Stephen Boyd was very busy making movies while I was flying, including: *Seven Waves Away* (1957), *Island in the Sun* (1957), *Seven Thunders* (1957), *The Night Heaven Fell* (1958), *The Bravados* (1958), *Woman Obsessed* (1959), *The Best of Everything* (1959), and *Ben-Hur* (1959).

HOPE LANGE

Hope Lange

On the same flight with Stephen Boyd was Hope Lange. She was a few years older then I, however she looked somewhat younger. She had a sweet personality, and I enjoyed her being on the plane.

I had seen Hope Lange in *Peyton Place*, which I remembered being an emotional movie. It dealt with the issue of abuse. I had never experienced such, so this movie opened my eyes, but it was so disturbing to me that I vowed I would never again go to any movie that would stir me into such emotional distress. The emotion it conveyed worked for Hope Lange though, because she received an Oscar nomination for her role in it.

ROBERT GOULET

Robert Goulet

Robert Goulet was so easy to visit with on that late evening flight. He was awake and I took the opportunity to visit with his baritone voice. His singing had won him American Grammy and Tony Awards. He also won the Theatre World Award. Two of his songs that are my favorites are "Do You Hear What I Hear" and "If Ever I Would Leave You."

DANA ANDREWS

Dana Andrews

Dana Andrews was an American actor in the 1940s and 1950s. He got on the plane and immediately crawled under his seat and went to sleep. I gave him a pillow for more comfort. This was before the jet days, and one could stuff oneself under the seats. Just roll into a ball with a pillow and blanket and you would be all set. He slept until I awakened him to sit up and belt up. He was pleasant.

Dana was an activist with moral conviction toward fighting alcoholism as a member of the National Council on Alcoholism. He spoke out against using one's body to obtain roles in movies. Since my brother, C. L., was involved with the industry at this time, I had heard something about that.

GENE TIERNEY

Gene Tierney

One evening, I boarded American Airlines in El Paso to find one of the most beautiful and apparently troubled ladies I ever met, Gene Tierney. After the seat belt sign went off, she walked up and down the aisle of the plane all the way to Los Angeles. I asked her if I could help and she told me that she was ill. Life had been hard for her, and she was very discouraged with her life. Her presence made me very sad. She was not arrogant or proud, just seemingly grateful for limited conversation. She was so beautiful and tender. I remember her being the most gorgeous actress on stage and in the movies.

ROBERT CULP

Robert Culp

Robert Culp was another actor I had with me on a flight from Los Angeles to El Paso. His agent asked if they could take my picture with him. I agreed, and after the photo shoot, the agent said, "Give me your address, and we will send a copy of the picture." I don't think I ever got it, but at least he has my picture!

DALE ROBERTSON

Dale Robertson

Dale Robertson was an actor who made his name in television Westerns in the 1950s and 1960s. He was another passenger whom I got to know on a casual level. He often flew on American Airlines to go to horse races at the Ruidoso Downs Race Track. He was a really nice man.

Dale was on my flight once when we experienced a real life drama. One evening, flying back from El Paso to Los Angeles, I boarded to find a problem with one of the passengers who had gotten on the flight in Houston. She was eager to tell me her story. She had fallen in love with a man of another faith. They had met in Europe that summer and had planned a marriage. She had gone to Houston to meet his parents. While visiting, the parents announced that they would disown their son if he married her. She reported that it was because she was not of the family's faith. So the love of her life put her on the plane bound for Los Angeles. She was very despondent and took a lot of pills.

About half way to Los Angeles, she got up and came to the buffet where I had positioned myself, across the aisle from where she was sitting. Dale Robertson was sitting in the seat in front of the buffet. The lady lunged for the door of the plane, pushing me out of her way. Immediately, Dale came to my rescue, helping me get the lady back to her seat.

He calmed her and sat with her the rest of the trip. After reporting the situation to the pilot, he came back to the cabin to assess that we had the situation under control. The captain radioed ahead for help, and she received help when we landed. From this experience I learned that religion can destroy as well as weld relationships depending on how it is used. So sad!

DEAN MARTIN

Dean Martin

I loved watching Dean Martin and Jerry Lewis as a musical and comedy team, so it was exciting to have them both on board separately after their breakup and to see that they had moved on with their developing talents.

Dean was an actor with John Wayne in the film *Rio Bravo*. He was traveling back and forth from Los Angeles to the Old Tucson Studios, just outside Tucson, Arizona. I was working the flights from Los Angeles to El Paso, and at that time American Airlines had a stop in Tucson. We talked on many flights. Dean and I became more than passenger and stewardess—I knew his name, of course, but he also knew *my* name. We visited, laughed, and connected with energy. During one conversation, he told me, "You will never be a singer because you talk through your nose." The nerve! I practiced talking, but he only reiterated, "Yep, you won't make it."

Dean invited me to go places a couple times, but I never did go. He invited me out to see the Old Tucson set, and he invited me to Las Vegas to see him in a show at the Sands Hotel. He was often accompanied by a Mr. Grey whom he introduced as his agent. I loved getting to know Dean Martin. Once he told me he drove by the Latter-day Saint Temple on Santa Monica Boulevard and told me that if he weren't what he is, he would be the same religion as I. Dean also told me once that the image he often portrayed of being a drunk was "only that; an image." Dean had a one of a kind voice. And he was a kind, sensitive gentleman with a tender heart. He reminded me so much of my brother—their personalities were so much alike.

Dean was a member of the "Rat Pack," a partying group of show business friends. I didn't follow their reputation, but knew they were out there somewhere ripping through the world of entertainment and enjoying themselves.

Dean carried his Italian-American charm into the movies and television, but for me, it was his voice that scratched my heart. I don't have a favorite Dean Martin song. I thrilled to all of them, though "Return to Me," "Memories are Made of This," "Everybody Loves Somebody," "Mambo Italiano," "Sway," "Volare," "Ain't That a Kick in the Head," and "That's Amore" are among the best of the best.

MAUREEN O'HARA

Maureen O'Hara

Maureen O'Hara was a famous red-headed beauty who acted and sang her way into passionate roles. I remembered her acting with John Wayne in *The Quiet Man*. There was a certain magic between the two. It didn't seem to be romance, but certainly a relationship between two good friends. I don't remember much about this beautiful lady on my flight; I didn't have much conversation with her. But the one thing that I remember is the energy which I felt as she walked down the aisle. There was nothing passive about her demeanor. I felt she was in charge!

GARY CROSBY

Gary Crosby

I met Gary Crosby, son of the famous actor and singer Bing Crosby and an actor in his own right, on another of my flights. He asked me out on a date, though he did not use his father's name as a way to get my attention. Our enjoyable date was during the Christmas season. The dress I wore was borrowed from my cousin. I picked it up in El Paso and returned it on a later trip. Gary and I went to the Palladium Ballroom on Sunset Boulevard in Los Angeles. He was light on his feet as we danced through the evening and was a gentleman in every way.

PIER ANGELI

Pier Angeli

Pier Angeli, an Italian actress, was on her way to Juarez, Mexico, to get a divorce from Vic Damone—at least that is what she told me when I visited with her. She was sad, with her green eyes looking even greener when filled with tears. She was a very, very pretty lady! I often felt like crying after visiting with sad people. I just tried to show them I cared as best I could for the few minutes I had with them. Pier was kind. I had heard of her movies but had not seen them. She had appeared in *The Light Touch* with Stewart Granger, who was also one of my favorites.

LEE MARVIN

Lee Marvin

Lee Marvin's white hair seemed to identify him. The roles that he acted demanded his six-foot-two stature and his well-known gravelly voice. These were roles that were notably heroic.

As Lee Marvin was deplaning my flight, an older lady was having trouble getting herself and her things together to get off the plane. Without hesitation, Lee didn't just offer to help—he took her arm, her things, and away they went. She was so pleased, and he was a gentleman in action. I thought, "This is the aggressive, tough actor?" I am certain that older lady had no idea who was helping her with her bags and was so concerned for her safety. I found that he was a dear man, such a real and caring person and one of the jewels I met during my flying career.

THE AMES BROTHERS

Clockwise from top:
Ed, Vic, Joe, and Gene

The Ames Brothers, Vic, Joe, Gene, and Ed, were handsome gentlemen, and they boarded the plane looking like they had just played a game of tennis: white shorts, tennis shoes, and racket in hand. I immediately fell for the tall one. The Ames Brothers were a singing quartet famous in the 1950s for their traditional pop music hits.

GENE FULLMER

Gene Fullmer

This world champion boxer was so nice. We had something in common: our religion. It was fun visiting with him. Eventually his nephew Troy Fullmer would become my son Randy's good friend.

JANE RUSSELL

Jane Russell

When I had Jane Russell on the flight, I was still shy about talking to VIPs. All I could do was smile and give my best service. If the passengers were not on the VIP list, it was easier for me to visit. Somewhat later, I realized that we are more alike than different and that service was the foundation of relationships. Everyone, no matter who, wants the pillow to be offered, not to have to ask for it. And once I'd served someone it was easier to talk.

I remember Jane Russell most for the movies she starred in opposite Robert Mitchum. Mostly because my first boyfriend when I was 15 years old looked a lot like Robert. She also starred with other famous actors such as Frank Sinatra, Groucho Marx, Vincent Price, Hoagy Carmichael, and Jeff Chandler. A couple of her films that were famous while I was flying were *Gentlemen Marry Brunettes* and *The Revolt of Mamie Stover*. Jane Russell was something else and a lot of it!

Other famous people with whom I flew include Billy Eckstine, a jazz musician whose music introduced me to other avenues of music; Jayne Mansfield, an actress who worked on Broadway and in Hollywood (she was another

Marilyn Monroe, only more glamorous—I felt sad when she was killed in an auto accident); The Bonaires, a singing group made up of Alan, Eddy, Tom, and Pat who harmonized Rock 'n Roll; The Mills Brothers, who released over 2,000 recordings and were probably the best singing group of their time ("Standing on the Corner" was my favorite;) and Gene Kelly, who will always be remembered for his incredible contribution to the public for entertaining us through dance and choreography.

What a thrill it was to get a glimpse into the lives of these people who made such a profound impact on American culture.

Billy Eckstine, The Mills Brothers, Jayne Mansfield, and Gene Kelly.

After a while, I became less concerned about myself and far more interested in the needs and feeling of our passengers. I became what I desired to become: a caring, connected, and unselfish person. As passengers boarded, I could feel the emotions they brought with them. Some were experiencing loss and sadness while some were on the usual business trip and preoccupied with the task ahead. Others were on an exciting journey for the first time, and some were frightened and scared. My heart reached out especially to them because I felt the same way during my first months of flying. It was not uncommon to say, "Hello," to an enthusiastic actor, actress, military man, or elderly person; a varied and colorful passenger wanting to be left alone or a lonely person desiring to talk to someone. No matter who it was I spoke to, we often found a common ground of conversation. It was an enthralling learning experience as my social maturity unfolded, and I learned that overall we have more in common than we have differences.

Top to bottom: A 707 in the air, photo courtesy of Beth Macatee Snyder, Captain Macatee's daughter; close-up of Argie before the inaugural flight; News clipping highlighting the crew of the inaugural flight, photo courtesy of Beth Macatee Snyder.

Chapter Nine
The First Jet Flight

Public relations appearances soon became part of my job. My supervisor Jeanne Folk was influential in giving me this honor, and I'll be forever grateful to her for having confidence in my ability to represent American Airlines. My first public relation (PR) experience was appearing at a monument which American Airlines was installing in Texas. It felt fitting for my first PR assignment to be in El Paso, right there in my own area of the Southwest.

I accepted invitations to represent American on many occasions such as telethons, Rotary Club meetings, high school career days, and the like. I enjoyed contributing in that fashion, never turning down an opportunity to serve. Meeting people and talking to them became second nature to me—me, who used to be so timid and lacking in confidence. I had to learn to talk with others, and it started with me learning to just move on and get over it or through it. And I found it was fun!

I also learned that if the attention is focused on me, I have a very difficult time with conversation. If attention is focused on others and what they know and are willing to share, then chatting is so very pleasant. Expressive language processing has always been a challenge for me, but receptive language is a gift sent from Heaven.

I was kept quite busy with PR assignments along with my regular stewardess duties. My journal from that time captures some of that—it is interesting to read it now. Some of these events, written down on ordinary days in my own handwriting, have proven to be historic.

American Airlines' monument atop Guadalupe Peak in Texas. The newspaper clipping contains the caption, "Monument to be put atop 8,751 foot high Guadalupe Peak, the highest mountain in Texas, by American Airlines honoring pioneer airmen and stagecoach drivers who conquered the dangerous pass, is pointed out by William E. Swift, El Paso, to Stewardess Argie Hoskins." The article that accompanied the picture is titled "American Airlines to Place Monument" and reads:

American Airlines today announced that it would place a monument atop Guadalupe Peak, the highest mountain in Texas, in honor of pioneer airmen whose courage and steel nerve, and devotion to duty at the dawn of commercial aviation contribute greatly to the development of the airline.

The monument will be dedicated September 29 [1958] at Pine Springs, Culberson County, Texas, which is located at the summit of Guadalupe Pass, approximately 55 miles from Carlsbad, New Mexico, and 115 miles from El Paso, on Highway 180-62.

Pine Springs is the site of the "Pinery Station" a stop on the Butterfield Overland Mail, whose 100th anniversary is being celebrated this year by an auto caravan that left Tipton, Missouri, September 16 to retrace the original route to San Francisco.

It will reach Guadalupe Pass the exact day (September 29) the first transcontinental stage coach rolled through there one hundred years ago.

The plaque on the monument reads: "1858 through 1958. Dedicated to the airmen who, like the stage drivers before them, challenged the elements through this pass with the pioneer spirit and courage which resulted in a vast system of airline transport known as American Airlines."

Although the airliner of today cruises high above the Guadalupe range, it was considered one of the most formidable obstacles encountered by the pioneer pilots of two of America's predecessor companies—Texas Air Transport and Southern Air Transport. The same was true of the stage coach driver in 1858.

Dignitaries attending the ceremony will include a number of AA pilots, company officials, local residents from the area, and members of the Butterfield Overland Caravan.

Guadalupe Peak is part of the 73,000 acre ranch of J. C. Hunter, Jr., of Abilene. Hunter and Walter Glover of Pine Springs owned the site of the Pinery Station.

THURSDAY, JANUARY 1, 1959:

The Rose Parade was really beautiful with flowers, flowers, and more flowers. One float had an American Airlines 707 jet model all decked out in appropriate colors. Go American Airlines!

In stewardess school we were trained to serve on various propeller airplanes, but soon new technology caught up with us—jet airplanes were the future, and we were soon all being trained to serve on the new 707 jets. Everyone was excited by the prospect of serving on such new and cutting edge planes. The group of stewardesses I trained with was not very large. We had a lot of intensive work to accomplish to serve on our new 707. We needed to know what was what, where it was, how to use it, and when. The *when* part was the most pressing of the training because jet flight is a lot faster than propeller flight, and we needed to get the meal served before we landed—time was so short! The flights were now in jet mode, and in our training I heard more than once, "Hurry up, we're landing!"

We had been told that the first transcontinental jet flight would take place on January 25 on the beautiful Boeing 707, Flagship California. It was to be an important day in history, and we were going to be prepared for it. We worked tirelessly on public relations with all the big businesses in the Los Angeles area to get the word out. But even as the energy and excitement for the first flight grew and I worked more and more on PR and learned the ins and outs of the 707, I had no idea that the honor of working that first flight would come to me. In fact, none of us knew which stewardesses would be on the flight until eleven days before the big day.

WEDNESDAY, JANUARY 14, 1959:

Supervisor Jean called and gave me a very special assignment, "You and Claire (a roommate) are going from Los Angeles to New York on the 707 on the 25th and the 29th," which meant that we had been selected for the crew of the first commercial jet flight in America. WOW!

Having gone through the training for the 707, I knew this honor didn't come lightly. Those chosen had shown commitment, focus, and discipline. This was an honor. Again, the thought came, as it often had, "How do I multi-task and sequence everything the job demands correctly? Can I do it?" And again, the words of my wind-miller, cowboy father came comfortingly to mind, "Get up and amount to something, Sister." And I remembered the words of American Airlines President, C. R. Smith, "We strive to treat every customer with dignity and respect to make each person feel like the most important person in the world." And I thought, "Yes, I can do that!"

In the days after that phone call I could find myself thinking, "Me! On that flight? Wow!" I recall someone saying that the passenger letters we had received in addition to our excellent checkrides, our relationships with our staff of supervisors, and our performance on learning the new aircraft had all pointed the finger in our direction for being chosen to be on the flight. I also knew that my supervisor Jean was very grateful for the job I did with PR, helping out wherever it was needed, even before the big push to jets began. I don't know who was ultimately in charge of the decision or what exactly made them choose me, but I'm sure all of that helped. And I'm so grateful and honored to have been chosen.

There were always the little errands to take care of—get my hair cut and styled, get my uniform cleaned, make sure my shoes were in good repair, and keep myself in shape. Another item on my to-do list was to avoid a migraine. I'd had a migraine before that made me miss a flight where I could have met Rock Hudson, and I wanted to make sure that didn't happen again! I could usually avoid migraines by avoiding sugar, eating well, and getting enough rest. Getting enough rest was tricky because I was very busy working on flights and various PR assignments in preparation for the big day.

> THIS AND THAT . . . Westwood Second Ward's ARGI HOSKINS participated in an historical event Sunday when she was selected from among American Airlines stewardesses to accompany the Los Angeles to New York jet flight inaugurating four and one-half hour cross country service.

My ward (my local church congregation) printed up this notice about me in their bulletin.

FRIDAY, JANUARY 16, 1959:

I have been very busy doing public relations for American. I went with one of the American Airlines sales representatives to meet and deliver models of the 707 to VIPs in the LA area: President of a Stock Exchange, President and Vice President of California Bank, President of Citizen's Bank, leading advertising businesses, and President of Pacific Mutual.

This day was very exhilarating as we made our way down Spring Street, the "Wall Street of the West." I was awestruck by the historical buildings and the beauty, strength, unity, and dignity of their architecture.

MONDAY, JANUARY 19, 1959:

Mr. Scroggins, an American Airlines representative, and I met with Mayor Paulson, the publisher of the L. A. Times, and many individuals, such as the President of Southern California Edison Co., and others who would be on the Inaugural Flight. I am lucky to be on the Inaugural flight!

TUESDAY, JANUARY 20, 1959:

Today, I drove to Huntington Park to meet Mr. Hall, a sales manager for American Airlines. From there we drove to Fullerton to meet Dr. Arnold of Beckman Scientific Instruments, who was a pioneer in his field.

To this day, I remember the generosity and kindness of Dr. Beckman. He and I connected in a very special way. Me, a girl from Animas Valley! He and his wife, Mabel, were the "real" thing. The California Institute of Technology (Cal Tech) alumni association has this short bio about Dr. Beckman:

> Arnold O. Beckman, chairman emeritus of the Cal Tech Board of Trustees, and founder of Beckman Instruments, Inc., achieved international recognition for his accomplishments in industry, science, education, and civic affairs, founding his company in 1935 with the development of a pH meter that has become an indispensable tool for analytical chemists. Beckman saw his firm become a major international manufacturer of instruments and related products for medicine, science, industry, environmental technology, and many other fields.

Back to Huntington Park to dinner with Jay Dickie and then to Pasadena to meet Sidney Small. We went to Jet Propulsion Laboratory and met with the Nuclear Physics core staff of our country, including Dr. William Pickering.

In 1958, as Director of the Jet Propulsion Laboratory (JPL), Dr. Pickering led the successful effort to place the first U. S. satellite, Explorer 1, into Earth's orbit. The Cal Tech Speech Reference Collection has this to say about the JPL and Dr. Pickering:

> In January 1959, JPL was assigned the responsibility for the robotic exploration of the moon and planets. Under Pickering's direction, JPL supervised the Ranger missions returning the first close-up, high-resolution pictures of the lunar surface; he also supervised the Surveyor

soft-landers on the Moon; the Mariner missions to Mars and Venus; and the first gravity assist mission to Mercury, via Venus.

The JPL also designed the Viking Orbiters to Mars and designed and built the Voyager spacecraft for their mission to the outer planets.

Along with Dr. Pickering was Dr. Al Hibbs, a physicist, Dr. Val Larsen, Dr. Frank Goddard who was the California Scientist of the Year, and a number others of the team. I presented Dr. Pickering and Dr. Larsen with a miniature Boeing 707 model.

The Cal Tech Reference Collection says this about Dr. Goddard:

> Alumnus Frank E. Goddard Jr. (PhD '57), assistant director for research and development at Cal Tech's Jet Propulsion Laboratory received the NASA Exceptional Service Medal for outstanding performance in advancing the technology of automated spacecraft design.

After pictures, we journeyed on to see a Dr. Fay who is a teacher at CalTech.

It is amazing that I brushed shoulders with these busy and very involved individuals.

FRIDAY, JANUARY 23, 1959:

For our jet flight, we stayed in class all day long. We had our food service procedures today, which meant checking the buffet area for all needed items, what to turn on, what to turn off, all the food and beverage items for the flight including table clothes, wine and food menus, cocktail napkins, stirrers in preparation for a several course dining experience with special appetizers, salad, entree, dessert, and fruit candy.

If something was missing, we needed to know who to contact. Prior to that Friday we had been briefed on the emergency procedures.

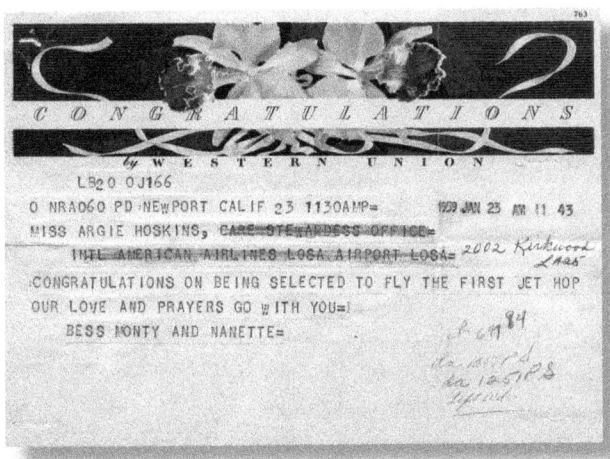

Telegram of congratulations from Beth, Monty, and Nanette Spain, the family with whom I lived when I first moved to California. It reads:

Congratulations on being selected to fly the first jet hop our love and prayers go with you,
Bess, Monty, and Nanette.

SATURDAY, JANUARY 24, 1959:

I went to the airport; we finally got on the jet after much delay. What an exciting day! I remember the feelings which flowed over me as I walked onto the aircraft. Thinking, "This is the real thing." Had my hair cut and fixed by Mr. Reid, very pleased. Came home after appointment and got ready for the flight.

This was the first time I had been on a real 707. We had practiced and been trained in a 707 mock-up. I was overwhelmed with its size. It was almost half the length of a football field. Knowing the next day would be the big one, I felt adrenaline rush through my being bringing an electrifying thrill.

On January 25, 1959, American Airlines became the first airline to offer coast-to-coast jet service with the Boeing 707. On this historic flight, I was

I still have my American Airlines Jet Training Boeing 707 card. It reads, "This certifies that Argie Hoskins is a qualified Stewardess on American's 707 Jet Flagship. Signed, Ralph Radcliffe, Director-Stewardess Service.

treated like a celebrity, being one of four stewardesses picked out of more than 2,000. It seemed as if the whole population was thrilled to be riding on the jet.

SUNDAY, JANUARY 25, 1959:

Claire and I got up at 5:30, dressed, had a bite to eat, and went out to the airport an hour and a half before the flight departure. While we were being debriefed, a newspaper man took our pictures.

Crew of American Airlines' Flagship California Boeing 707 Inaugural Flight, left to right: Flight Engineer Norman Rice, Stewardess Marilyn Rutkowski, Stewardess Edna Garrett, Captain Charles Macatee, Stewardess Argie Hoskins, Captain Lou Szabo, Stewardess Claire Bullock, and Flight Engineer Bill Duncan.

We boarded our aircraft and while having our pre-flight check, we had Governor Brown and Mrs.

Pat Brown, Red Moiser (an American Airlines Executive), President C. R. Smith, Miss Jane Wyman, and Mr. and Mrs. Hill plus others stroll through the plane. Mrs. Brown christened the plane, "Flagship California," with speeches by Governor Brown and C. R. Smith.

Not only was the event impressive, but Flagship California was graceful, sleek, and absolutely gorgeous with open hospitality for all who entered her doors. In her resplendent beauty she was far more than a ticket.

At this point Claire Bullock, who was my roommate and one of the jet stewardesses, was standing in the front of the craft. She was from the South and a totally dedicated fan of Elvis Presley. As she was standing in front of the plane, Elvis's agent handed her a photo of Elvis to accompany us on the first jet flight. Claire was thrilled. In different locations on the plane, bouquets of yellow and lavender flowers welcomed our guests. Oh yes, the stewardesses received orchids to wear. The entire flight was made up of very influential and successful people; newspaper people and cameramen, plus other wonderful passengers. Passengers were milling from one cabin to the other, Mercury to Coach. It was like a press conference and confusing for me. The task at hand was to serve our passengers beverage and food with first class service in a very informal atmosphere as one big happy family. I gave Miss Wyman my flight topper to wear, that being the dress we wore during the food service. Everyone

A close-up of Claire with her orchid.

was having a grand time up in the "dream of sunshine and clouds." It was a magnificent experience and lots of hard work.

A memorable highlight of the day was when I met President C. R. Smith as he walked the aisle during the flight. One could feel the strength of his character. He had the skill of looking you in the eye and connecting with you on a level which left you feeling like you were important to American Airlines. I knew that he appreciated me as a stewardess.

I remember giving Jane Wyman my flight topper to wear, and she was filmed while she had it on. Flight toppers were worn while serving a meal. We had our choice as a crew to either wear or not wear the topper. It made a more appropriate dress for the food service if we did, though. One of the important reasons for the cover-up was that it kept the uniform clean. It was flattering to me that Miss Wyman wore the same size as I wore. She was very pleasant to be around. In the movie *Three Guys Named Mike*, she played the part of an American Airline stewardess.

Jane Wyman with Captain Macatee and an accompanying news article about the flight.

Breathless

Actress Jane Wyman is ecstatic over her Los Angeles-New York 707 Jet Flagship flight as she chats with Capt. Charles A. Macatee following arrival at Idlewild. The airplane, Flagship California, zipped from coast to coast in four hours and three minutes to set a record for commercial transports on the route. The airplane left Los Angeles International Airport at 9:01 (PST). Hundreds turned out at Idlewild to welcome the first transcontinental jet nonstop trip.

On the passenger list, Mr. G. Wright was listed as 89 years old; I think that made him the oldest person on the inaugural flight. Mr. and Mrs. L. Barnett brought their little son who was two and a half years old, making him the youngest passenger.

A souvenir coin we gave all the passengers to commemorate the flight.

Also on the flight was Dr. Arthur L. Klein, an aeronautical engineer and legend designer. Dr. Clark Millikan was also on board. He was one of the nation's foremost pioneers in aerospace research and development. He was also a pioneer in the development of multi-engine, high-altitude airplanes, jet propulsion, and guided missiles. I had this gentleman on an earlier flight, and I had enjoyed his friendliness and his usual enthusiasm for his projects. In the 1950s a new facet of aeronautics came into view with the ideas of satellites and spacecraft, and he worked right at the forefront of these ideas. I had met him a second time on a PR assignment, and now this flight was my third meeting with him. It was always exciting to meet people over and over.

We arrived in New York 4 hours and 3 minutes later. A band was playing when we opened the door and bright lights were shining with people taking pictures. Our debriefing after the flight was interesting. We are helping work out all the things which need to be changed with the Boeing 707 stewardess procedural operations. We were so tired, Claire and I said, "Never again."

The flight was overwhelming; however, our training kept us calm and poised. We had the knowledge to be self-sufficient and to make decisions that affected our passengers. In a crisis we could rise above the everyday requirements of passenger service. We were tired yes, but we were prepared. After a good night's sleep, we put in our bids to work the 707 flights again and again.

Not only was it a privilege to have the greatest passengers walk through our American Airlines doors, but we also had crews who were marvelously skilled behind the wheels of our fantastic aircraft. The captain of our flight was Charles Macatee. He had years of experience flying. Frank Brady's book, *A Singular View*, begins with just one of Captain Macatee's experiences—successfully landing a hit plane in the crash that cost Brady his eye. Brady writes:

> I have no memory of being hit. I recall only a dazed awareness that something was wrong, very wrong... that [Charles Macatee] was swinging our plane into position for a landing... asking the tower for runway lights... calling for an ambulance to meet the plane.
>
> Then Tom Wright, the third man aboard, was helping me out of the cockpit, where I had been flying copilot, and onto a couch so that he could take my place and assist in the landing....

Our plane, a research DC–3, had been on the last leg of a flight from Chicago via Washington that April evening. We'd been skimming over Long Island after sunset and were preparing to land at Grumman Field when the craft was struck. Captain Macatee (who later was to pilot the first scheduled jetliner across America) had no idea what had hit us until after landing, when he found a five-pound mallard duck in the cockpit.

It was little wonder why American Airlines chose Charles Macatee to captain the inaugural flight.

Captain Macatee in uniform and his plaque commemorating the historic flight. Photos courtesy of Beth Macatee Snyder.

The Astrojet News published an interview with Captain Macatee 10 years after the inaugural flight. In it, he says that piloting this flight "was and had to be his biggest thrill in 30 years of flying."

> The preparations had begun years before. "Paper jets" had begun "flying" daily New York–Los Angeles and Chicago–Dallas trips in July 1958.
>
> But the big moment was 8:45 a.m. Pacific Coast Time Sunday, Jan. 25, 1959.
>
> With Capt. Macatee at the controls, First Officer (now captain) Lou Szabo beside him, and 112 passengers aboard, American's first Jet Flagship lifted off Runway 25L, at Los Angeles International Airport and headed for New York.

FIRST TRANSCON FLIGHT

It was commercial aviation's first transcontinental jet flight, a flight that brought east and west coasts three hours closer together and revolutionized an airline, an industry and the nation's transportation system.

"We got off 20 minutes late because of the ceremonies at Los Angeles. But we were fortunate enough to catch tailwinds that at times were in excess of 150 knots. We arrived at New York on schedule, exactly four hours and 3 minutes after takeoff." ...

Hundreds of people, including a 25-piece brass band, turned out at Idlewild to welcome the first transcon jet (more than 25,000 had seen it off at LAX). Newsmen, government officials and movie stars were aboard, including actress Jane Wyman ("who for some reason I kept calling Mrs. Lyman," Captain Macatee recalled).

C. R. Smith, also aboard, told AAers in a special issue of Flagship News to "take a bow to history, for you are a part of it today. The piston-engined airplane will retain our affection, for it has done so much for us and for air transportation. Today, we have a new area of expectation, for the bright promise of what the turbine-powered airport will bring lies ahead of us."

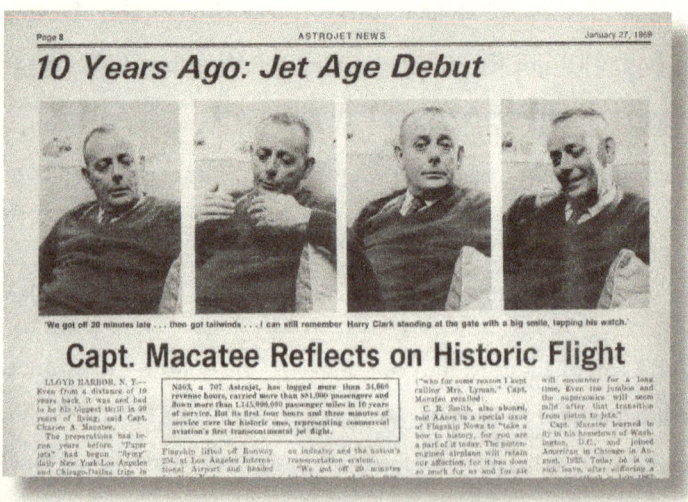

Astrojet News vol. 24, no. 2, January 27, 1969. Photo courtesy of Beth Macatee Snyder.

In the article Captain Macatee also reflected upon the historical significance of this first transcontinental jet flight. He and Captain H. C. Smith, who flew the return trip, had flown the 707 without passengers for about 200 hours before this historical flight with passengers. The article states that for Captain Macatee, this flight was "biggest thrill in 30 years of flying," and Captain Macatee concluded his comments by saying that while he had many special memories of flying "those four hours three minutes were the big ones for me. They always will be."

Captain C. A. Macatee

Close-up of Captain Macatee before the flight; copy of Captain Macatee's bio, courtesy of Beth Macatee Snyder.

Captain C. A. Macatee retired on September 1 after flying for American Airlines for 30 years.

Charlie Macatee's flying experience started back in 1928. Since that time he has flown a wide assortment of airplanes in a wide variety of activities. Before coming to AA in 1939, he flew with Air Service, Inc. in Washington, D. C., he flew with Pennsylvania Airlines for a time and he spent four years as the Assistant Manager of Washington Airport.

His flying career has also encompassed stints with the ATA as an Engineering Pilot, an assignment as a special Technical Consultant to the U. S. Navy, and an assignment on the Research and Planning for AA's Turbine Training Programs. Charlie served in Flight Management for a number of years, as an Assistant Superintendent and Superintendent of Flying Operations. Except for brief periods in Chicago and Cincinnati, he has been New York based through most of his AA service.

Among Charlie's many other distinctions is the fact that on January 25, 1959 he flew the first commercial jet aircraft, nonstop Los Angeles to New York, in a record time of 4 hours and 3 minutes.

The Macatees live in Huntington, Long Island. They have a son, Charles, and two daughters, Marianne and Elizabeth. Charlie's basement is rigged out with a complete machine shop, where he's already deeply engrossed in his hobby of inventing and building an infinite variety of gadgets.

Born November 7, 1909
In Huntington, West Virginia
Passed away October 17, 1983
In Boxford, Massachusetts

Started with American Airlines August 7, 1936
As of June 1, 1938 his flight time was 2559:48
Retired from American Airlines September 1, 1969

Captain Charles A. Macatee had an outstanding aviation career. He holds the distinction of flying the first American Airlines Jet, a Boeing 707 non-stop from LAX, Los Angeles to IDL, New York in 4 hours and 3 minutes on January 25, 1959, thereby opening the "Jet Age" to American Airlines.

His first professional position was as a Congressional Page in Washington at age nine, where he attended the special school for the pages of Congress.

In 1927 he worked at Hoover Airport, then the largest airport in Washington. He called himself the "handy man" and was involved in the making and developing of the first landing lights there, the construction of the tower and managing improvements.

In 1928 he bought his first plane, a Waco, getting his pilots license later that year. Six years after he soloed he was a co-pilot for Pennsylvania Airlines flying Boeing 247s.

In 1936 he joined the Naval Reserve and was hired by American Airlines, both based in Chicago. In June 1942 he was called to active duty in the U.S. Navy. He went to the newly formed Naval Air Transport Squadron, VR-1. He was an Ensign, stationed at Norfolk and later Patuxtent River Naval Air Station. Charles, in VR-1 flew the first bomb supply flight over the Atlantic to Iceland and into North Africa. He was a technical advisor, became Engineering Officer and was involved in testing aircraft. Charles, a Navy Commander, returned to American Airlines after WWII.

Charles' flying career also encompassed work with the ATA as an Engineering Pilot, an assignment as a special Technical Consultant to the Navy, and an assignment on the Research and Planning for AA's Turbine Training Programs.

Charles served in American Airlines Flight Management for a number of years as an Assistant Superintendent and Superintendent of Flying Operations. After AA retirement he continued his great interest in aeronautics as a consultant to Sperry and General Electric and continued as a private pilot.

Another bio about Captain Macatee courtesy of Beth Macatee Snyder.

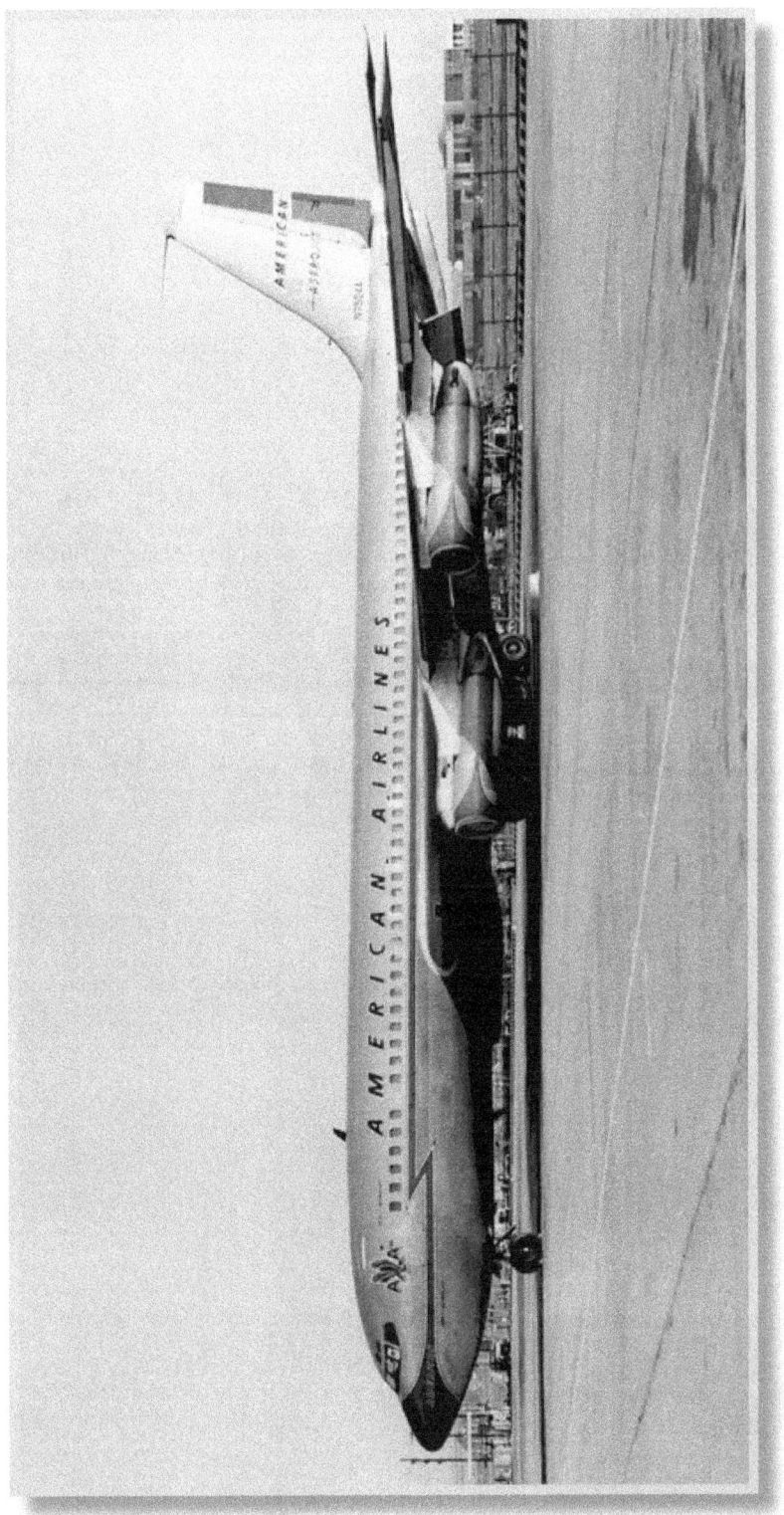

Photo of a 707 jet by Bob Proctor. © Jon Proctor.

707 jets © Jon Proctor
The night time shot of 707-123B N7503A was Flagship California before conversion to turbofan power. This is the Inaugural Flight jet.

707-123B N7503A, Flagship California, on her way to be scrapped. When I first saw this photo, it pulled at my heart strings. I cried tears of joy having known it and tears of sadness that it's gone. © Brian Lockett, Air-and-Space.com.

Passenger List for the First Jet Flight across the USA

These people were more than passengers. They quickly became friends as we shared this historical moment in time. President C. R. Smith set the example as he strolled the aisle connecting with the passengers with cheer and good wishes. I, also, felt the association as we smoothly flew through the clouds of time. Time and space seemed to be flying through another dimension. Through the years it has been my pleasure to continue or renew some of these honored relationships.

MERCURY SECTION MANIFEST

Mr. and Mrs. Robert Adamson	Aviation Department, Shell Oil Company
Carrell Alcott	CBS Radio News
C. Babcock Jr.	
Mr. and Mrs. Joseph Binns	Executive Vice President of Waldorf Hotel
Mr. and Mrs. Frank Bull	Sports Announcer
Meuschki	NBC Monitor
Wilbur Clark	Owner of Desert Inn Hotel, Las Vegas
W. C. Collins	President of Northrop Aircraft
Henry Dreyfuss	Architect-Designer
M. Epley	Long Beach Press Telegram
Will Fowler	American Airlines Public Relations
J.A. Frabutt	President of Int'l Telephone and Telegraph
Charles Fry	Vice President of Austin-Field-Fry
I. Grainger	President of Cera Exchange Bank N. Y.
Rex Metz	Cameraman
Mrs. Cordel Hicks	L. A. Times
William Hogan	Sr. Vice President and Treasurer of American Airlines
Alex Jacome	President of Jacome Department Store
Frank G. Jamison	President of Pacific Automation
J. Paul Kirk	President of Morris P. Kirk Company
E. D. Kraugh	L. A. Herald Express
Mr. and Mrs. Abe Lastfogel	President of William Morris Agency
Miss Maryon Lears	Merchandise Manager Silverweeds
Paul Levitan	CBS T. V. News
Dr. and Mrs. Majer	Physician
Mr. and Mrs. Lee Mytinger	Corp. Secretary and Co-owner of Mytinger and Casselberry
Mr. and Mrs. M. Pollard	Airport Commissioner L. A.
A. H. Power	Partner Ernst and Ernst
Henry Reiger	United Press
C. R. Smith	President of American Airlines
Revel H. Smitter	Sales Manager Waugh Engineering
Mr. and Mrs. R. A. Stabler	President of Filmasters, Inc.
Dr. Frank Stanton	President of CBS
Sam Stewart	Coplay Newspapers
Herace Stoneham	President of San Francisco Giants
William Summer	Pasadena Star News & Independent
Bill Thomas	L. A. Mirror News
Mr. and Mrs. Karl Weber	Chair of Board Weber Aircraft
Elmer J. Weis	Executive Vice President of Pacific Pumps, Inc.
P. G. Winnett	Chair of Board Bullocks
Mr. and Mrs. G. Wright	89-year-old gentleman with his wife
Miss Jane Wyman	Actress
Mr. and Mrs. Glen Wallichs	President of Capital Records
Dr. Clark Millikan	Cal Tech
Dr. Arthur A. Klein	Professor of Aeronautics at Cal Tech; Director of the Society of Automotive Engineers

ROYAL COACHMAN SECTION MANIFEST

Mr. and Mrs. L. Barnett	President of Music Corp. of American
Norman Barnett	Vice President of Barnett Int'l Forwarders
Miss Margaret Bassetti	Single lady booked by travel agency
Phil Bath	American Airlines Photographer
Franklin G. Berlin	President of Beemak Plastics
Robert Blodgett	American Airlines Admiral
H. E. Bowers	Executive of J. E. Haddock Company
E. Buller	Mayor of Atwater, California
Mr. and Mrs. William H. Burgess	Electronic Specialty Company
R. J. Caverly	Head of International Division Hilton Hotels
Enoch Christophenson	Past Mayor of Turlock, California
Dr. and Mrs. Walter	Optometrist & Designer
John Elmore	Prominent Farmer, Brawley, California
Michael Feitler	Manager of Oakland Realty Company
Neal Galloway	Merced County, California
W. L. Gore	Vice President of Aerojet Corp.
G. Gundell	Vice President of National Dairy Association
Mrs. E. H. Haag	Wife, Sales Manager Air Products Company
John H. Harris	President of Ice Capades
Gilbert Havas	Credit Analyst of Bank of America
R. M. Johnson	Western Regional Manager General Controls
Dr. J. B. and Dee Jones	President of Abundavita
Mr. and Mrs. William Koda	World's largest rice grower
Mr. Fritz Larkin	Vice President Security Bank
Mr. G. Lavender	Railway Express Driver
Mr. Lee Little	Radio KTVC
Lunn	National Dairy Association
David MacMorris	DCA Eastern Rep. Sunstrand Turbo Div.
Wayne McGrew	Vice President of Partlow Company, E. Hartford, N. Y.
N. O'Conner	Vice President of N. W. Ayer & Son NYC
Allen Parkinson	President of Sleep-Eze Company, Inc.
Howard Partlow Jr.	President of Partlow Company, E. Hartford, N. Y.
Lawrence E. Patterson	President of Pepsi Cola, Santa Ana, C. A.
Jack Ray	Vice President Sales, General Controls
E. E. Rubel	Partner, Roemer & Rubel Buick
M. Rubin	President of California Jersey Mills
Russell Smith	President of Avery Label
Roger Stebbins	Pacific Coast Executive - Sears
Tingdale	American Airlines Operation Service
Miss Alice Toner	Nurse - Larry Barnett Family
T. Watson	Vice President of N. W. Ayer & Son N. Y. C.
Gordon Way	Vice President of Bechtel SFO
Bernard Willett	Vice President of Space Tech. Lab., Greenwich Div.
John Wolff	Sales Manager, Heating General, Control
Dr. John Froehlich	Jet Propulsion Laboratory
Dr. Allen	Jet Propulsion Laboratory
Dr. Lombardi	Jet Propulsion Laboratory

AMERICAN AIRLINES
CABLE ADDRESS AMAIR
100 PARK AVENUE · NEW YORK 17, NEW YORK

January 25, 1959

This Letter
Made Postal History

It commemorates the inauguration of Jet Air Mail Service across the country -- a milestone in U.S. postal history.

If you'll glance at the postmarks and backstamps on the outside of this First Flight Cover, you'll notice that it travelled coast-to-coast -- and back -- within twelve hours. A simple, yet effective demonstration of jet travel's capabilities.

Historically, the U.S. Post Office Department has been quick to take advantage -- and make maximum use -- of fast, new transportation methods. At American Airlines, we're proud to be part of this momentous "First"...proud that our Jet Flagship Service will help America enjoy the fastest airmail service ever.

It is our pleasure to be able to supply this commemorative First Flight Cover...our hope that it will gain an honored place in your collection.

Sincerely,

B. E. Sherwood
Director -- Mail and Express

bes/pod

This letter speaks for itself.

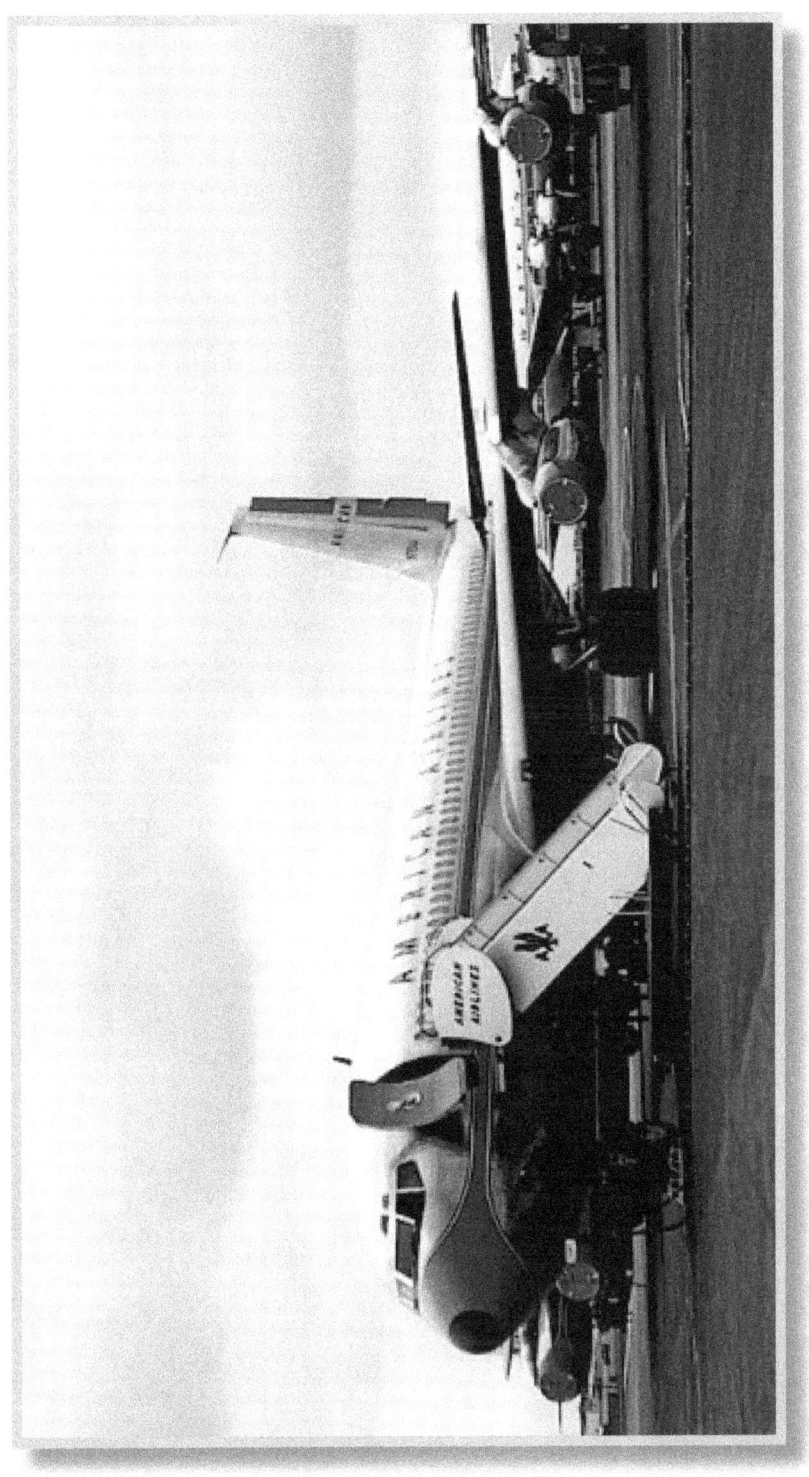

"Straight-pipe" American 707-123 N7504A, Flagship New York, is in position at the gate for its next load of passengers. Photo taken by Bob Proctor. © Jon Proctor

Left: Claire, Barbara, me, and Gerry checking in with Crew Schedule; this is where we assured the crew that we were ready and raring to go. After reading the memos to update us on procedures, we hurried on to the planes.

Below: Claire, me, Barbara, and Gerry in full stewardess uniform in the front room of our bungalow.

Chapter Ten

Four Friends for the Jets

The cottage that Claire, Barbara, Gerry, and I shared was near Century City in the Westwood area of Los Angeles. We had all been trained at the same time, and soon we were all flying together on the beautiful Boeing 707. One time Barbara and Claire were traveling East to West at the same time that Gerry and I were traveling West to East on the jets. As we approached each other, the captain announced that "the roommates" were passing in the air. It was so thrilling! I looked out the window, and I could see the other plane not too far away.

My roommates and I all jumped at a chance to fly together. So we put in our bids for the same jet trip to New York as often as possible. Our togetherness created an atmosphere of fun, warmth, and love. Lucky passengers! When I didn't bid this trip, I bid the El Paso trip. I usually got that one—seems that not everyone had an Aunt Boo in El Paso. It was always a moment of expectation when the assignments for the month appeared in our boxes—sometimes filled with anticipation and sometimes with disappointment. Echoing through the room I would hear, "Will he still be there?" "Why didn't I bid the other trip?" "I have plans for the trip I bid! I will need to trip trade." "I like to fly with that crew." "I don't like to fly with that crew." "I am so pleased that I got what I bid." "Dallas again!" "Gerry, we are flying together!" "Yea! We all got the same trip to New York." And on and on through the whole range of emotions.

STEWARDESS SCHEDULE TIMES EFFECTIVE 10/1

TRIP	EQUIP	LANDINGS	DEPT	ARVL	TIME	LAYOVER
2	707	LAX IDL	0845	1640	4:55	14:50
1	707	IDL LAX	0845	1120	5:35	
6	707	LAX IDL	1600	2355	4:55	15:35
5	707	IDL LAX	1545	1820	5:35	
76	707	LAX BAL	0800	1535	4:35	25:10
75	707	BAL LAX	1800	2005	5:05	
78	707	LAX BAL	2355	0730	4:35	26:15
77	707	BAL LAX	1100	1305	5:05	
30	707	LAX ORD	0730	1310	3:40	:35
35	707	ORD LAX	1545	1745	4:00	
32	707	LAX ORD	0915	1455	3:40	1:35
37	707	ORD LAX	1745	1945	4:00	
38	707	LAX ORD	2330	0510	3:40	1:35
31	707	ORD LAX	0800	1000	4:00	
24	707	LAX DAL	1100	1550	2:50	1:25
25	707	DAL LAX	1830	1920	2:50	
28	707	LAX DAL	1730	2220	2:50	10:00
27	707	DAL LAX	0935	1025	2:50	
776	DC7	LAX STL	0755	1520	5:25	19:45
775	DC7	STL LAX SAN	1220	1720	6:35	2:25
774	DC7	SAN LAX	2100	2145	:45	
774	DC7	LAX CLE	2220	0800	6:40	26:00
773	DC7	CLE LAX	1115	1530	7:15	
950	DC7	LAX ELP	0705	1055	2:50	3:15
961	DC7	LAX SAN ELP SAN ELAX	1525	1800	3:15	
960	DC7	LAX SAN ELP	2250	0325	3:15	15:05
953	DC7	ELP LAX	1945	2130	2:45	
622	DC6	LAX SAN PHX MDW	0605	1650	7:55	17:11
731	DC7	MDW TUS PHX	1115	1637	5:57	
731	DC7	PHX LAX	1715	1745	:45	
112	DC6	LAX TUS ELP MAF ACF	1300	2210	6:05	18:40
695	DC7	ACF LAX	1805	2120	4:55	
908	DC7	LAX SAN DAL	2315	0630	4:55	22:45
211	DC6	ACF ELP DUG TUS PHX SAN LAX	0630	1305	6:54	
28	DC7	LAX DAL (THRU 10/6)	1730	2355	4:24	12:25
167	DC6	DAL MAF ELP TUS SAN LAX	1335	1935	6:35	
902	DC6	LAX DAL	0850	1555	5:05	16:25
27	DC7	DAL LAX (THRU 10/6)	0935	1205	4:30	
902	DC6	LAX DAL (EFFEC 10/7)	0850	1555	5:05	20:25
167	DC6	DAL MAF ELP TUS SAN LAX	1335	1935	6:35	
966	DC6	LAX ELP DAL	2215	0605	5:25	14:50
903	DC6	DAL SAN LAX	2210	0205	5:35	
694	DC7	LAX DAL	2350	0615	4:25	19:35
655	DC6	DAL LAX	0305	0520	5:15	
746	DC7	LAX PHX	1815	2050	1:35	9:20
621	DC6	PHX SAN LAX	0725	0905	2:20	

WEEK-END FREQUENCY

622	DC6	LAX SAN PHX MDW	2650	7:55	17:11
731	DC7	MDW TUS PHX			13:33
621	DC6	PHX SAN LAX			

Papers detailing Stewardess's flying assignments; we received papers like this all the time. These specific papers are the October 1959 schedule.

STEWARDESS' FLYING ASSIGNMENTS EFFECTIVE OCTOBER 1, 1959

51-1. Sanford
51-2. Adams, S.
52-1. Hass
52-2. Holsinger
53-1. Salyer
53-2. Ward
54-1. Troy
54-2. Fiedler
55-1. Demarinis
55-2. Winzer
56-1. Banding
56-2. Derrig
57-1. Kramer
57-2. Guy
58-1. Hanson
58-2. Jenkin
59-1. Amante
59-2. Rogers, M.
60-1. Olson
60-2. Hite
61-1. Goodwin
61-2. Tsoumides
62-1. Warren
62-2. Deboard
63-1. Wightman
63-2. Brazee
64-1. Sorenson
64-2. Freeman
65-1. McMenamin
65-2. Kueneman
66-1. Boyce
66-2. Vandersteen
67-1. Hurst
67-2. Lee
68-1. Baker, S.
68-2. Farrall

Cole
Elward
Fisher, M.
Halls
Fairly
Tanner
Starke
Walker
Ladwig
Shockley
Sager
Harward
Bishop
Wheelan
Ray
Howard
Mowery
Mick
Gillis
Micholson
West
Crawley
Boyer
Dansby
Burt
Scofield
Engelman
Allison
Slater
Fricioni
Szabo
Uitts
Laparne
Perry
Secord
Horton

96. Luft
97. Hawley
98. Qualen
99. McRoberts
100. Gingles
101. Williams, G.
102. Boland
103. Baker, M.
104. Collins
105. Birge
106. Henderson
107. Prosch
108. Rowe
109. Hallett
110. McLagen
111. Curvan
112. Hudson
113. Hicks
114. Brown
115. Rogers, B.
116. Knowles
117. Martin
118. Ascher1
119. Whitesell
120. Eaton
121. Barrett
122. Toman
123. Hinners
124. Cavenaugh
125. Hoskins
126-1. Ladou
127-2. Gronefeld

Dartt, Sharon
Dartt, Sandra
Ogden
Fitch
Adrian
Pruette
Dwyer
Farko
Currlin
Chevalier
King
Davis, S.
Schneider
Wilcox
Connearney
Berry
Jennings
Henry
Brence
Kennedy
Browne
Crane
Linden
Nyberg
Sundstrom
Fischer
Anderson
Beuscher
Davies, C.
Powers
Curley
Raymond

RESERVES
128. Davis, J.
129. Sherwood

The United Aircraft Corporation published a trade magazine quarterly called *Bee-Hive*. In spring 1959 they published an article by Emily Watson entitled "Four Jills for the Jets" that detailed our lives as stewardesses in the jet age. I felt like a celebrity as she was working on this article—Miss Watson followed us around with cameras for a few days, and it was so fun to read about us in print.

> When the jet age in United States transcontinental air travel dawned last January 25 with the flight of an American Airlines Boeing 707 from Los Angeles to New York, the household probably most directly affected was that of a "family" of four stewardesses who live in a bungalow in West Los Angeles.
>
> Two of the girls—Argie Hoskins and Claire Bullock—were stewardesses on the inaugural flight; the others—Gerry McMasters and Barbara Whaley, assigned to later 707 trips—distributed 707 models to herald the new jet service.
>
> Since that flight, the four stewardesses have been averaging some 40,000 miles of jet travel a week from Los Angeles to New York and back. Their experience in these early days of jet travel is helping to establish the pattern of service aboard the jets.
>
> THEY PRACTICED IN A MOCKUP
>
> Although the four girls each had two years of flying experience, they virtually had to re-learn their jobs when they were assigned to jets. During their qualification schooling, they acted out in a 707 mockup the parts they were to play in jet flight. They learned where supplies were and how doors opened, lights operated and seats reclined. They learned that new equipment, such as pop-out oxygen masks, is carried on the high-flying 707. They replaced the phrase "miles per hour" with the word "Mach" in their vocabulary; "thrust" took the place of "horsepower" as they learned the rudiments of the operation of the airplane's four Pratt & Whitney Air-

craft commercial J–57 engines. They became familiar with the names and functions of the parts of the airplane visible from cabin windows—such as the vortex generator—which might arouse a passenger's curiosity.

They had to know their jobs well. They would be performing more services for more people in fewer hours. There would be no time for faltering, fumbling, or finding out.

For their part in the inaugural flight, Claire and Argie even memorized the names of the 106 passengers who would be aboard, in the hope that they could make this the signal day it should be for each of the first-flighters.

... There was little time for the leisurely conversations they had enjoyed with passengers on previous trips. What snatches of chatting they managed, however, were unusually pleasant in the quiet, vibrationless cabin....

A lot of changes have taken place in the stewardesses' job since that first flight. With an increased number of passengers requesting first-class accommodations, the bulkhead on the 707 was moved back so that three of the airplane's four stewardesses work in the front section with 68 passengers, and one in the aft with the remainder. The serving of the meal and beverages and the other routines in the jet cabin have undergone changes as Claire, Barbara, Argie, and Gerry, along with other jet stewardesses,

Barbara and Claire checking in with operations before a flight. Note their nicely manicured nails.

Clockwise from top left: Barbara handing out magazines; Claire handing out magazines; Barbara tending to a passenger; Barbara and Claire on the boarding ramp; Claire boarding the plane with a child.

have studied their own capabilities on the flights, the passengers' requirements, and the most efficient way to use the 707's cabin equipment.

TIME BECOMES CONFUSING

Problems of time differentials, always existent on transcontinental airplanes, are especially acute on the jet, moving as it does quickly from time zone to time zone. When the stewardesses are asked for the time, they, too, are confused. Does the passenger wish to know the time relative to his departure point, the point over which they are passing, or his destination? The girls notice, too, a variation in appetites, a returning New Yorker's stomach being geared for lunch when a Californian may be ready for breakfast. They recommend compromises as to serving time.

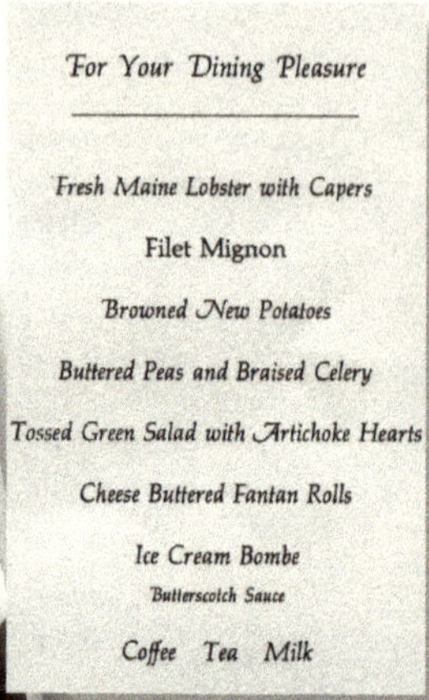

For Your Dining Pleasure

Fresh Maine Lobster with Capers

Filet Mignon

Browned New Potatoes

Buttered Peas and Braised Celery

Tossed Green Salad with Artichoke Hearts

Cheese Buttered Fantan Rolls

Ice Cream Bombe
Butterscotch Sauce

Coffee   Tea   Milk

Left to right: Claire and Barbara preparing to serve the passengers; one of the menus we handed out; Barbara taking a passenger's order.

It really did get confusing! I recommended that we look at the food schedule and think, "be flexible," and see what the passenger's wanted before it was set in concrete. That was one of our responsibilities—to give feedback to the airlines about customer preferences. Sometimes suggestions were workable.

Changes are difficult, be they good or bad. I always had a feeling of excitement and anticipation as I quickly walked through the terminal to be on my way. Flying on the Boeing 707 was a different experience and a new adventure. I was thrilled and excited with this revolutionary mode of transportation; however, I felt a tremendous loss in many ways with passenger contact. I did not have the time to visit as I had once enjoyed. I struggled with this. I did my best to hurry up and get procedures accomplished so I would have time to engage my guests.

The four stewardesses do a lot of high living as they hurtle busily back and forth across the nation five times a week at an average altitude of 30,000 feet. That schedule adds up to the fact that relaxing is one of their favorite occupations. Their lives, once they hit sea level, are relatively quiet ones.

Minutes after a 707 whines onto the runway at Los Angeles International Airport and passengers stream from both ends of the big jet, Claire and Barbara, who usually fly together, hurry down the ramp, rush into a field office to check in an electric razor used by passengers on the flight, dash to stewardess headquarters to do their paperwork, check their mailboxes and crew schedules. Then, suit-

Claire and Barbara returning home.

cases and heavy overcoats in hand, they scurry to the parking lot where Claire's middle-aged Pontiac awaits them. . . .

Argie, who has just tidied up the house, greets them. Gerry is out with her steady boyfriend, a UCLA student. Barbara likes soft music. She puts a record on the hi-fi which Gerry's father built and contributed to the household. They sit down to read their mail.

After they get into something comfortable, they spend the afternoon at restful activities. Argie knits; Gerry sews when she's home; Claire and Barbara may go bowling. . . . The beach is a good place for relaxing, and now and then the stewardesses pile into one of the cars to head for Santa Monica for surf-bathing. Rose Marie Reid, the famous swim-suit designer, is a neighbor and friend of the stewardess family. They occasionally would swim in her pool.

Left: C. L. relaxing in the pool.

Right: Claire, me, and Barbara enjoying the pool.

Barbara climbing out of the pool.

There are sometimes small parties in the bungalow and always friends (mostly other stewardesses) dropping in—Donna Folkers, for instance, who frequently flies with the girls and spends her spare time modeling for various Los Angeles, San Francisco, and New York stores.

At lunch with my housemates and Donna Folkers.

Argie's brother, C. L., is like a member of the household. A bona-fide cowboy, he appears in Western roles on television. The girls proudly call him "the actor of the family."

C. L. in some of his publicity photos for his television roles.

Argie, a Mormon, works in the information center of the Mormon Temple during some of her off-duty time.

I enjoyed going to the temple whenever I could and helping in the information center. Helping visitors feel welcome there wasn't much different than helping the passengers on a plane.

All the girls enjoy reading, especially poetry. They patronize the public library and have large library of their own. A few medical tomes belong to Gerry, who once was a nurse. Some Spanish books come in handy when the stewardesses fly to a border town. But the bulk of their library was gathered from scores of passengers who left the books they had read en route behind for the stewardesses....

Before the four stewardesses moved to their bungalow, Claire, Barbara, and Gerry lived in a Hollywood apartment. "We would often get home at 1 a.m. from a flight and feel like playing records," Barbara recalled. "That's not ideal when there's just a wall between you and your neighbors. We decided a house would be perfect for people who keep such strange hours." The three stewardesses moved into their two-bedroom cottage . . . , and Argie moved in with them. The four cars joined the household immediately; the stewardesses no longer had to take the limousine from Hollywood to the airport.

Clockwise from front seat left: Barbara, me, Claire, and Gerry.

Much of our time was spent in getting ready for the next day's trip, arrangements for who takes which car and who picks up the uniforms at the cleaners. We shined our shoes and polished our nails, checked the time and arrived at crew schedule.

In our cottage two of us smoked and two didn't. Gerry and I chose to be roommates because we didn't smoke. Having grown up in a home with smoking, it did not seem like a big deal to have smoke all around me. We regularly gave our passengers packs of cigarettes—an extra stash. It is funny to think of it now, with the *No Smoking* signs right next to the *Fasten Seat Belt* signs. Back then, each passenger's seat had an ash tray built into the arm rests. Smokers would light up as soon as the sign went off. Talk about secondhand smoke. My hair was a filter. The first thing I did when arriving home was wash my thick hair that was thick with smoke. Even now, I can still taste and smell the smoke.

Top: Claire bidding me and Gerry farewell from our cottage near Century City Studios.

Middle: Me and Gerry walking down the front walk on our way to the airport.

Bottom: Barbara wishing me and Gerry well by the car for our jet trip to New York.

The bungalow costs the stewardesses $195 rent a month. Each girl pitches in $10 a week for food and pays her share of utilities. Their phone bill is a big item, running around $60 a month. The telephone rings almost constantly and often their calls overflow into the home of an accommodating neighbor.... Many of their calls concern business—such things for instance, as a "trip trade."...

An exceptionally congenial group, all four of the stewardesses regret that they can be together only about one day a week. Their training in working as teams on the jet airliner helps them to work well together on the household chores. All the girls like cooking and especially enjoy barbecues on their patio. At vacation time, the quartet still sticks together....

Here we are enjoying time together on our patio.

They visited the Hawaiian Islands on their two weeks' holiday. Their current ambition is to maneuver their schedules on the jets so that all four can fly on the same airplane. "We could all go to the airport in the same car, and think of the gas we'd save!" one girl remarked. This would also give them more time at home together, and, of course, company in New York.

A night in New York, the girls regard as pretty routine. Arriving late in the afternoon, they check in at their quarters in the Belmont-Plaza Hotel, rest awhile, and go out for dinner. Now and then they attend a show. More often, they turn in early to be rested for the trip back the next morning.

Arriving in The Big Apple, New York City, was an exciting place of hustle and bustle from museums, theater, and music to taxi cabs, Saks, the garment district, and interesting cemeteries. Honk! Honk! Hurry! Hurry! It was so fun to be in the heart of the city.

Top: Claire and Barbara in the snow on the streets of New York.

Middle and bottom: How we celebrated Christmas in the bungalow.

Packing for such a jaunt is no problem. An extra sweater and skirt usually is all they need. Each of the stewardesses owns but one uniform. They patronize one-hour cleaners at both ends of the line.

In our toppers, Gerry and I are mixing drinks. They didn't need to worry about us sneaking drinks off the plane; neither of us drank.

We regularly paid $1.25 or $1.50 to have our uniforms cleaned. I never went to bed without hanging it on a dresser drawer or in the closet. Good habit! We all had our rituals before jumping into bed.

My memories of this time are golden. As of this writing, Barbara and Claire have gone to their eternal home in the sky. Time passes so quickly; tomorrow steps into yesterday with life stepping into eternity. Enjoy the todays and tomorrows with love and commitment, and appreciate the footprints of history, because they direct our footprints toward the future.

This book by Martin Caidin—an authority on aeronautics and aviation—was published after I finished flying and mentioned our roommate Barbara. To the right is the page she's mentioned on. She gave me a copy. The note she wrote inside reads:

To My Dear Roommate—
 Ours will be the times to remember forever.
 I've so enjoyed our friendship and know it will continue even though we are many miles apart. Remember good old "American" Arg, and remember me.
 Love You Much,
 Barbara
 P. S. Page 179 you can't forget.

Documents We Often Found in our Mailboxes

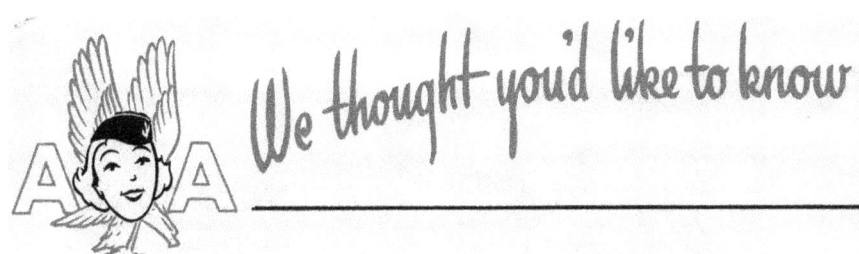

September 16, 1959

AA 707 Stewardesses:

No small part of the success of American's 707 jet service must be attributed to the performance of the World's Finest Stewardess Corps. More particularly is this commendable in view of the operational delays normal with the introduction of new equipment.

Your Company and your fellow employees recognize the added burdens of unusually long duty hours and intensified customer service these delays have occasioned for you. The thanks and appreciation of all of us go to you for the patience and extra effort you've given so generously during this important transitional period.

So that you may know that we will soon be able to put some of our mutual problems behind us, I am outlining below the nuisance situations (none having any bearing on airworthiness) we've encountered on the 707 and what is being done to overcome them. Until these fixes have all been achieved and we have attained a consistently normal operation, we are confident we can count upon your continued complete cooperation to the end that American's customers will be assured again and again of our constant action in their best interests.

Following are the problems that many of you have heard of or have experienced.

<u>Landing Gear - Hydraulic System</u>

These 2 have hit the headlines more than once. Structurally, the landing gear is more sound and stronger than Fort Knox. We have experienced quite a few problems with the hydraulic system, none of which affects airworthiness. Problems in lowering of the gear were caused mainly by pump casings, seals, a few lines, filters. All of these have been identified and fixes made. The mechanical system is more than adequate in case of any hydraulic failure. Our airplane is newsworthy and the press loses no opportunity to give every incident, no matter what, the full treatment.

<u>Air Conditioning</u>

Passengers and crews really felt the impact of these problems. Hot and cold Biggest problem was overheating. A reset switch was relocated so that the Flight Engineer can check and reset if the freon system kicks out. Installation of new air ducts and modification of air outlets now gives better air flow in the cabin.

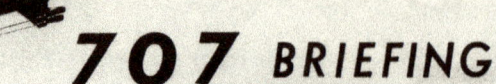

707 BRIEFING
Stewardess Service Division

Briefing Bulletin 37-59

September 16, 1959

To: Boeing Stewardesses

Subject: Changes in Current Patterns of Service

September 27 West Coast cities (only) will return to Standard Time. On that date several changes will be made in Patterns of Service for Boeing flights serving Los Angeles and San Francisco. These will continue until Eastern cities return to Standard Time. All flights serving LAX or SFO not mentioned below will leave or arrive at these cities one hour earlier and will maintain their present schedule at the other end of the line. Patterns of Service for flights departing from LAX will be moved up one hour earlier (Pacific Standard Time). The changes are as follows:

Flights 2, 6, 23, 76 and 78 will retain their present LAX departures and arrive one hour later at Eastern cities. Since Patterns of Service are based on departure Time, no change will be made.

Flight 7 leaves IDL one hour later (7:45P EDT) and arrives at LAX on its present schedule (9:20P PST). The new Pattern of Service for this flight is as follows:

MERCURY CABIN	ROYAL COACHMAN CABIN
8:00P - Set up Service Carts	8:00P - Set up Buffet for Dinner
8:15P - Cocktail Hour	8:15P - Royal Coachman Dinner
9:00P - Set up Buffet for Dinner	
9:15P - Mercury Dinner	

```
              Arrive LAX 1:20A (EDT)
                         9:20P (PST)
```

WORLD'S FINEST STEWARDESS CORPS

Briefing Bulletin 38-59

P. 2

Extra Coffee - Transcontinental Nonstops

Many of you who have been flying the transcontinental nonstops have requested that extra coffee be supplied on these trips. As the hot plates are inoperative for the time being, a shortage problem is created by having to throw away cold coffee. Therefore, effective immediately and continuing until further notice, caterers will provide one extra bag of coffee for each buffet on the coast-to-coast nonstops.

- - - - - - - - - - - - -

Deadhead Liquor Bottles

On certain Boeing flights operating into DAL, miniature liquor bottles are stored in Buffet Annex "D." Some of you have reported that passengers are pilfering these bottles. To alleviate this problem, caterers will tape a paper cover over the bottles so that they will not be visible to passengers.

Second Stewardess will be responsible for this deadhead liquor and will fill out and sign the liquor inventory before boarding passengers. The inventory form will be placed on top of the special liquor storage drawer. It will be necessary to untape the paper cover to count the bottles and then retape it.

List: 1607

Briefing Bulletin 37-59

P. 3

Flight 40 leaves SFO at 7:45A and arrives at ORD at 2:45P. Breakfast will replace cocktails and lunch presently served.

MERCURY CABIN	ROYAL COACHMAN CABIN
Leave SFO 7:45A (PST)	
8:00A - Set up Buffet for Breakfast	8:00A - Set up Buffet for Breakfast
8:15A - Mercury Breakfast	8:15A - Royal Coachman Breakfast
Arrive ORD 11:45A (PST)	
2:45P (CDT)	

- - - - - - - - - - - -

Flight 75 leaves BAL one hour later (7:00P EDT) and arrives LAX at 8:05P PST and arrives LAX at 8:05P PST. The new Pattern of Service is as follows:

MERCURY CABIN	ROYAL COACHMAN CABIN
Leave BAL 7:00P (EDT)	
7:15P - Set up Service Carts	7:15P - Set up Buffets for Dinner
7:30P - Cocktail Hour	7:30P - Royal Coachman Dinner
8:15P - Set up Buffets for Dinner	
8:30P - Mercury Dinner	
Arrive LAX 8:05P (PST)	
12:05A (EDT)	

NOTE TO STEWARDESSES:

The departure time for this trip is very late in respect to the normal dinner hour. However, this will only be the case for a one-month period. Therefore we will not change the service for this short time. It is evident that Stewardesses must accomplish the cocktail and meal service in the shortest possible time. Tablecloths will be placed in the seatback pockets prior to passenger boarding. Do not delay getting started immediately after take-off. As soon as the "No Smoking" sign goes off, change into toppers.

When distributing menus and wine lists, Stewardesses will see if any of the passengers prefer to have dinner immediately. Should they prefer to pass up the cocktail, they will serve these passengers their meals as soon as possible.

In order to offer all passengers their dinner at a reasonable hour, dinner will not be served in courses on this flight. All items, including entrees and desserts, will be placed on the tray at the buffet. Beverages will be served as passenger requests.

- - - - - - - - - -

Patterns of Service for all flights not mentioned above are contained in Briefing Bulletin 32-59.

707 BRIEFING

Stewardess Service Division

Briefing Bulletin 38-59

September 22, 1959

To: Boeing Stewardesses

Subject: 1. Condiment Cups
           2. Extra Silverware
           3. Extra Coffee - Transcontinental Nonstops
           4. Service Carts
           5. Deadhead Liquor Bottles

Condiment Cups

We have received occasional reports of passengers breaking the plastic condiment cups and spilling or spraying the contents on their clothing. Therefore these cups have been redesigned. Provisions have been made to strengthen the walls of these containers so that this type of accident will no longer occur.

For your information, the condiment cups are disposable and are never reused by the caterer.

- - - - - - - - - - - - - -

Extra Silverware

As soon as possible, 3 extra sets of silverware will be provided in the Royal Coachman Buffet "C." These will be stored in the cup drawer.

- - - - - - - - - - - - - -

Service Carts

As a result of your OP4s, corrective measures are being taken to remedy the squeaking wheels and other problems on the 707 Service Carts.

In the future, if you should find a Service Cart that is any way inoperative or in need of repair, please report this on an OP3 (Stewardess Request for Fixed Cabin Equipment Repair), and give this to the Flight Engineer. This will insure that the need for repair is brought to the attention of the ground personnel responsible. Although this equipment may be classed as "removable," it is unnecessary to tag it with an OP6 as the carts are not removed from the aircraft.

- - - - - - - - - - - - - -

WORLD'S FINEST STEWARDESS CORPS

Briefing Bulletin 37-59

P. 2

NOTE TO STEWARDESSES:

The departure time for this trip is very late in respect to the normal dinner hour. However, this will only be the case for a one-month period. Therefore, we will not change the service for this short time. It is evident that Stewardesses must accomplish the cocktail and meal service in the shortest possible time. Tablecloths will be placed in the seatback pockets prior to passenger boarding. Do not delay getting started immediately after take-off. As soon as the "No Smoking" sign goes off, change into toppers.

When distributing menus and wine lists, Stewardesses will see if any of the passengers prefer to have dinner immediately. Should they prefer to pass up the cocktail, they will serve these passengers their meals as soon as possible.

In order to offer all passengers their dinner at a reasonable hour, dinner will not be served in courses on this flight. All items, including entrees and desserts, will be placed on the tray at the buffet. Beverages will be served as passenger requests.

- - - - - - - - - -

Flight 10 will have a Deluxe Sandwich Snack. Refer to Boeing Stewardess Manual, Section 7, page 42, for Deluxe Sandwich Snack Service procedures. Services will be offered as follows:

MERCURY CABIN	ROYAL COACHMAN CABIN
Leave LAX 10:30P (PST)	
10:45P - Set up Service Carts	10:45P - Coffee Service
11:00P - Cocktail-Deluxe Snack Service	1:30A - Set up Buffet for Breakfast Snack
1:30A - Set up Buffet and Cart for Breakfast Snack Service	1:45A - Breakfast Snack
1:45A - Breakfast Snack Service	
Arrive IDL 3:25A (PST)	
7:25A (EDT)	

Flight 30 leaves LAX at 7:30A and arrives ORD at 2:10P. Breakfast will replace cocktails and lunch previously served.

MERCURY CABIN	ROYAL COACHMAN CABIN
Leave LAX 7:30A (PST)	
7:45A - Set up Buffets for Breakfast	7:45A - Set up Buffets for Breakfast
8:00A - Mercury Breakfast	8:00A - Royal Coachman Breakfast
Arrive ORD 11:10A (PST)	
2:10P (CDT)	

- - - - - - - - - -

Left to right: Howard Duff, Ida Lupino, Jack Paar, Perry Como, Herb Shriner, Pat Weaver Jr., Jose Ferrer, John Ford, Ricardo Montalban, and Porfirio Rubirosa.

Chapter Eleven
VIP Passengers after Jet Travel

Once jets were introduced, propeller airplanes were gradually removed from service. I still occasionally served on the DC-6 and DC-7 planes—which I loved because I really, really enjoyed my passengers—but I loved flying on the 707. Here are some of the VIP passengers with whom I flew after the jet service began.

GARY COOPER

Gary Cooper

I was surprised to see Gary Cooper walk through the door of my airplane. The name on the VIP list was Frank Cooper—which I hadn't known was his real name. I didn't recognize many of the stars because I didn't follow them or their movies, but I recognized Gary because he was one of my favorites. I perceived Gary as a cowboy with the grit and grace of a gentleman. He won an Academy Award for his acting in *Sergeant York* and then again for *High Noon*.

PORFIRIO RUBIROSA

Rubirosa was well known as "The Last Playboy." Yes, I walked by and brushed Rubirosa's shoulder on board American Airlines and had the audacity to ask, "Name and destination, please." To which he gave the appropriate response and that ended our interaction.

HENRY J. KAISER

Henry J. Kaiser

The happy smiling face of Henry Kaiser greeted my day on Friday, January 30, 1959. He had the most infectious smile. I felt positive energy flowing from him. Mr. Kaiser was a well-known industrialist to all of us who had lived in the World War II years. Because of his steel plants, he gained the title of being the father of American shipbuilding.

HELEN KELLER

Helen Keller

I consider having been touched by Helen Keller a privilege indeed. As she got off the plane, I thought about what it means to see and hear. She made me think twice when I was feeling down or felt the urge to whine. I would think of her—deaf and blind since she was 19 months, yet a successful leader and powerful force of hope and inspiration—and my concerns would not seem so weighty. What an example of overcoming tremendous obstacles. It was a blessing to be able to brush shoulders with her and with so many really great people, and I am thankful for how they have influenced my life with the lessons of their lives.

RICARDO MONTALBAN

Ricardo Montalban was a Mexican-born actor, very good looking, and suave (see his photo on page 150). He didn't talk a lot on my flight, but he was successful in radio, television, theatre, and the movies. He was a gentleman along with being a family man. His wife died after 63 years of marriage, and it is reported that his Catholic religion was the most important thing to him.

ALFRED HITCHCOCK

Alfred Hitchcock was an English filmmaker and producer, famous for his suspenseful mysteries. He became an American citizen and was very successful in Hollywood. One article says he was unquestionably the greatest filmmaker to emerge from Britain. It continues,

Alfred Hitchcock

> Hitchcock did more than any director to shape modern cinema, which would be utterly different without him. His flair was for narrative, cruelly withholding crucial information from his characters and engaging the emotions of the audience like no one else. (Richard Avedon, "The top 21 British directors of all time," *The Daily Telegraph,* April 14, 2007.)

Alfred Hitchcock asked me to get him change for a 20 dollar bill to pay for his taxi cab after the flight. Someone in the cockpit had the change. As he sat there flying on the 707 Jet, he had a look of wonderment, and I couldn't help but wonder what unique plot he was creating.

HUGH O'BRIAN

Hugh O'Brian

Hugh O'Brian was a popular television actor, staring in the ABC TV series *The Life and Legend of Wyatt Earp* (1955-1961). He was also my could-have-been opportunity to date an actor. This is how it all happened:

I had been to a church meeting in Westchester, California, where Charlotte Sheffield, Miss USA 1957, was one of the speakers. She had told of the Miss USA festivities and her escort, Hugh O'Brian, who had graciously respected her standards as a member of The Church of Jesus Christ of Latter-day Saints. She spoke of him as being a gentleman.

Straight from that church meeting, I went to the airport for my assignment to New York on a 707, and Hugh O'Brian's name was on the VIP list. When he boarded the plane I took his name and told him that I had just heard Charlotte Sheffield tell the congregation what a gentleman he was. We conversed over the coincidence that here he was on my flight to New York.

During the cocktail service he surprised me again. I offered him the drink, and he said, "Since today is Mormon day, I will have tomato juice." I smiled. Later I asked him if he'd like "coffee, tea, or milk?" "Milk" was the returned answer. We were having fun.

After the meal service, Hugh came to the buffet area and visited. He was on his way to New York to judge the Miss Rheingold Beer contest. He said he had some time while there and would like to call me and we could get together. I was flattered, but I had other plans. He asked me to call him if I changed my mind, but I never called.

After the crew got in a taxi, ready to go to our hotel, I got my knitting out for the trip into the city. As I sat there knitting, the captain said, "Who in this car is that man trying to get their attention?" I looked up, and there was Hugh, waving and looking at me. All the way to town, we played that game, waving to each other each time our cars passed. It was fun.

I had told him I had other plans, but the truth was I had not brought any extra clothes with me and had no money to go out and buy something "just right" to wear. I had not planned on an exciting date. I have found that often we have a reason for why we do things and then there is the *real* reason. They are not always in concert. I have always wanted to tell him my *real* reason, and it was not that I was rejecting him. He was a fun and nice person. In retrospect, I wished that I had made do with what I had and met him for some conversation and entertainment to continue the playful scene that had unfolded on the airplane.

LUCILLE BALL

Lucille Ball

I worked the trip from New York to Los Angeles on the day before the Oscars and the late night trip from Los Angeles to New York after the Oscars. I had a lot of well-known movie people on those flights, and Lucille Ball was one. She was a neat lady. After having one trip with her, she acted like we were old friends. The night flight back to New York, she took me up and down the aisle introducing me to the passengers she knew—and she knew many of them! That was a blast! Don't we all love Lucy?

HENRY PLITT

Lucille Ball introduced me to the president of ABC Films, Henry Plitt, who gave me his card and invited me to come to his office to see him. He said that I reminded him of the actress Carolyn Jones. I didn't think I looked like her, and I never did go to see him, but he was courteous with manners that showed respect. On our planes, passengers could be more relaxed than in an office with scheduling deadlines. That was always an advantage that stewardesses had when visiting with very busy people. They were guests, and we had the opportunity to be pleasant and sociable.

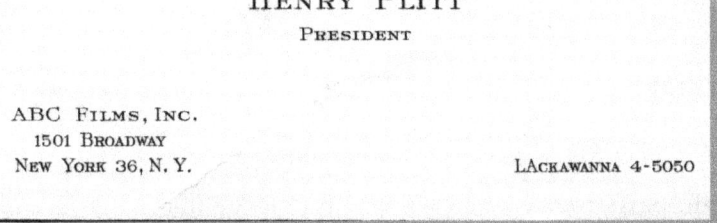

PEGGY CASS

Peggy Cass

I had Peggy Cass on the same flight with Lucille Ball the night of the Oscars. She was so friendly. She was an American actress, comedian, game show panelist, and announcer, and she was very funny. That Oscar night flight will never be forgotten. What a blast. Party, party, up and down the aisle, with Lucille Ball acting like I was her good friend, introducing me to everyone. Little wonder that Peggy Cass acted also like we were old friends when I saw her again on the same flight with Mrs. Arcaro and Keely Smith.

MRS. EDDIE ARCARO AND KEELY SMITH

Keely Smith

Mrs. Arcaro had a lovely feathered hat which she gave to Claire and me. We had been complimenting her on her hat, and she said, "I won't be wearing it next year; you girls take it." Mr. Arcaro was one of the greatest jockeys on the scene. He is in the American Thoroughbred Horse Racing Hall of Fame. On the same flight as Mrs. Arcaro was Keely Smith, an American jazz and popular music singer who enjoyed popularity in the 1950s and 1960s.

VELCRO MAN

I can't remember his name, but I was standing in the first class section of the plane in the buffet area when a gentleman came up to me and got my attention with a small piece of something that I had never seen. I studied it as he ripped it open and snapped it closed and explained that it had been registered in the USA the year before. He asked me if I thought it would sell. To which I replied, "Interesting." I didn't want to hurt his feelings by asking my real question, "How could that *something* sell?" Little did I know!

VAN CLIBURN

Van Cliburn

Van Cliburn could paint a picture with music that touched the soul. He was a great pianist. Every time I hear the notes of Liszt, I think of him.

I met Van Cliburn in the Mercury Section of the 707. He sat on the left side of the plane facing the cockpit near the buffet area. As we visited, he asked me where I was from. We were flying west to Los Angeles and when I replied, "Animas Valley, New Mexico," Van summoned me and pointed, "You are from down there." He was right. If we were to fly due south, there Animas would be in all the glory of an arid desert. I was impressed that he knew where Animas was and would point it out to me. He was interested in the world and connected with it.

JACKIE COOPER

Jackie Cooper was another really nice person on board American Airlines. I met him as an adult, but he played the boy Jackie in the TV show *Our Gang*. At about the age of nine, Jackie Cooper was nominated for the Academy Award for Best Actor.

Jackie Cooper

LEO DUROCHER

Leo Durocher

It was fun to have Leo Durocher on my flight because his wife, Laraine Day, was in my Sunday School class at church. Leo Durocher was an infielder and manager in Major League baseball. When I was a young girl he was managing the Brooklyn Dodgers. In the Hoskins home, many hours were spent listening to the radio as the Brooklyn Dodgers played the New York Yankees.

My Daddy was a Dodger fan, and we all rooted for the defeat of those "Damn Yankees." Yes, that is the way it was in Santa Rita, New Mexico, where western music was priority. Except when the Dodgers played, sorry western music.

MAX SHULMAN

Max Shulman

Max Shulman was an American writer who wrote humorous things. After he was on my flight, I recorded in my journal, "*Rally Round the Flag, Boys* is a book that I should read." Shortly after that, I went to the movie based on it. It was enjoyable.

CHARLES SCHULZ

Charles Shulz

Charles Schulz, best known for his comic strip *Peanuts*, was one of my favorite passengers because he interacted with the world around him. He had the gift of connecting with his very presence. He reached out in such an engaging way that I knew he was watching the world in an interesting way. I loved getting a glimpse of how he saw everything. He could explain life in a way that no other could. I am pleased that I had the opportunity of saying, "Thank you, Mr. Schulz, for flying with American Airlines."

DR. HOWARD "HOWIE" LAITIN

Howie worked at a high level job for the Rand Corporation. They were fortunate to have Howie's intelligence, energy, and commitment. He did a lot of flying with American Airlines, and as we visited on the plane, I knew that he was an honorable person. Howie has influenced my life with his knowledge and good values. I was fortunate to enjoy some jazz spots with him. We went to the Limelight where they featured Dixieland music. Howie was fine company for an evening out on the town and for stimulating conversation. When I think of intelligence, I think of Howie Laitin. I am still in contact with him and consider him to be one of my best friends.

JERRY LEWIS

Jerry Lewis

It was always nice to have an entertainer on board. The trip went faster and the crowd loved it. With childlike behavior, Jerry Lewis entertained the crowd in the Mercury Section with American Airline balloons. He kept everyone laughing as he entertained himself.

VIC DAMONE

Vic Damone

What a voice! Frank Sinatra even said that Damone had "the best set of pipes in the business." The stewardess who was working the flight with me brought a baseball on every flight for the VIP passengers to sign. I remember Vic Damone signing it for her. I thought this was a novel idea of hers, and I imagine she enjoys the collection. It was fun to see Vic Damone in person since it was his voice that serenaded my first sweetheart and me as we listened, sang, and danced together, making memories. Some of my favorite songs of his are "An Affair to Remember," "Do I Love You," "It's Magic," "My Heart Cries for You," "My Truly, Truly Fair," "On the Street Where You Live," "Take My Heart," "Tell Me You Love Me," and "You're Breaking My Heart."

DINAH SHORE

Dinah Shore

Dinah Shore was another phenomenal voice with a warm personality and a delight to have around. What I remember about her was her contagious smile. She was an American singer, actress, and television personality. She was most popular during the Big Band era of the 1940s and 1950s. Her story is inspirational. Dinah failed at auditions, but kept trying and trying until she made it to the top.

EDWARD EVERETT HORTON

Edward Everett Horton

Edward Horton was an American character actor on television, movies, and radio, doing voice work for animated cartoons such as the series "Fractured Fairy Tales." Bruce Eder's *All Movie Guide* says that "few actors were more beloved of audiences across multiple generations—and from more different fields of entertainment—than Edward Everett Horton." But Edward Horton hardly smiled that day on my flight. He seemed serious with a contemplative countenance.

MARGE AND GOWER CHAMPION

Marge and Gower Champion

These two were a sensational dance team. Marge Champion was also an American dance choreographer. On my flight they were so personable. I can see their smiling faces still as they conversed with the stewardesses.

GENERAL AND MRS. GAVIN

For me as a young adult having General Gavin as a passenger was and is an inspiration. His life was one of determination, hard work, and leadership. He showed endurance with principle which made him a hero for me to admire and respect—he was a man of honor. General Gavin was a World War II commander. He continued in the Army after the war and rose to become one of the top leaders. The *New York Times* gave this summary of his background:

> James Maurice Gavin was a native of Brooklyn who was orphaned in childhood and reared by adoptive parents in the coal country of Pennsylvania.

He left school after the eighth grade and worked at odd jobs until he joined the Army at 17.

Setting his sights on West Point, the young private took after-hours courses to gain a high-school education and passed a competitive examination to win appointment to the United States Military Academy.

(*New York Times*, "Lieut. Gen. James Gavin, 82, Dies; Champion and Critic of Military" by Glenn Fowler, February 25, 1990)

But what impresses me most about his life is what follows after he joined the military:

General James Gavin

The career of Lieutenant General James M. "Jumping Jim" Gavin was outstanding. He began his service to the Army as a private and rose through the ranks on the basis of ability and drive to be a three star general. He led the 82nd Airborne Division through some of its toughest fighting in World War II.

At the pinnacle of his career, with a fourth star and probable selection as the Chief of Staff of the Army, General Gavin suddenly retired. The crux of his decision to end his illustrious career was bound up in this notion of HONOR. As a senior member of the Army team, he was bound to support the leadership. If he in all good conscience disagreed with policy, he had only two honorable choices—resign or support.

General Gavin honorably chose the former. The news hit the Army with the impact of a major caliber round, and most Army personnel who know the general were saddened that so notable a talent would leave on the brink of the crowning achievement of his career.

Today in a world that believes in expediency, General Gavin's honorable gesture would be ridiculed. In the so-called Me Generation, all that counts is getting ahead. If General Gavin were alive today and in the same position, he could have just kept quiet with his views and changed the whole situation when he became Chief of Staff. But Gavin came from the old school that still believed "honor" was important. His entire life had been bound up in this notion.

The one individual that Gavin had to, in the end, account for his actions was Gavin HIMSELF. He could not stand by and see the Army adopt a doctrine he thought wrong. But to undermine the position from within was not honorable. The only way he could live with himself was to retire first, and then speak out. It was certainly not an easy choice. But it was a most honorable one. (Compiled by the U.S. Army Quartermaster Corps Historian, Fort Lee, Virginia, "General Gavin: Man of Honor.")

General Gavin's story epitomizes the general attitude of American culture at the time, not necessarily for each individual, but it was the tone of our great country. Our citizenry generally didn't think in terms of "me first," but knowing well that there were values and principles guiding us into higher thinking than ourselves. General Gavin's life motivated me, and continues to motivate me, to be what American Airlines was looking for when they looked for stewardesses back in 1957, "a contributor, a giver. Not a taker." It is the desire of my heart that my attitude will be one of selflessness, honor, and bubbling patriotism as exemplified by General Gavin's life.

MILLIE PERKINS

Millie Perkins

Millie was a model and international cover girl. She did not seek to be an actress. When she was pursued by director and producer George Stevens for the title role in *The Diary of Anne Frank*, she resisted at first. I'm so glad she decided to do it though; I appreciate and respect the message of the movie. Millie was a lovely young lady. I remember thinking as she boarded the plane, "I will never make it as a model if I need to look like Millie." She was a beautiful girl. She was on my 707 Boeing flight of March 24, 1959 with George Stevens's son, George Stevens, Jr., who also became a successful director like his father.

MITCH MILLER

Mitch Miller

Mitch Miller was well known for being a musician and singer. I enjoyed his TV series *Sing Along with Mitch*. On my flight, Mitch Miller entertained us as we served our meal. Up and down the aisle, he was hosting his own *Play Along with Mitch*. After excusing myself to get on with the task of serving a meal, he continued the need to party. So, to make a statement that it was time to get serious, I pulled his beard! I can't believe I did that, but my journal doesn't lie. He responded with good humor, as did the passengers.

DANNY KAYE

Danny Kaye

This man saved our bacon. Bless him! Here we are in the Mercury section of American Airlines Boeing 707. It was a beautiful, happy day and we had Danny Kaye on board the flight from Los Angeles to New York. We thought we had checked all the latches in the buffet area. On takeoff, we sat down across from some passengers. Up, up into the sky we went, and down, down the aisle rolled the rolls, the silverware, and salt and pepper. Oh, glory! We were so embarrassed! It could have been the end of American Airlines stewardesses on that flight.

When the seat belt sign turned off, Danny Kaye absolutely turned the place into a party. He danced up and down the aisle helping us pick up the rolling stuff. Teasing us, laughing with all the other passengers, he played around. My journal says, "Kissed us in the buffet area and tickled us as we served our meal." He was such a party clown. It was one of the best trips I ever had! The passengers loved it. Talk about turning a lemon into lemonade; it happened!

CONRAD N. HILTON

Conrad N. Hilton

Conrad N. Hilton owned the Hilton Hotels chain. I had been an occasional guest in Hilton Hotels, and I was excited to see him on our flight where I could now graciously serve him as our guest. I felt a kinship to him since we both were born in New Mexico. His father owned a general store there. We both had lived in primitive adobe dwellings. The points for conversation with him were already in place. I was impressed with his humble spirit. The Conrad N. Hilton Foundation records sum up his life thus: "Hard work, faith in God, an abiding patriotic confidence in the United States and the capacity to dream as large as his imagination would allow were the cornerstones of Conrad Hilton's life." After I had him on my flight, I never desired to stay in another hotel name. It will always be the Hilton for me.

PETER LAWFORD

Peter Lawford

Peter Lawford was an English actor, member of the "Rat Pack," and brother-in-law to President John F. Kennedy. I will never forget the flight he was on. It was an evening of panic. I was on reserve, which meant I had to stand by for a call from Crew Schedule for the opportunity to fly. The phone rang. I answered, and a panicky voice at the other end said, "Hurry!" They thought the flight had a stewardess scheduled, but something had occurred, and there was no stewardess. The plane door could not close for takeoff until a replacement was in place. Oh, dear! "We need you now, because it has passengers on board and the plane is ready to push off." Being thirty minutes from the airport, I surely wasn't ready when they called; I panicked. Usually, we had more notice to get ourselves going. Hurriedly, I threw on my uniform, drove like fury, and made it quickly through operations and up the stairs to the plane. A gentleman greeted me at the door of the plane with a welcoming kiss, hug, and salutation. That gentleman was Peter Lawford. The passengers responded to the theatrics of the moment, and the flight was a delightful time from Los Angeles to New York, even though we got there late.

JEAN PAUL GETTY

Jean Paul Getty

Jean Paul Getty was an American industrialist. His formula for success was to rise early, work hard, and strike oil. He became a billionaire and collected art and antiquities. His collection was the foundation for the J. Paul Getty Museum in Los Angeles, California.

It wasn't until after my flight with Mr. Getty that I realized who he was and that he was between marriages—he was ending his fourth; he has been quoted as saying, "A lasting relationship with a woman is only possible if you are a business failure." As he was reaching out for a smile from me, I thought, "He's another man trying to secure an invitation to dinner." His presence was filled with energy. He was friendly and seemed to be always in the aisle. "Excuse me sir."

CARY GRANT

Cary Grant

Cary Grant was my favorite actor. He played the part well as he boarded the Mercury flight in Los Angeles. Immediately after I had shown him to his seat, he took off his shoes, slipped on doe skin slippers, and watched us for the rest of the flight. I hadn't lived until I had Cary Grant watching me for four hours. It was difficult to remember my lines.

Other celebrities I flew with include: comedian and TV show host Herb Shriner and his wife (I remember my grandpapa enjoying him because, as Grandpapa said, "The kids don't have to cover their ears."); Puerto Rican actor and director Jose Ferrer; the president of NBC, Pat Weaver, Jr.; famous movie director John Ford; comedian Jack Parr (Claire, Barbara, Gerry and I went to Jack Parr's show in New York), and American actor Howard Duff and his wife, actress Ida Lupino (see their photos on page 150).

I could go on and on. There were so many wonderful people and memories. I have been so blessed to meet such varied and accomplished people. I remember them with fondness and hope someday to meet them all again. I served them the best that I knew how to serve, and service is the foundation of relationships.

A DC–6B from my friend Jon Proctor. He said, "This is one of my favorite shots. The sun was just perfect on Flagship Oklahoma City, one of American's DC–6Bs, as it waited clearance for takeoff at Lindbergh Field, bound for Los Angeles. What makes it special for me is the fact that my dad (Heath Proctor) was aboard. This was the origination of American/Delta Interchange Flight 902, headed for Birmingham, Alabama via Los Angeles, Phoenix, Dallas and Atlanta." © Jon Proctor

Chapter Twelve
Final Flights

Transitioning from props to jets didn't happen overnight. Jets were introduced, but we still worked the other equipment the whole time I was flying.

One evening, we were deadheading a DC-6 plane back to Los Angeles when an engine caught on fire! I remember looking out the window and thinking, "Wow, that is really pretty." We made an emergency landing, but I was not one bit concerned. The flying crew knew what to do! I didn't need to wonder any longer why we were deadheading that particular plane.

Another evening, flying between El Paso and Douglas, the pilot picked up a UFO on radar. Being on a collision course, he quickly dove the plane to a lower altitude. It was in the evening, and I remember I was walking up the aisle when all of a sudden I was on my knees! This made me a bit nervous because a few flights before on an all-night flight to New York when all the passengers were asleep, the flight engineer had made his way to the lounge in the back of the plane for a short conversation with us. It was a beautiful night—the moon was reflecting on the clouds, and they were not a threat to a smooth ride. Our chit-chat resulted in him telling me about the UFOs he had seen and that he enthusiastically believed in the reports he had read about others seeing them. I didn't know exactly how to take such enthusiasm. My own, brief "encounter" with them left me wondering, "Are they real or unreal?"

My journal details many more of my adventures while flying.

Another photo of a DC-6B taken by Jon Proctor. About this picture he says, "These were the days, when you could walk right out onto the ramp in order to grab a picture. An American DC-6 receives attention on its transit stop. In the background, a PSA billboard advertises 75-minute flights to San Francisco for $19.85 plus tax." © Jon Proctor

FRIDAY, JANUARY 30, 1959

During our landing approach in Los Angeles, we descended so rapidly that our speed brakes were used and believe me, was I ever scared because the plane really made noises and jerked like nothing before, honest to goodness. Another debriefing after the trip.

MONDAY, FEBRUARY 2, 1959

Coming home from Fort Worth, we had to hold over Los Angeles because of traffic problems. I have never seen anything so tremendous as "our" city. The atmosphere was so clear and visibility very good that one could see for miles and miles. Captain Kreamer banked so steeply that you really felt like you are walking on Cloud Nine. Never in a long time, twenty months, have I been so excited about the view: diamonds, emeralds, onyx, everywhere, glory be!!

You can tell I was grateful that we were in a holding pattern, circling the airport to be cleared for landing.

TUESDAY, FEBRUARY 3, 1959

We arrived (Stewardess MaryLou Parkes and I) in Phoenix at about 12:30 a.m. Two and a half hours before we landed, a new American Airlines Lockheed Electra, Flight 320, crashed into the East River while on approach to LaGuardia Airport in New York. Three crew members survived, First Officer Hlavacek, Flight Engineer Cook, and Stewardess Zeller. I feel so empty. Our crew came unglued. We may be here today and gone tomorrow.

Photo of a DC–7 by Jon Proctor, "American's DC–7B "Royal Coachman" flights were still passing through SAN. N343AA pulls into Gate 6." © Jon Proctor

SATURDAY, FEBRUARY 7, 1959

I drove out to the end of the runway and watched a 707 jet take off.

I had driven Barbara to the airport for her jet trip and wanted to see her plane leave. Interestingly enough, although we flew on 707s often, we didn't see them take off. This was a first for me, and it was thrilling!

THURSDAY, MARCH 12, 1959

After having had an extended layover in New York City because of a wicked snow storm with continuing cold and gray skies, the following was not an emergency; however, it could have been. We left New York City for the airport in a cold snowy mood, and we had a time getting to the airport. On the way we had a flat tire. From operations to the hangar we had more car trouble. The car stopped and we had to take another car. We loaded our passengers in the hangar because of something about keeping the plane de-iced. Little did I know that in spite of the working snow plows, the runway conditions were still icy. Unbeknownst to us, the ice on the runway was peeling the aluminum off the belly causing it to roll up. The noises on takeoff didn't seem much different from other icy, snowy takeoffs, but the peeling created additional drag so on takeoff we cleared the blast fence by only two feet! Kinda close. Hmmmmm. The crew did some very quick and skillful flying to leap us over the fence. As I deplaned, the Captain and his crew were talking and taking notes as they studied the rolled up metal on the belly of the plane. I suppose this rolled up metal on the fuselage was caused by ice on the runway. I wanted to see that report.

Oh, yes, Barb, Claire, and I worked the forward cabin, Mercury Section. This we did all month.

My PR assignments continued as well. Claire and I participated in the "Stop Arthritis Telethon." Will Fowler and Bill Phillips of American Airlines Public Relations wrote to my supervisor Jeanne Folk thanking her for our participation on the KTTV-TV telethon.

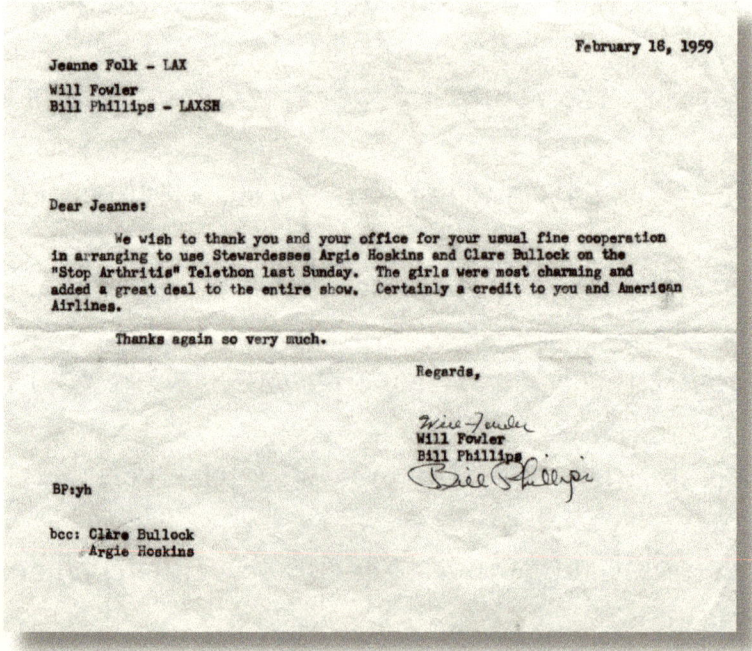

William Fowler was in his early eighties and worked for six years as a public relations representative for American Airlines and then became the news director for KTTV-TV Channel 11.

SUNDAY, FEBRUARY 15, 1959

My friend Bob Cawley said the NBC control

unit in his particular studio was watching the telethon Claire and I had been on. There were lots of people on the program such as Jane Russell, Jerry Lewis, Lucille Ball, Billy Eckstein, John Smith (actor in *The High and Mighty*), Kathy Nolan (actress), Terry Moore (actress), and the MC, Uncle Miltie Berle. Oh yes, should I forget, Claire Bullock and Argie Hoskins.

Peter Pitchess had been in charge of the telethon. He was the Los Angeles county sheriff. One newspaper reported him as being the sheriff "who transformed the nation's largest Sheriff Department from a rustic cowboy agency into a modern professional law enforcement organization" (Myrna Oliver, "Peter Pitchess, Sheriff Who Modernized Agency, Dies," *The Los Angeles Times*, Monday April 5, 1999).

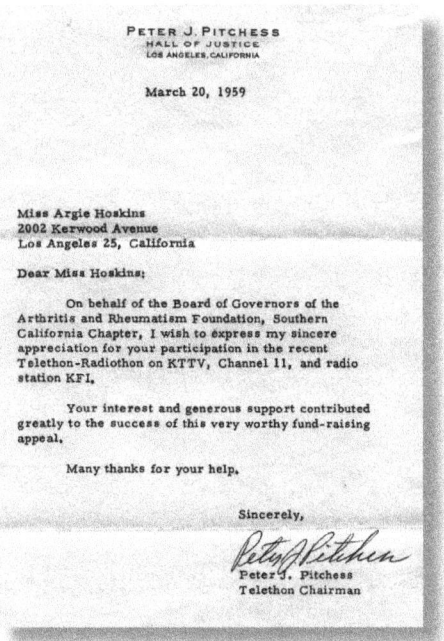

A letter from Peter Pitchess thanking me for helping with the Telethon.

As I reflect on many of the passengers I enjoyed, I feel a sense of loss that their names are gone from my mind, but their faces still appear in my memory bank. Their personalities remain intact in these snapshots I carry in my memory. As I write this, a couple from New York pops in my mind. Their only child, a son, had died of a boating accident. They were Jewish and lovely people. As the flight drew to completion, they gave me a hug and said that I was the kind of young lady who they had wanted for their son. Even if I were not of their faith, they would welcome me. Relationships are the most wonderful moments on earth.

Passenger letter from flight number 960 from San Diego on February 21, 1959. It reads:

A very pleasant flight, cleanliness of plane impressed me; one of the stewardesses was particularly gracious without the usual obsequiousness. I am recommending your line to my friends.
 Signed, Emm [Emmett McKowen]
The note from my supervisor at the top reads, "Argie, for your info. Has been credited to your file, Dottie."

The note from Emmett McKowan was written on Continental Airline stationery because sometimes we used Continental planes if a particular flight was to continue on through. Also, Western and Eastern had a deal with our equipment.

Passenger letter from flight number 681 from Chicago to Los Angeles on February 2, 1959. It reads:

I travel by air a great deal but not too often at all by coach. The flight has been very pleasant in spite of a large number of passengers due to the very efficient and courteous service by the two stewardesses Miss Hoskins and Miss Flynn. Miss Hoskins particularly has been outstanding.
   I congratulate you on your selection and personnel training.
   Signed, Mr. Kenneth G. Woolley
The note from my supervisor on the side says, "Thanks again Argie. Another credit. Dottie."

Passenger letter from flight number 609 from Phoenix to Los Angeles on February 25, 1959. It reads:

Dear Mr. Sadler,
 Two weeks ago on this flight my Stewardess was Miss Argie Ella Hoskins. Being my first flight after a near mid-air crash, I was very upset.
 Miss Hoskins put me at ease—and with many little efforts (coffee—reading material, etc.) made my trip the finest in twenty years of airline travel.
 Miss Hoskins is the finest example of "service with a beautiful smile". I'll keep flying American.
 Signed, Mr. Robert M. Cawley NBC-TV Sunset and Vine, Hollywood 28, California.
The note on the side is from my supervisor, Betty: "Argie, this is absolutely wonderful! All our thanks for all your efforts! Betty."

Bob Cawley was a director and producer for NBC-TV and taught at the acting school in Hollywood where C. L. attended. Bob started helping C. L. with his dream to get into pictures. I had gotten to know Bob on this and other flights, and C. L. met Bob through me. Bob had also asked me if I would like to take some acting classes. I would have like that very much, but my plate was full of other things at that time in my life.

In some ways, I feel that acting is what I have done all my life—I am what my heart desires to be. Ultimately, we get to choose who we become, so I've always tried to act like the person I've wanted to be, and, eventually, that is who I became.

C. L. didn't have the resources to continue his movie and TV adventure. C. L. joined the Army so he could get out of debt and have an income. Not long thereafter, Four Star Playhouse sent him an invitation for a contract in a series, but it had come too late.

Left: Me, C. L. in his Army uniform, and Barbara.

Right: C. L. in his suit looking dashing.

Passenger letter from flight number 3 from Idlewild to Los Angeles on April 3, 1959. It reads:

This is my first experience in jet flying (not, however, my first in the air), and I find it superior to any other form of travel. It is a clean, pleasant, precise, and most delightful trip. The courtesies afforded by the stewardesses (Miss Meek and Miss Hoskins) make it a completely comfortable and memorable flight. Since the service is superb, I have no suggestions to improve it.
Signed, Mrs. A. C. Hershatter

A letter from passenger Joseph T. Martin on April 6, 1959. It reads:

Dear Miss Hoskins:
This is just to tell you that you certainly did everything you could to make our trip from Los Angeles to New York on the Mercury 707 most enjoyable, and it surely was.

It was nice to have had the pleasure of meeting you, and I do hope we shall have the good fortune to ride with you or see you sometime in the not to distant future.

With kindest personal regards.
Very sincerely,
Signed, Joseph T. Martin.
The hand-written note on the bottom reads, "You are a little darling"

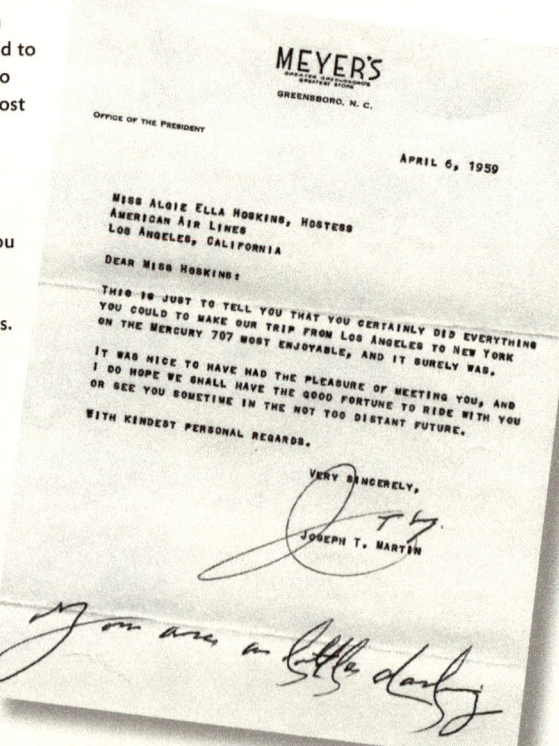

Joseph Martin was a prominent businessman. His leadership led Meyer's Department Store to become one of the most successful retail businesses in the South. He was also "one of the fathers of commercial air travel in Greensboro, [North Carolina,] as he pushed for the expansion of the Greensboro-High Point Airport, providing leadership that allowed it to become one of the largest airports in North Carolina." (MSS Collection #91, Joseph Martin Papers, 1918-1982. 4 boxes (169 folders), c. 450 items.)

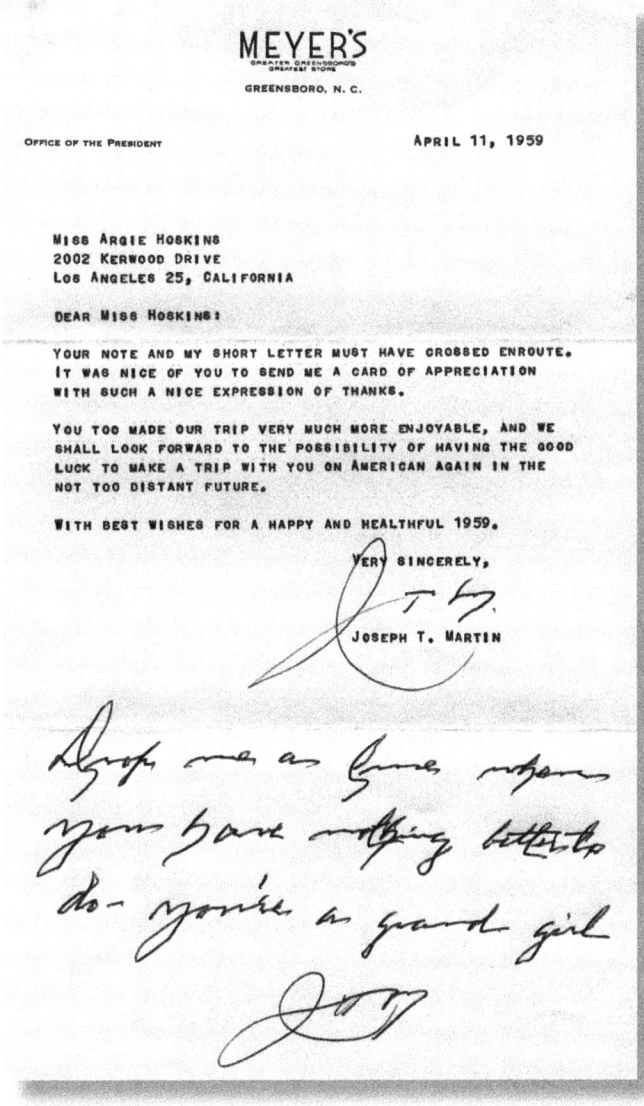

Another letter from Joseph Martin on April 11, 1959. It reads:

Dear Miss Hoskins:
 Your note and my short letter must have crossed en route. It was nice of you to send me a card of appreciation with such a nice expression of thanks.
 You too make our trip very much more enjoyable, and we shall look forward to the possibility of having the good luck to make a trip with you on American again in the not too distant future.
 With best wishes for a happy and healthful 1959.
 Very sincerely,
 Signed, Joseph T. Martin

The hand-written note on the bottom reads, "Drop me a line when you have nothing better to do. You're a grand girl, J. T. M."

Passenger letter from a flight from New York to Los Angeles on May 12, 1959. It reads:

Miss Argie Hoskins is a very capable, courteous stewardess. She made the trip very enjoyable.
  Signed, Mrs. Helen Goldschmidt
The note from my supervisor below reads, "Argie, look at all these nice words about busy you! Many thanks for all your interest. Betty."

This lady was so kind and such a pleasure to have on board; my home on American Airlines. I never experienced a difficult trip with guests. And that is how they were treated, as guests.

> **PASSENGER LETTER**
>
> Dear Mr. Sadler:
>
> I am flying with American From New York to Los Angeles
>
> On Flight Number 3   Date 5/12/59
>
> This is my first flight by airplane or jet, which I have enjoyed very much. It was a smooth and pleasant flight. Your Stewardesses efficient. The services was excellent.
>
> Thank you.
>
> Miss Elmira Sears
> 323 Lark
> Albany 10, New York
>
> *Argie — wonderful letter! Please add this to your collection. Many Thanks, Betty*

Passenger letter from flight number 3 from New York to Los Angeles on May 12, 1959. It reads:

Dear Mr. Sadler:
   This is my first flight by airplane or jet, which I have enjoyed very much. It was a smooth and pleasant flight. Your Stewardesses efficient. The services were excellent.
   Thank you,
   Miss Elmira Sears
The note from my supervisor reads, "Argie, wonderful letter! Please add this to your collection. Many thanks, Betty."

This flight from New York to Los Angeles was on a Mercury 707. It was boarded in the hangar after a delay because of the threat of more weather and a lasting snowstorm. The crew had transportation trouble reaching the terminal. In spite of the challenges for passengers and crew, we had an enjoyable trip. Life is so much more enjoyable when challenges are met with hope and optimism.

A passenger letter from flight number 30 from Los Angeles to Chicago on June 16, 1959. It reads:

This is my first flight on a jet plane, and I am very well pleased with the service.
The stewardess is doing a very fine job, and everyone is very well pleased with her service. If I might make a recommendation; some type of altitude and speed meter would be very good for passengers' enjoyment of the flight. Thank you for your time in looking at this note. I will be looking forward to flying American Airlines again as soon as I can.
    Signed, Mr. P. A. Romero
The note from my supervisor on the side reads, "Argie, here is another one full of praise about you. Many thanks, Betty."

Receiving another passenger letter was always exciting, but the real reward was in the service and how pleased my new friends were as they deplaned. It was always a joy to welcome them again and, sometimes, again and again.

Flying with American Airlines was so fulfilling for me. I was constantly thrilled with the beauty of the sky, the penetrating images that were as real as real. Flying through misty grey clouds to tails of frosty scrapings, and feeling stuck in the high, white, wispy clouds on a sunny day was absolutely fascinating. Going from having a scared feeling to a feeling of peacefulness as the clouds danced across the sky was everyday life in the sky. It was an honor to fly on planes captained with old World War II pilots; from the props to the jets, they were the greatest! Just knowing the skill of the men at the wheel was a comfort.

Bob Merritt

Crew members watched out for each other. I remember one time when Captain Clarke, Stewardess Jennings, the copilot, the flight engineer, and I were together on a flight deadheading from El Paso to Los Angeles. We were all of the same faith, and Captain Clarke said, "Let's take this flight to Heaven." We had a fun time. Captain Clarke was a wonderful man. On one flight from Los Angeles to San Diego, Captain Clarke had seen me visiting with a young Annapolis graduate, Bob Merritt, who had become a navy pilot. After the flight, the American Airlines crew had several minutes in the crew lounge before working the trip back to Los Angeles, and Captain Clarke said, "Argie, go out and visit with that young man." So, I went out to a concession area and continued my visit with Bob. He walked me to the gate and a wonderful relationship began to unfold. Bob and I became great friends.

One day, I was in the stewardess office just hanging out, chatting with my good friend Kay Hansen. She worked in American Airlines' corporate offices and in the administrative end of the stewardess program. I didn't see her often, so it was neat to have this time with her, and I loved learning from her wisdom. She was so dedicated to American Airlines and her position with Flight Operations. Her wit and her inexhaustible spirit were her personality hallmarks. You might say that she was "on the go" all the time. Somewhere in our conversation that day she said, "We need to have a retirement home for American Airlines pilots and stewardesses, so they can sit around and tell each other about their varicose veins." We had been talking about the importance of staying in our seats until the seat belt sign went off to protect us from experiencing g-forces on our body, which somehow creates varicose veins. I didn't understand the physics of the force, but I had felt the impact.

Historical American Airlines' Kiwi monument

But Kay was serious. That little idea about a home where American Airlines relationships could continue grew under Kay's indomitable spirit and untiring support. She was always thinking of others and was a guiding influence in organizing the Kiwi Club as a service organization of present and former stewardesses and flight attendants. The goal of the club was to be an honorable organization for women of common interest and to provide for social and charitable activity. Now there is a community where the wonderful friendships of the past can continue thanks to Kay's invaluable advisory contributions in the Kiwi Club's founding.

Another stewardess I always enjoyed conversing with was Bettye Harris. She was my supervisor, but she was also my good friend. Bettye gave me encouragement as well as direction. She said someday I would be a successful supervisor. Her words motivated me to continue to do my best when times were difficult. Bettye was quite accomplished. She had studied at Arizona State College at Tempe as a psychology major. While there, she was a member of the traditions committee and the student governing board. She was a cheerleader and was chosen a battalion sponsor for the ROTC. She also was a champion swimmer. She had always loved to travel and so was interested in aviation as a career. When she saw the film comedy *Three Guys Named Mike*, based on experiences of an airline stewardess, she decided to apply for a similar position (see pages 200 and 201 for more information about her).

My history takes me to the day when I sadly walked into Bettye's office, laid my head on her desk, and through my tears announced that I was terminating my service.

"No, not you, why?" Her question rang in my soul. My desire was to marry and have children, and I didn't feel in concert with myself because at that time American Airlines stewardesses could not marry.

American eventually changed their policy, but at that time the wall seemed too high to jump, and to climb it seemed impossible. As I packed Autumn Leaves and hugged my friends, my heart kept reverberating Bettye's statement, "Not you."

But as I pulled away, a new sense of adventure grew in my heart. I started a new chapter, one which has brought me the joy of four sons who have delighted my heart. It is a choice I have not regretted. Sometimes I still dream of being that stewardess supervisor—I would have loved to inspire the dream of "doing what we do best" in those souls of the serving and caring faces that greet you at the door. But I suppose that as a wife, mother, and grandmother, I will always be that kind of supervisor.

I'll be forever grateful for the privilege of being associated with American Airlines during the golden age of flying. Truly, it was more than a ticket.

Me and my sons around 1972.
Left to right: Christopher, me, Randy, and on the floor Daniel and Bradley.

Me in 2002, standing in front of the centerpiece of the C. R. Smith Museum, the lovingly restored 1940 Douglas DC–3, Flagship Knoxville. The museum is located in Fort Worth, Texas, and was named after the president of American Airlines during my time, C. R. Smith. The funds to build the museum came from fundraising efforts of various American Airlines employee and retiree groups to honor C. R. Smith's accomplishments and leadership.

Above: American Airlines gave me this charm.

Left: My sons gave me this American Airlines 707 jet model as a Christmas gift.

Part Two
On Wings of Time

Above: Heath in front of a Pitcairn mail plane in 1928. © Jon Proctor

Right: Heath in 1937. Captain W. H. Proctor remains an American Airlines icon for whom we have utmost respect and appreciation for all the hours at the wheel through the storms and the beauty as he skillfully flew his journey through the clouds of time.

Willis Heath Proctor

AMERICAN AIRLINES PILOT AND TRAINER, 1927–1957

This memoir is written by Heath Proctor's son, Jon, who shares the excitement of living with a historical icon. Jon is an airline industry journalist and historian, who has authored several books. Jon's photos are inspirational. They are technically outstanding and emotionally rewarding.

I come from an American Airlines family. My father was a pioneer airmail pilot and flew the first westbound mail across the state of New York in December 1927, with Colonial Western, which eventually melded into American Airlines. Dad's American Airlines payroll number was 02! I still have Dad's AA retiree ID card, with employee number 02 on it. Here's a little bit of American Airlines' trivia, employee 01 was Goodrich Murphy, a ground employee who won a contest with his American Airlines eagle design suggestion that was adopted as the corporate logo. From Dad's initial assignment to the Buffalo domicile, he flew out of Newark and Cincinnati before relocating to Chicago in 1936.

During World War II, Dad served in a number of capacities including commander of the Air Transport Command facility at La Guardia Airport and Commanding Officer of the India Wing in the China-India-Burma (CBI) Theater. He retired as a Colonel and was nominated for promotion to General in the Reserves, but he declined as it would have meant more time on active duty. Instead he flew out his career with American.

Dad became the first pilot in the United States to reach the mandatory retirement age of 60 in May 1950, although back then it was company policy rather than law. LIFE Magazine published a tribute to him, and TIME also covered the milestone.

> **The First Grey Eagle Convention**
> 1962 November 15–17
> Sheraton Hotel, Chicago, IL
>
> President: W. H. Proctor
> Convention Chairman: W. H. Proctor
>
> Attendance: 67
> Membership: 162
>
> Highlights: Formation of Grey Eagle by-laws. Harold Ames (Director, American Airlines) gave a cocktail party for entire convention (38 Grey Eagles and 17 wives) at the Prudential Plaza. C. R. Smith was the guest speaker at the banquet on the evening of 17th. (Note: Room rates $8.85 single, $14.00 double. Mixed drinks 65 cents.)
>
> Quotes from C. R. Smith's speech:
> "We find that in the 'past the middle' years of life we do not form new friendships with the ease of our more youthful years and new friends do not wear as well; they seem more like acquaintances."
>
> "We hold up the fingers to count our real friends, all fingers may not be up. The truth of the matter is that good men are scarce and good friends hard to come by."
>
> "The Village advice was 'to stick by the home town girls'. It is good advice for us as well. Grey Eagles has many worthy purposes but none more worthy than to encourage good men to continue their friendships and to enjoy them."

Minutes on the Grey Eagles' formation.
Reprinted by permission of Jock Bethune, Grey Eagles Pilot Association.

Dad stayed with American as Head of Pilot Training at Chicago-Midway until his retirement in August 1957, so he was right down the hall from the stewardess training department. He was also a founder of the Air Line Pilots Association (ALPA), and the first president of The Grey Eagles, American Airlines' retired pilot association.

To further illustrate the charm of American Airlines I found the following quotation from the article "Friendly Skies? A Cultural History of Air Travel in Postwar America" by Anke Ortlepp Research Fellow, GHI.

> Captains were featured as their airlines' most precious asset.... He was a reliable partner to his copilot and a fair and compassionate boss to his female in-flight crew.... [In general] he was a family man who longed to get home to his wife and children after spending demanding hours or days on the job. As part of this job, the captain took care of his passengers, whether they were a group of business travelers or a boy travel-

ing alone. He was a knowledgeable person even beyond his high-tech expertise, and a patriot on top of that. American Airlines Captain W. Heath Proctor, an ad stated in 1953, spent his summer vacation in the American Southwest to learn lessons that he could later pass on to his passengers via the plane's communication system: "Good morning, ladies and gentlemen, this is your Flagship Captain speaking." "From high in the sky," the ad continued, "his detailed descriptions of points of interest made the whole trip seem like a personally guided tour. Scenic highlights and historic landmarks—Indian chiefs and pioneer heroes—Proctor wove them all into one fascinating American history lesson that thrilled thousands of travelers." It portrays the captain's efforts as an expression of the care he invested in his passengers. He wanted them to experience the landscape they traveled across not only as something remote and abstract but as a real space that had layers of meaning.

Heath on retirement day.

Dad was close to and a friend of Kay Hansen. Kay worked at American Airlines' corporate offices in the administrative end of the stewardess program. In addition, Dad and C. R. Smith, the president of American Airlines, were very close, having flown together in the Air Transport Command during World War II. I was lucky enough to meet C. R. once, and I treasure the experience.

Like many pilots, Dad died relatively early, at age 74. I still miss him.

Left: Heath and his wife in front of a Ford Tri-Motor in San Diego in 1963 when they visited on a country-wide tour. Heath actually flew this very airplane, NC9683, with American. It now resides in the National Air & Space Museum in Washington, D. C. Photo courtesy of Jon Proctor.

Below: A Fairchild FC–2 that Dad flew with Colonial Western, an American Airlines predecessor. Photo courtesy of Jon Proctor.

Above: A Sikorsky S38, taken July 15, 1929, just before the first departure of the Toronto-Buffalo air mail service. Heath Proctor is on the top of the plane's float on the left, accepting the mail bound for Toronto.
Photo courtesy of Jon Proctor.

Right: A DC–4, photographed by Bill Proctor at Chicago-Midway. © Jon Proctor

A DC–3, photographed by Bill Proctor at Chicago, Midway. © Jon Proctor

Middle: A DC–6, photographed by Bob Proctor at Chicago-Midway, was last type of plane Heath flew. © Jon Proctor

Bottom: A Curtiss Condor Heath flew in the mid-1930s. Photo courtesy of Jon Proctor.

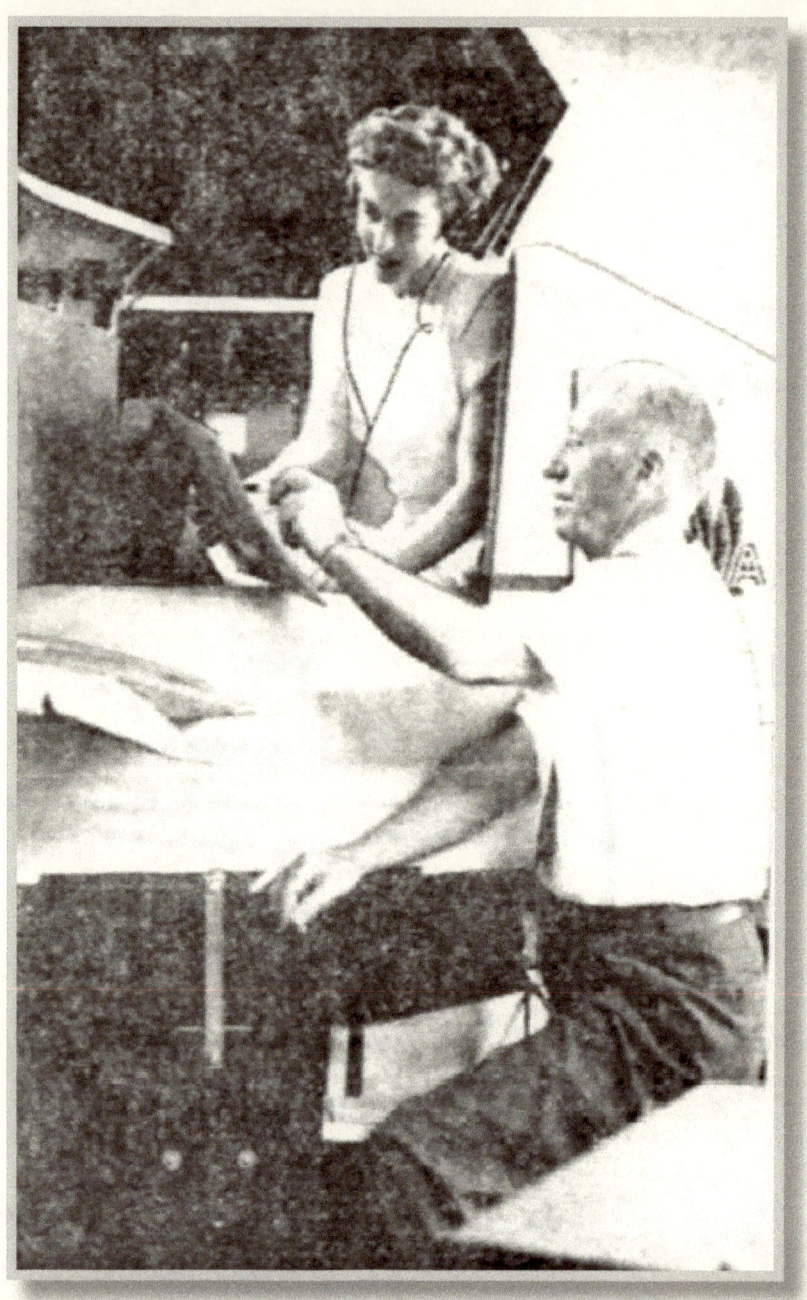

Heath Proctor training Bettye Jean Harris. This photo was in a newspaper article highlighting Bettye's graduation. The caption in the paper for this picture reads:

UP IN THE AIR
Miss Bettye Jean Harris learns the answers to "What makes a plane fly?" during her recent training as an American Airlines stewardess. She gets instruction in the fundamentals of flight from Captain Willis H. Proctor, a multi-million-mile pilot and head of the company's Link Training Department.

PHOENICIAN BECOMES STEWARDESS

Poise, education, physical fitness, beauty—all are requirements for airline stewardesses.

Pretty Bettye Jean Harris of Phoenix qualified under these rigid rules and graduated recently from the American Airlines Stewardess Training Center at Chicago Midway Airport.

Daughter of Mr. and Mrs. H. B. Kegler, 1810 E. Culver, Bettye Jean received her silver wings in a graduation ceremony which climaxed four weeks of intensive training.

Because she loves travel, the Phoenician was interested in aviation as a career. Then she saw the film comedy *Three Guys Named Mike* based on experiences of an airline stewardess—and decided to apply for a similar position.

During the course in Chicago, Bettye Jean studied flight operations, flight control, meteorology, radio, personal grooming, company routes, policies and emergency procedures, sales, air freight, air cargo, maintenance, and public relations.

Bettye Jean studied at Arizona State College at Tempe as a psychology major.

At the school, she was a member of the traditions committee, the student governing board, was a cheerleader, and was chosen a battalion sponsor for the ROTC. She was also a champion swimmer.

Movie talent scouts named her Miss Panchromatic of 1949. In conjunction with her academic studies, Bettye Jean served as an occupational and recreational therapeutist at the Arizona State Hospital.

The 63 young girls who were graduated with Jean were from every section of the United States and Canada.

They met the basic stewardess requirements of being 21 to 28 years old, between five feet two inches and five feet seven inches tall, weighing not more than 130 pounds, having a university degree or adequate business experience and being physically fit and attractive. They also qualified for requirements of character, personality, and the desire to be helpful to people.

Roy Jacobson working on a prop as a mechanic for American Airlines.
Photo courtesy of Roy Jacobson's son Curt Jacobson.

Roy G. Jacobson

AMERICAN AIRLINES MECHANIC AND FLIGHT ENGINEER, 1941–1984

This memoir is written by Roy G. Jacobson's son Curt Jacobson who connected with me through my blog.

As a little kid, when we came home from my grandmother's, my father would always drive us through the JFK airport. Before the airport was named John F. Kennedy Airport, it was Idlewild Airport. It is located on Jamaica Bay in the southeastern section of Queens County. The airport is located about 15 miles by highway from midtown Manhattan.

I'll never forget the smell of jet fuel and seeing all the planes and the times we would go with my father to clean out his mail box or pick up his bid sheets. We would go through the hangars and look at the planes.

When we went on vacation we would go up to the cockpit to look around. I will never forget the hot fudge sundaes they served on the plane; they were the best. I still think of them anytime I get ice cream today. Wherever we went, my father would always meet people he knew. American Airlines was really like a great big family back then.

We would always see my father go when he left, and run to the door when he came home from his trips. I remember how happy we were when he came home. Excited! I can still picture him standing there in his uniform. I was so proud of him and thought he had the best job there is.

My father worked for American Airlines for 43 years from 1941 to 1984, at LaGuardia and then Kennedy airport in New York. He started as a mechanic on the DC-3s a prop plane and finished as a flight engineer on the 747, a jet plane out of NY, during the glory years of the airlines. He flew the Convair 240, DC-6, DC-7, Lockheed Electra, Boeing 707, Boeing 720, Boeing 727, and the Boeing 747 airplanes.

He flew the 707 for over 20 years and the 747 for the last 6 years. He really loved the 707; it was reliable and a real work horse. I think he said that in all the years he flew the 707 they only had to shut down an engine one time. My father loved his job and American Airlines.

Roy Jacobson. Photo courtesy of Curt Jacobson.

Above: Picture of a Convair 990 taken at the Convair plant in San Diego. The people in the picture are a training class. This is when American first got the 990. Roy Jacobson is the sixth person from the right in the front row. Photo courtesy of Curt Jacobson.

Below: A Boeing 707 © Jon Proctor

Stewardess MaryLou Parkes

Below: The Electra Team admiring a model; Bill Hall, MaryLou, and Jim Shires

MaryLou Parkes Whipple

AMERICAN AIRLINES STEWARDESS, 1955–1959

MaryLou and I happened to get the same flight. Seniority and knowledge of the equipment is everything with airlines. I happened to like to fly to Texas and could hold that bid line. More often than not, I would fly with different stewardesses. Some months the pairing would be more compatible than others, and MaryLou and I were very compatible. We had a lot in common and became friends.

Approximately fifty-five years after the events of my years with American Airlines my memory is extremely weak. Only some awkward thoughts come to mind because I have no journals or records, and the years are a blur to me. In 1955, I believe we had to be 21 to fly. I was first accepted by Western Airlines to join their Stewardess program, but then they went out of business. A secretarial job opened a few miles from home with American Airlines' engineering office which I took and loved. I never wanted to leave.

Right: An American Airlines Electra in flight. Photo © Bob Garrard

Left: MaryLou modeled for a promotional about the new, beautiful Lockheed Electra. Before MaryLou was a stewardess she had a secretarial job with AA's engineering office that interfaced with the Lockheed engineers.

More pictures of the Electra team looking at the latest model.

American Airlines bag tags and Electra matches that we would give passengers.

Left: Newspaper clipping advertising for stewardesses.

Below: MaryLou's acceptance letter into stewardess school.

MaryLou was ready to be an American Airlines' stewardess.

At that time Lockheed was building an Electra (a turbo prop) for American Airlines, and I helped with some promotional work for that.

I had such a glorious time at the newly built stewardess college in Fort Worth, Texas. I remember strutting around in bathing suits with so many beautiful girls around the pool with instructors' eyes upon our every move, the entire time there. The instructors knew everyone's name the moment we entered. They were fantastic women. Their eyes followed us along the cafeteria line and every other move we made. They had to make sure we did things just right. Emergency training was the most critical. What was it, six weeks? Whew!

The moments in those weeks when a student disappeared from our view were especially sad. Their bags had already been packed for them, and they were led to the awaiting taxi. We had a wonderful dormitory, big classrooms, gorgeous grounds, and a beautiful huge main hall with a wide curving staircase where we would meet our guests. Elvis Presley was dating one of the girls. We all hung over the balcony to see him and his friend come to pick up their dates! Silly us.

There were so many procedures to ready the flight for passengers. We'd been well trained, so by the time we flew even the little details such as counting the bottles of liquor was no biggee. Today, I can't imagine serving so much coffee and tea and carrying it up and down the aisle. All the training we went through led up to our being able to "work" a flight along with a regular crew. Oh the thrill and anticipation of our first experience in flight, of where we would be assigned, and of learning to use different types of equipment in a timely manner.

Unfortunately, I am a very independent person, and I tried so hard to fit in with a group, or with my roommates, or whatever. I determined to wait with my roommate to go down to the field with her. She was a gracious Southern girl, but slow. I managed to go with her, only to learn that I missed my flight! Surely, I would be sent home, I thought! Luckily, they gave me another assignment. From that moment, I became myself again: independent, on-time, and successful, but often a loner.

Graduation time was beautiful. We had received our uniforms: dark blue for winter, tan for summer, all measured to fit to our body shape perfectly. There were military pressed creases, even in the blouse underneath our suits.

Local newspaper clipping announcing MaryLou's graduation.

MaryLou's graduating class. She is on the back row on the stairs, the fourth from the bottom.

We also had a flight topper to put on when we served food and a heavy, heavy beautiful dark blue wool coat for winter locations. Our shoes were spectators, tan and white, as I recall. I remember getting my shoes. I flew from Fort Worth to Los Angeles for a day's shopping. My dear sister Kay met me at the airport, and we found the perfect shoes in an expensive Beverly Hills store, as I recall, then back I flew. Of course the Army-style caps over very short hair topped off our uniform. Our hair had to be above the collar—a must!

Our class made up a fun song to the tune of the music from *The Bridge over the River Kwai*, a 1957 British World War II film. Unfortunately, I can't remember the lyrics we used for the last line.

> **Today we're going to march with you,**
> **Today we make our grand debut,**
> **Soaring, forever soaring,**
> **Ta da-da-da-da; da, da-da, de-do!**

MaryLou's graduation certificate; MaryLou and stewardess friends on graduation day.

We sang as we marched through circling pathways to the graduation grounds! I can almost hear it ringing in my ears right now.

The other big hubbub was about where we would be located. I was thrilled to receive Los Angeles as my base. It is my birthplace. As it turned out, if I had a few days off, I could be at home with Mom and Dad in North Hollywood. That was the best! If I had a quick turn-around, I had a nearby apartment with other American Airline Stewardesses. It was a little tricky when I served on standby and had to be at the Los Angeles Airport (a small little airfield) in an hour. My uniform stayed ready to jump into when I drove from North Hollywood. Once I forgot my jacket, and Daddy drove it down to me when I was almost already in the plane. There were no freeways then, it was city streets all the way! There were also no jetways in those days. We had to cover our heads with the American Airlines scarf and walk out across the windy tarmac to our flight.

I served as Stewardess in mostly DC-6s and DC-7s (Douglas Aircraft Company planes). They allowed about 100 passengers tops, and it was an eight-hour flight from coast to coast. I remember spending all-night flights hoping to visit with a passenger and not sit and just look at the Exit sign and take coffee to crew.

On those LAX-NYC flights we usually always had movie stars on board. The one I remember best was Dick Powell as he sat back in the lounge with me on an all-night flight. He was wonderful to visit with!

MaryLou on a plane.

On one NYC-LAX flight, the usual fog rolled in over Los Angeles, and we had to actually land in Burbank. As I lived close, I had some great young movie stars drop me off at home from their rental car as they drove on to Los Angeles. If I remember correctly, Tab Hunter was among them. Hollywood tours were always offered to us. We met Pat Boone and other show people. It was a great life.

MaryLou (far right) with stewardess friends and Pat Boone (center).

In the East, when it was cold, the passengers entered and gave us their coats as we welcomed them on board. We had to tag their coats with seat numbers and hang them up for them, returning each one to the correct person just before deplaning. Whew!

Here are some highlights that come to mind about flights and layovers: bidding vacation replacement, which meant I had four flights to New York a month! I loved seeing the sights, five star hotels, walks all over Broadway, and seeing the high rises! The Empire State Building was the tallest! I also loved my three-day layovers in Chicago where the Museum of Science and Industry became my weekly stop over. On June 19, 1933, the Museum of Science and Industry opened its great doors for the first time. It was the first museum in North America to feature interactive exhibits.

Anytime we wanted a short leave it was available to us; I was off to Mexico every other month. I had a special blood doctor in Mexico City of whom I was fond. His name was Enrique (my father's name) Hurtado. I shared a flat there with a girlfriend and her brother, the Brianos from San Luis Potosi. It was past the bull ring, and we could walk there on dirt paths from downtown Acapulco (on the beach). She worked at Las Brisas. We knew all the hotels, the morning and afternoon beaches, and every other place in town. I remember water skiing every day and jumping the ramp occasionally. I would ski until the very last second I needed to catch a taxi to the Acapulco Airport, practically flying in my bathing suit.

The run from LAX to Fort Worth was delightful as there were some fine young men who took us water skiing on Lake Arlington! The rental car companies treated stewardesses very well and gave us cars. In fact, everyone treated us like royalty. In Dallas, a pink Cadillac limousine would take us shopping.

It was the crews in the LAX to Dallas runs that were the best: We went bowling! What a lot of fun with the whole crew and then huge steak dinners for just $1 or $2. The prices were out of this world, and shopping was great at Neiman Marcus. I did all my Christmas shopping there; no sales tax. Sorry, California, but I don't like tax.

The best part of those LAX to Texas flights was flying over the Grand Canyon—what a sight that was from the air! It was exciting for the passengers to hear the Captain's voice point out places of interest.

In the summer in St. Louis the big outdoor park had Broadway productions, great musicals, and the powers that be put in extra chairs up front just for us stewardesses. No charge, of course.

In the propeller planes we didn't reach the heights they do now, and it was not unthinkable to occasionally get tossed about and have sudden drops because of the updrafts and downdrafts due to weather with exciting cloud activity. In coach class one time, I had 19 babies and rough weather. After the meal service, all the babies got sick, then their mothers, and then me, running into the bathroom to throw up in an air sickness bag. Those were a *must* on our flights. What an awful feeling and smell with no escape.

The short hops were not quite so exciting—San Diego, Douglas/Bisbee—but sitting in the cockpit in an early morning into Phoenix was the biggest thrill to watch the sunrise. One flight out of New York into Tucson with a plane load of snow birds, was horrible. It was snowing in Tucson, probably for the first time ever. What a lot of grumbling passengers.

I enjoyed going to Detroit and attending church there. We usually always included a ferry trip over to a city in Canada, I believe. It was quite an experience. One of the best parts of my benefits was having mother and dad travel a bit. Other than Mexico, American only flew in the United States, so Mom and Dad did have great travels in Mexico City, attending the Ballet Folklorico de Mexico with dazzling costumes that kept them in another world of music and dance. We also visited the pyramids, Xochimilco, Taxco, Guadalajara, and Acapulco, where we stayed at the beautiful Majestic Hotel overlooking the bay and had huge fruit plates for breakfast. Daddy had fun swimming in the pool and shopping for his grandchildren. I got terrible sunburns. We hit all the sights, and then Mom and Dad took a grand train trip to the other coast and enjoyed many other cities, including Vera Cruz. They even met some Mormon missionaries there.

Another really memorable trip on American Airlines was to Boston. I walked the historical city and saw the opening release of *Around the World in 80 Days*. It seemed like we were doing just that. Then on down the coast to New York, Washington D. C., the White House, Lincoln Memorial, Washington Monument, then crossing the Potomac to Washington and Jefferson's plantations. Arlington Cemetery with its Tomb of the Unknown Soldier was one of the most outstanding memorials at the time. I think we all had one of the best experiences of our lives.

Then the jets came. I met Argie Hoskins who flew as stewardess on the Boeing 707 Inaugural Flight. She is a delightful girl and the only Mormon I met in the business. We were doing what we do best! Does that sound familiar? We were the best! I'm so happy to have happy, exciting memories with the carrier of our choice, American Airlines.

MaryLou in front of a Lockheed Electra.

Following my career with American Airlines, I continued to live with a spirit of adventure. I went on to earn a bachelor's degree in Humanities and a master's degree in Communications from Brigham Young University. After that I worked as an office manager for the prolific Hollywood producer Albert Zugsmith in addition to teaching in the Los Angeles Unified School District. I eventually retired as manager with the Walt Disney Company and decided to serve a mission for my church, The Church of Jesus Christ of Latter-day Saints. My call was to Melbourne, Australia, and I loved it. One will find me now "living on the edge of the sea" in La'ie, Hawaii.

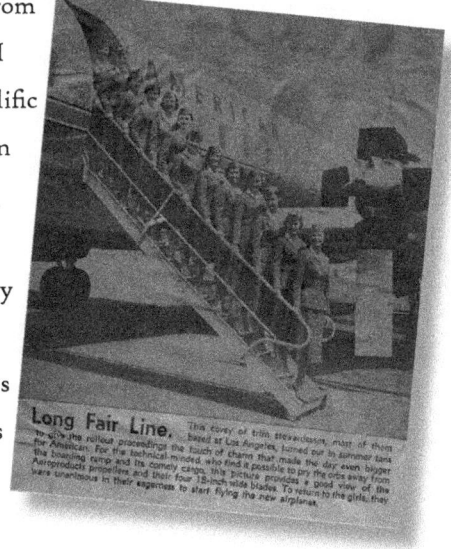

A newspaper clipping about American Airlines. MaryLou is the fourth from the bottom.

Passenger letter from flight number 2 from Los Angeles to New York on August 25, 1958. It reads:

The flight has been enjoyable in every way, particularly because of the efforts of the hostess, Miss Parkes. She has been very helpful and friendly. Her service has been unobtrusive, as the best always is. Yet her manner conveyed a warmth that immediately put us at our ease. She did everything possible for us to ensure a comfortable, pleasant trip.

Signed, Miss Joann M. Baumert

Passenger letter from flight number 3 from New York City to Los Angeles on August 26, 1958. It reads:

My wife and four children flew from LA to NYC on flight 2 July 31. When putting my family on the plane, I recognized the 2 hostesses as ones with whom we had flown previously. My wife reports that, as always, the hostesses were most courteous and helpful with the young children.

I should like to express our gratitude to them, and our appreciation to the company for the selection of such excellent personnel.

Signed, Mr. M. S. Marvin

Passenger letter from flight number 731 from Chicago to Tucson on November 20, 1958. It reads:

On this flight there were two blond young ladies, both very efficient. But may I say the Miss Parkes was most gracious and kind.
  Signed, Mr. and Mrs. Julius M. and Gertrude L. Schoen

Passenger letter from flight number 76 from Los Angeles to Cincinnati on August 15, 1958. It reads:

Air travel is a new experience to me and a delightful one. This is an enjoyable flight with American. Your stewardesses are most concerned for passenger comfort and happiness. I find them superior to stewardesses on other air lines. They are charmful and helpful young women. I shall look forward to other trips, flying with American.
  Signed, Mrs. Dean Brill
  P. S. I liked having a choice of drinks. Some other airlines do not.

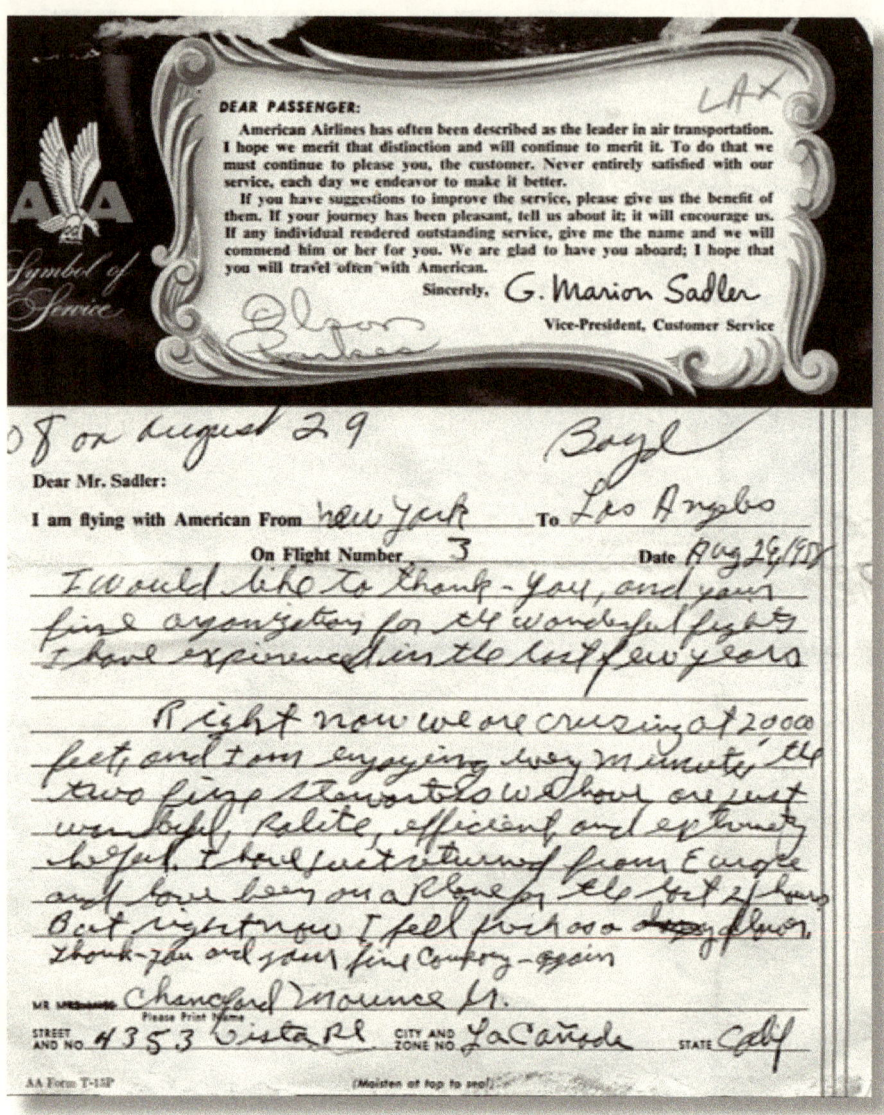

Passenger letter from flight number 3 from New York to Los Angeles on August 29, 1958. It reads:

I would like to thank you and your fine organization for the wonderful flights I have experienced in the last few years.

    Right now we are cruising at 20,000 feet, and I am enjoying every minute. The two fine stewardesses we have are just wonderful, polite, efficient, and extremely helpful. I have just returned from Europe and have been on a plane for the last 21 hours, but right now I feel as if it has been one hour. Thank you and your fine company again.

    Signed, Mr. Chancford Morence Jr.

Passenger letter from flight number 76 from Los Angeles to Cincinnati on October 24, 1958. It reads:

Dear Sir: I would assume most of these memos are complaints, however, I wish to express my opinion relative to the services rendered on this flight. Personnel very courteous and accommodating, food excellent, public consideration very good. It is appropriate to commend Miss Jerry Coher and Mary Lou Parkes for their passenger consideration and courtesy extended on this flight. They make a fine team worthy of their assigned responsibilities.
Signed, Mr. Forest F. Duwe

Passenger letter from flight number 2 from Los Angeles to New York on August 25, 1958. It reads:

I wish to call to your attention the excellent manner and efficiency displayed by one of your hostesses on this flight, Miss Parkes. I do a great deal of flying, and she stands out in my mind as being the best hostess I have seen.
 Signed, Mr. Martin Tahse
Note from supervisor in red reads, "MaryLou, our sincere thanks to you for being such an asset to the Stwd. Corps! Jan E."

The following information came from MaryLou to me, Argie, after a long stay in an old box on her shelf. She had pulled it down and ventured a look inside. These treasured bits of information were there, having been stored and gathering dust for some 55 years. MaryLou knew I would appreciate these deteriorating treasure and sent them from Hawaii to me in Utah so that I could share them here.

Excerpts from American Airlines' brochure "Welcome Aboard"

FEELING UNDER PAR?

Should you feel ill at ease for any reason, by all means press the call button to summon your Stewardess. She is well trained to serve your needs.

Motion and Emotion

Modern airplanes have made "airsickness" almost obsolete. That's because they usually fly at altitudes where the air is smooth, because radar helps them avoid most turbulence, and because they're quieter, more comfortable and better ventilated. Also, of course, there is virtually no vibration in the 707 or the Electra. And like the DC-7, they are air-conditioned both in the air and on the ground.

Nowadays only a small fraction of one percent of all air passengers ever feel any sense of discomfort. These are generally folks who tend to feel somewhat squeamish in a few hours in any type of conveyance whether it's a car, boat, train or plane.

Should you feel slightly queasy, don't hesitate to call your Stewardess. She has a most effective motion sickness preventative. If it seems too late for such a remedy, you'll find a special receptacle in the seat pocket ahead of you. No need to be embarrassed — you're not the first, and you'll soon be feeling as good as new!

Colds and Ears

Today's planes have also eliminated most ear discomfort. That's because your pressurized cabin maintains its own comfortable atmosphere, regardless of how "high" the air is outside.

If unusually sensitive, you may still notice a mild ear popping due to a change of altitude. Such "elevator ears" are quickly cured by yawning or swallowing. Should you suspect that your baby is experiencing this sensation, just offer a sip or two of his formula.

Mention any cold symptoms to your Stewardess when boarding the plane. She can make suggestions and supply simple medications to ward off discomfort in flight.

RELAX YOUR WAY FROM HERE TO THERE

Favorite Pastimes: Reading, Writing, Playing Cards

Feel like reading? Your Stewardess has a wide selection of current magazines . . . also special magazines for the youngsters. If you want to catch up on correspondence, she'll supply you with stationery, and there are picture postcards right in the back of this booklet. Should you be more in the mood for playing cards, she'll provide you with a deck and suitable table.

Whatever pastime you choose, you'll find the overhead light convenient. Just snap it on, and you automatically have the right amount of illumination pre-focused on your book, paper or playing cards.

Maps for the Do-It-Yourself Navigator

You will find a supply of handsome American Airlines route maps in your seat pocket. You may enjoy tracing the progress of your flight across the land, or locating the points of interest your Captain calls to your attention.

Heavenly Opportunity to Take it Easy

Maybe you'd prefer just to lie back and relax. You'll find your seat reclines to almost any position when you touch the armrest button. If you'd like to sleep, call for a pillow . . . a blanket too, if you like.

Saving the Sights — on Film

There's no better way to get a comprehensive view of the countryside than to "flight-see" it from your Flagship window. Sometimes your Captain will point out particularly interesting landmarks over the public address system. You get a wonderfully wide view . . . especially from a Jet Flagship.

Often you may want to take snapshots to record it. We recommend holding your camera at an angle to the window or shielding its lens to avoid reflection, but don't rest the camera directly on the window or its frame. Use haze filter against cloud glare, speeds of 1/100 to 1/200 in bright sunlight. Even if you're a serious fan who knows his exposure like a pro — the daylight up here is brighter than you think! Use your meter, or cut down a stop.

How to Word a Wire

Send a telegram? Your Flagship carries telegraph blanks. The Stewardess can advise you about sending it at the next stop, and you may have telegrams charged to your home telephone number. When telling someone of your arrival, you'll avoid confusion if you specify in your wire American Airlines, flight number, and scheduled arrival time.

Those Wonderful Washrooms

You'll find Flagship washrooms clean and well-equipped. There's a plug for any standard AC-DC electric shaver, and your Stewardess will provide a Remington Electric Shaver on request.

There are two lavatories in the front of every DC-6 and DC-7 cabin. In Convair and DC-6 "Commuter" Flagships, lavatories are to the rear. On the Electra, they're located opposite the carry-on baggage rack.

On the 707 Jet Flagships there are four lavatories — two forward and two aft.

POINTERS ON PERSONAL BELONGINGS

Hints to Help With Your Baggage

Naturally all baggage must be weighed . . . it's part of federal regulations. You can take 40 pounds of luggage free anywhere in the United States and Canada. The allowance to Mexico is 66 pounds . . . on Aircoach flights 44 pounds. If you are traveling on a ticket also covering a foreign leg of your journey, you are of course given the overseas allowance of 66 pounds.

Your baggage will be efficiently checked through to your destination. You'll find the airport's self-claim system both quick and convenient . . . and when you arrive from a 707 Jet Flagship or Electra Flagship journey, American's new Baggage Expediter system will enable you to claim your bags and be on your way sooner than ever before.

If you like, you can carry smaller luggage on board with you, and stow it under the seat (not in the overhead racks, please). Limiting size: 21" x 13" x 8".

In addition, the Electra and the Convair offer air commuters in a hurry the extra convenience of full size carry-on racks, should you not wish to check any of your luggage. There is no restriction on size of your luggage in this rack.

Hats and Coats

The overhead rack is reserved for your hat and coat, not for luggage, as noted above. Should you wish, your Stewardess will hang your coat in the wardrobe and return it to you just before you arrive at your destination.

Miscellaneous Tips

Be sure to tighten the caps on all liquids, as bottles filled on the ground sometimes leak because of lower pressure at flight altitudes. And a full bottle is safer than a partly empty one. The same holds true for fountain pens, so be sure yours is completely filled and that you open and close it carefully. Matches and cigarette lighters should be in a pocket or handbag, never a suitcase.

Excerpts from Joseph Payne Brennan's "20,000 Feet over History"

During your air journey today, between Texas and California, you will travel across half the breadth of the United States, all within a few hours.

There were other travelers before you in time. Underneath the wings of your airplane are the dim trails of yesterday, slowly worn into the earth during a period when extended travel took weeks or months and often involved both uncertainty and danger.

The route over which you will fly parallels or crosses the historic trails of early America. Spanish priests and explorers knew some of these trails two centuries before the Declaration of Independence. El Paso, known as The Pass to the North, was a travel crossroads before the first white men established settlements on Manhattan Island.

In your imagination you should be able to see the early travelers beneath you today: the Conquistador with his sword and cross; the Indian with his horse, or dog and travois; the prospector searching for precious metal; the blue-coated cavalryman trailing marauders; the cattleman looking for good grass and the farmer seeking fertile soil.

I feel sure that any thoughtful person traveling high above this historic route will often say to himself: "I wonder what happened below?" The purpose of this booklet is to tell you something about the history of the land beneath you, by arranging for your choice a selection of the true stories of this region.

We hope you will enjoy reading these narratives. If you do, we would be happy to have you keep the booklet as a pleasant reminder of a journey across a land which is rich in the history of America.

C. R. SMITH,
President,
AMERICAN AIRLINES, INC.

---

passenger revenue (excluding commuter) and was second only to the Pennsylvania Railroad among all forms of transportation. In 1951 it even led the Pennsylvania for several months and became engaged in a nip and tuck race for supremacy.

In the face of the burgeoning traffic the airlines were hard-put to maintain the standards of service they had established for themselves. In a few short years they outgrew magnificent prewar airports optimistically designed to handle the traffic for decades to come. More and bigger airports had to be built. Prewar procedures creaked and groaned under the load.

Reservations became a particular problem. To solve it, American turned mechanical, and came up with the Reservisor, a pushbutton system of handling reservations. The first was an electrical device installed in Boston in 1945. This was not the complete answer, but experiments and development continued until, in 1952, the company unveiled the Magnetronic Reservisor, an electronic "brain", installed at LaGuardia Airport. This machine does all of the calculating and recording of more than 1,000 flights in a ten day period out of the New York area and gives ticket and reservations agents quick and easy access to the inventory of seats.

By this time air transportation had earned an undisputed place, not only as a great industry, but as a growth industry. Few industries had ever come so far in so short a time. Few were going ahead so fast.

Dramatically underscoring this is the fact that the pioneers who nursed the industry up from the pastures are men still in their prime, still pioneering. Working with men of 20 to 25 years' service in American Airlines, you are working with men who were there when it started. They embody the history of air transportation — and of American Airlines.

HISTORIC "Firsts" FOR AMERICAN

A glance at the milestones that mark the history of air transportation shows there must be a close relationship between being *first* and being a leader. Only through enterprise, imagination, and a program devoted to continual improvement could any airline lead the way as has American.

Here are some selected American "FIRSTS":

FIRST to introduce Sleeper Planes

FIRST to offer the Air Travel Plan — now used by all major airlines

FIRST to develop AIRfreight

FIRST to introduce full-feathering propellers, now standard equipment for commercial aircraft the world over.

FIRST to use reversible propellers as landing "brake". Other major airlines followed suit.

FIRST to use Magnaflux to detect hidden imperfections in magnetic materials. Later, CAA ordered all airlines to use it.

FIRST with Family Fare Plan.

FIRST to introduce Magnetronic Reservisor, electronic "brain" for making reservations.

Excerpts from American Airlines' Stewardess College Brochure

The American Stewardess

The life of a stewardess is as rewarding as it is demanding, as varied as it is complex, and often not as glamorous as many believe. Yet the prestige a stewardess enjoys makes it a highly desirable career for thousands of American girls.

Only about 600 of the countless young women who apply annually at American Airlines hoping for a stewardess career manage to meet American's high standards. Of those selected, all are between 20 and 26 years old, single, between 5'2" and 5'8" in height, attractive, healthy, diplomatic, and possess sense of responsibility. Qualified young ladies receive a specialized education in the art of the stewardess that requires approximately six weeks to complete.

Your average American Airlines stewardess has about two years of college, though her roommates may range from high school graduates to PhD's and registered nurses. She is 24 years old, weighs 113 pounds, and is 5' 4½" tall. She flies with American about 28 months. During that time she will be in the air some 1,900 hours and on duty on the ground for 1,100 hours. During her career, she will assist some 15,000 passengers, play with 1,000 children, serve nearly 8,000 meals, and make 3,500 landings and takeoffs. She may become a supervisor or instructress if she remains over two years. But 85 per cent of those who resign do so to marry; most of them marry the "boy back home."

Being a stewardess—as many will tell you—is obviously one of the most stimulating and fascinating careers a young woman may have today.

It's an Art

Stewardesses are something special. Not only must they be young and attractive, they must also possess a unique blend of personality, poise, imagination, courage, knowledge and the desire to serve.

Being a stewardess, obviously, is an art—a very special art, as thousands of American's stewardesses of yesterday and today can attest. Just as a painter must know his palette and technique, so an American stewardess must know human nature and the air world.

Therein lies the art of the stewardess. It is an art that has been taught successfully for some 20 years. And in the decades ahead American will continue to refine and transmit that art to the stewardesses of tomorrow who dedicate themselves to air progress through service.

The Heart of the Matter

Even after such careful selection by American, a stewardess can be only as good as her education has qualified her to be. The emphasis at American, therefore, has been, is, and always will be on the quality of stewardess education.

It has four basic objectives:
1. *Development of personal confidence in the high level of air travel safety.*
2. *Development of skills in the use of all types of passenger service equipment.*
3. *Development of knowledge regarding the psychological handling of different types of people.*
4. *Development of the desire to maintain an outstanding level of personal performance.*

Attainment of these basic objectives through education provides the American Airlines stewardess with an appreciation of the fact that air travel today is one of man's most dependable forms of transportation, and she acquires the ability to transmit that knowledge and assurance to her passengers by her every action.

At the conclusion of her training every stewardess is able to recognize and please many different types of people. Her education makes her self-sufficient. She needs to be. For the nature of the stewardess profession often requires her to stand alone, to make her own decisions and to be motivated constantly by a desire to "please through service."

Stewardess Audrey Radziwon

Right: A close-up of Audrey in the Class of 57–6 birthday party picture.

Audrey Radziwon McGinty

AMERICAN AIRLINES STEWARDESS, 1957–1967
AMERICAN AIRLINES FLIGHT ATTENDANT, 1972–1976

Audrey and I met in stewardess school. We were in the same graduating class, 57-6, back when the school was housed in a hangar at the Midway Airport (see chapter 3).

About two and a half years ago, a retired Captain friend of mine sent me the link to a blog written by an American Airlines' stewardess. I was completely surprised when I checked it out and recognized my Class 57-6 picture. I discovered Argie Hoskins, the author, had been in my stewardess class. There was also a picture of the class helping me celebrate my 21st birthday with a cake.

Argie and I have been in occasional contact, and she has asked me to write about my career. After graduation, I was sent to Buffalo (BUF) in May 1957, along with about four other stewardesses. I was from Buffalo, so I returned to living with my parents. Unfortunately, I do not remember the other gals. I do remember being met by Betty Evans, the base supervisor.

World Airport Code:	
BUF	Buffalo
MDW	Chicago Midway International
LGA	LaGuardia
BOS	Logan International
ROC	Greater Rochester International
ORD	Chicago O'Hare International
STL	St. Louis International
SFO	San Francisco International
DAL	Love Field
LAX	Los Angeles International
SAN	San Diego
GSW	Greater South West

From BUF I flew the Convair 240 all over the Ohio Valley, Chicago Midway International (MDW), LaGuardia (LGA), Logan International (BOS) and other cities in New York. My first trip was a round trip to BOS with lunch at Durgin Park. It is still a great place to eat.

I still remember flying trips out of Rochester, New York, (ROC) in the Convair and the crew throwing out Girl Scout Cookies from the window to the local pheasant. It would wait at the end of the runway and as the plane started to roll, it would run alongside. The Girl Scout Cookies were in our first aid kit.

That airplane did not have a door to the cockpit; it had a curtain. It was gear-up and arm-out for coffee. I used to keep a log of the coffee preferences of the different crew members and took pride in my speedy service.

I had my long-time BUF friends, and did not live with stewardesses. I spent many summers living with my friends across the bridge from BUF, in Fort Erie, Canada. The custom agents knew me and it was no problem crossing back into the U. S. in my convertible sports car for my trips.

Being an American Airlines stewardess opened many doors. We hosted special events. Three of us had a ski trail in Holiday Valley Ski Resort in Ellicottville, New York, named "The Stewardess Cut" in our honor. I was also crowned the Resort's Ski Queen in 1960. Two of us BUF stewardesses were active skiers and one of the highlights for us was meeting and skiing with five of the original seven astronauts.

Audrey boarding a Convair 240.

Working the Convair was not easy. We had short segments and long days, a real challenge in a wool suit, blouse, full slip, girdle, stockings, gloves, and hat while being responsible for 40 passengers without help.

We had wonderful travel opportunities in those days. We were offered all sorts of deals to lure us to places all over the world. It was an unusual opportunity for a single girl.

I transferred to Chicago O'Hare International (ORD) in the early 60s. I flew out of there for about two years. I had the opportunity to travel to the West Coast, and my favorite place to visit was San Francisco. My favorite trip was a San Francisco International (SFO) turnaround in a Convair 990, working three on and four off.

I missed my hometown friends and returned to BUF. American Airlines started to hire new pilots in the fall of 64. We were flying a Greater South West (GSW) DC-6 trip with Love Field (DAL) pilots. We stayed in the same hotel (Western Hills Inn) as the new-hire pilots who were in training. The trip went senior because of all the new single blood in GSW. As soon as we entered our room and turned on a light, the phone would ring. It was a real fun time for the BUF gals.

I was working an early 0600 sign-in trip with a DAL crew in July 1965. I was the senior stewardess, and it was my duty to meet the Captain. In doing so, I met the rest of the crew, including a new hire. Our trip had a field break in St. Louis International (STL) that sent the crew to a motel for five hours. It was July and hot. The new hire, Doug McGinty, and I spent the time in the pool. Our trip continued on to ORD for a layover, and Doug asked me on a date. I had made plans for a visit with an ORD stewardess and told Doug that I would call him when my visit was over. I did and we went out for an evening and got acquainted.

Doug transferred to ORD and started bidding DC-6 trips that we were able to fly together. I was based in BUF. I used to pass out pillows to the passengers, telling them my boyfriend had the next landing, and he would make a hard landing. It seemed to always happen, having me on board, he just could not land as smoothly. He got lots of teasing. The Airline was family in those days, and we were at home.

Doug and I continued dating, fell in love, became engaged in December 1965, and were married July 2, 1966. I continued flying for the six months that our new contract allowed after marriage. My career ended at the end of January 1967.

Audrey and Doug

On January 30, 1967, I filed a complaint with the New York State Division of Human Rights charging that American Airlines denied me equal terms, conditions, and privileges of employment because of my sex, in violation of the Human Rights Law of New York State. I appeared at a hearing in New York City at the office of the State Division of Human Rights sometime in 1970.

I continued on with my life as a wife and mother. We had two children. In January 1972, we moved to San Diego.

In the meantime, others had filed grievances against American Airlines and had finally won and were recalled. I was pregnant at the time and did not get recalled, but in the fall of 1972, after the flight attendants won the case to fly pregnant, I was recalled. We had lost a child before we moved to San Diego, and my husband felt that returning to American Airlines would be good for me.

I was lucky to get San Diego (SAN) as a base and flew from fall of 1972 to March of 1976. I had left as a stewardess and returned as a flight attendant. It was an interesting experience, but the job was changing and the experience was different.

I had the opportunity to work the DC-10 and even worked the 747 a few times. My husband and I worked the 747 together to celebrate a dear friend's last flight before retiring.

I made the choice to end my career in March of 1976. I had a wonderful trip, and our daughter Lara joined me. I made many flight attendant friends, with many of whom I still keep in contact. I am an active Kiwi, presently belonging to the two SAN Kiwi clubs: San Diego Kiwi Chapter and Bay Cities/San Diego Kiwi Club. I am the vice president of the Bay Cities/San Diego Kiwi Club.

My husband, Doug, retired in July 1993, and I was able to join him on a Los Angeles International (LAX)/ Heathrow flight. It was a thrill for me. He was the senior international pilot in LAX. We had the special opportunity to have our picture taken inside the engine of the 767/300.

One of my stewardess friends from ORD was on Doug's flight to London, and two of my SAN buddies worked the flight back. Doug's co-pilot was Captain Barry Brannan, a special friend who flew on his own to London and got permission to work the flight back to LAX. Doug greased that last landing, one I will never forget.

Our SAN friends met us when we landed at the International Terminal in LAX, all dressed in spoof airline uniforms. They had arrived on a charter bus from SAN.

Our daughter Lara wore my original airline uniform. They carried Doug on a stretcher into American Airlines' operations. I cleared the whole event with the company and all were invited into operations to share the cake. It was possible because it was before 9/11.

American had been a huge part of my life. It was most of my adult working life, the door that opened for wonderful travel opportunities and many wonderful friends, best of all my husband and our daughter. I have seen the job change, my original era was the golden era when we were special and were treated that way. American Airlines instilled in me the desire to serve and it has stayed with me all my life.

Left: Doug's retirement party.

Below: Audrey's daughter Lara in Audrey's original airline uniform.

Fifty-seven years later I still get the comment, "Once a stewardess, always a stewardess." I naturally am more sensitive to the needs around me. I am most grateful for all the experiences I have had. It has been a great ride.

Doug and Audrey McGinty

Top: Gerry as a nurse before stewardess school.

Bottom: Gerry after stewardess school in full uniform.

Gerry McMasters Lockhart

AMERICAN AIRLINES STEWARDESS, 1957–1959

Gerry and I got to know each other when we worked a month of Dallas trips together. We ended up renting a cottage on Kerwood Avenue in West Los Angeles with two other friends (see chapter 10). Gerry and I had a lot in common. Our values and how we looked at the world were very similar. We were both committed to doing a super job for American Airlines and having good old-fashioned fun while serving our passengers. If a passenger didn't eat their meal, Gerry and I shared the bounty. It was with Gerry that I was caught with my shoes off behind the buffet curtain (see chapter 7). One of the most endearing and memorable things about Gerry is that she called everyone "Sweetie." I would choose her to be my stewardess any day.

During the year 1956, I completed my nurse's training at Mt. San Antonio College in Walnut, California, around 15 miles from where I grew up in El Monte. Just as I was entering my adult life, I got a job at the Pomona Valley Hospital.

Shortly thereafter, my older sister Grace noticed a newspaper advertisement. American Airlines was seeking candidates who wished to become airline stewardesses. Now that was interesting! Before activists and lawyers got into the act, the airlines had the right to hire stewardesses whom they believed reflected the image of their airline. American Airlines stewardesses had to be female, between the ages of 21 and 32, and single. They had to weigh an ideal weight for their height, they had to wear red lipstick, they had to cut their hair above the collar, and they had to courteously represent the airline. Once hired, they had to maintain these standards or they would be suspended from work or dismissed. Well, for me this was a tall order.

At my sister's urging, I went to be interviewed by American Airlines at the Los Angeles Airport. I was really nervous when I arrived because the other girls waiting to be interviewed were wearing business suits, high heels, gloves, and some were wearing hats. I was wearing a broomstick skirt and sandals. All of a sudden, I did not consider myself glamorous enough for this type of job. I was more like the girl next door.

The man who interviewed me was very pleasant. He made me feel comfortable. Except when he asked me why I wanted this job and I answered, "Because I love to fly." This was not exactly true, since I had never been in an airplane before. I was pleasantly surprised when they told me I was accepted, and then they arranged for me to report for training at the American Airlines Stewardess School. In 1957, the world's first special facility for flight attendant training was built in Dallas/Fort Worth, Texas. It was like a resort where you go for relaxation or pleasure, with recreation facilities. Little did I know when I arrived of the stress and pressure to earn the silver wings.

Training was an exciting experience. I saw big aircraft, engines, mock-up passenger compartments, etc. And I met some terrific fellow trainees. We were overwhelmed with the time pressure of getting prepared to be the perfect ladies in the sky and serving with dignity and grace. In addition, among the first things we did when we got on the plane was Listerine the pilot's microphone and see that the restrooms were clean and well stocked.

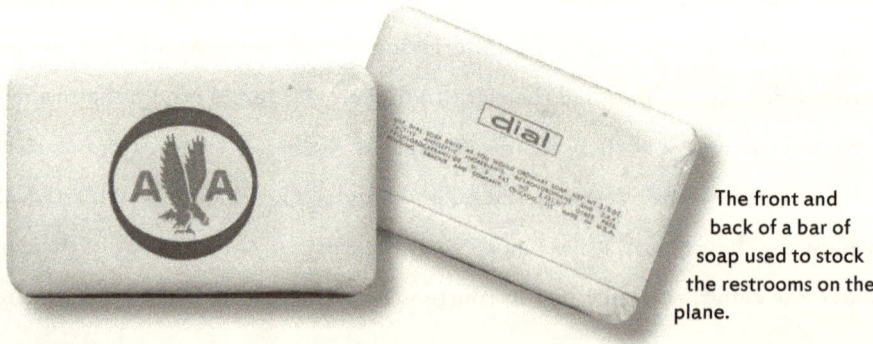

The front and back of a bar of soap used to stock the restrooms on the plane.

ARTICLE 2—DEFINITIONS

As used in this Agreement:

(a) "Stewardess" means an employee of American Airlines, Inc., who services passengers while in flight and whose duties include performing or assisting in the performance of all enroute cabin service or ground service duties related thereto in accordance with Company regulations and prescribed procedures; and who may be requested to participate in publicity and promotional and other special assignments.

(b) The term "employee" shall mean stewardess unless otherwise specified.

(c) "Month," as used herein, means the period from and including the first day of a calendar month to and including the last day of such month except that for purposes of determining service with the Company a month shall mean a period from and including a given date in a calendar month to but not including the same date in the following calendar month.

(d) "Service" shall mean the period of time assigned to active duty as a stewardess with the Company unless otherwise specified.

(e) "Run" shall mean that part of the Company's air routes over which a stewardess is regularly scheduled.

ARTICLE 3—COMPENSATION

(a) Stewardesses shall be paid minimum monthly salaries based on length of service as a stewardess in accordance with the rates shown below

1st six months of service	$285.00
2nd six months of service	300.00

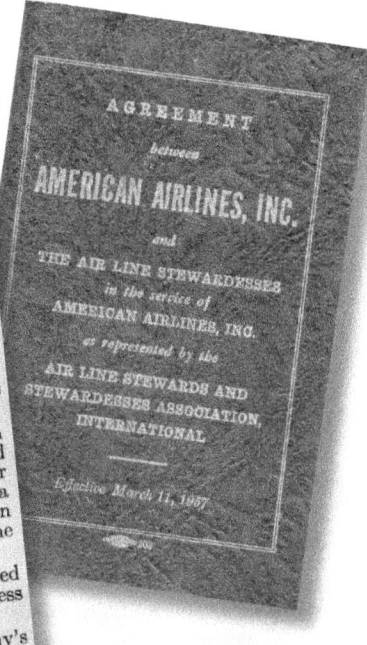

Copy of the booklet explaining the agreement between American Airlines and their stewardesses and a couple examples of the articles contained therein.

ARTICLE 5—UNIFORMS AND ACCESSORIES

(a) Stewardesses shall wear standard summer and winter uniforms in such manner and as prescribed in Company regulations at all times while on duty and such other times as may be required.

(b) The expense of uniforms and accessories shall be borne by the stewardess, except that the Company shall continue its present policy for the life of this Agreement of furnishing that portion of the summer uniform consisting of:

- 1 Jacket
- 1 Skirt
- 3 Blouses
- 1 Hat

(c) Effective April 1, 1957, the Company will furnish original Company insignia required to be worn by stewardesses. Replacements shall be made by each stewardess, as required.

(d) The recommendations of the Association will be considered by the Company before making any change in the style, color or material of the uniforms.

And yes, we also looked for stowaways! Our goal was to represent American Airlines absolutely and without a doubt, the most super service ever. We were on top of the world.

Students studying a prop engine. Gerry is sitting on top of it.

After training, I was assigned to the Los Angeles Airport as my home base, from which I worked on flights to Dallas and New York. When our Los Angeles assignment began, American Airlines put us up at the Roosevelt Hotel on Hollywood Boulevard across from Grauman's Chinese Theater (the place where movie stars make imprints of their hands and feet in cement.) A limousine brought us there and took us back to the airport between flights. This was a temporary arrangement until we could find our own place to live. I met Bea Keiser, and together we found a place right around the corner from the hotel. From there we could still take advantage of the limousine.

At Bea's request, she was transferred to San Francisco, and I had to find another roommate. Fortunately my friends—Barbara Whaley, Claire Bullock, and Argie Hoskins—and I got together and rented a cute little cottage in West Los Angeles next to a major movie studio. This place was also close to the Los Angeles Airport. By then we had our own cars and, believe it or not, in those days parking was close to the airport and it was free. In 1956, airline flights were slower than today's jets. A flight from New York to Los Angles took approximately seven hours. Night flights were a challenge because we had to stay alert, answer the pilots' calls, and keep an eye out for passengers' needs and wants, which included crying babies and sleepless teenagers, not to mention traveling military personnel who were away from home for the first time. I felt like a mother!

Most of our flights were predictably routine, but some were punctuated by unexpected excitement. One of the most dramatic experiences occurred when I saw a fireball, known as St. Elmo's Fire, roll across the wing and through the fuselage of our aircraft. St. Elmo's Fire is a plasma made of hot, ionized gas that forms during thunderstorms around pointed, raised conductors. It usually forms after the worst of the storm has passed and the voltage in the air is very high. Although they usually form on pointed things—like church steeples or

Picture of Gerry and Jerry Lewis with Claire standing behind them. Gerry and Claire were flying together to and from New York.

airplane wings or propellers—they can also be non-attached, rolling balls of fire. It was quite a sight to behold, at once both awe-inspiring and unnerving.

On another occasion, we looked down and saw a tornado working its way down the runway at the Dallas/Ft. Worth Airport. Nature is powerful to say the least. Perhaps the most scary experience occurred in Buffalo, New York, the day we heard our landing gear knock down the fence at the end of the runway as we landed. This was in the middle of the winter, and the Captain explained there was ice on the wings which made the aircraft a little heavier than expected. Wow, you might call this a *near miss*.

In 1957 my friend and fellow stewardess Jiggsie Voswinkle had a party to welcome Jim Lockhart to California. Jiggsie was a very young widow. Her husband, Paul, was a pilot for the 66th Fighter Squadron in Alaska when he was killed. Jim also flew for the 66th Fighter Squadron and knew Paul and Jiggsie. Jim had left Alaska to attend U. C. L. A. He was living at a small hotel, and while talking to the owner discovered that the owner knew Jiggsie. The hotel owner called Jiggsie who immediately called Jim and invited him to a party where he could meet some nice girls (aka, airline stewardesses). I was at the party and met Jim. We fell in love, and as soon as he graduated and got a job, we got married. This (getting married), of course, ended my career as an airline stewardess.

Our roommate Claire got married two months prior to me. Since Jim and I had very little money, Claire was very generous in letting me wear her wedding gown (size 5—wow!) The girls and I have never stopped being friends and have always kept in touch.

Top: Gerry picking out things for her wedding.

Bottom: Jim and Gerry the Christmas after they were married.

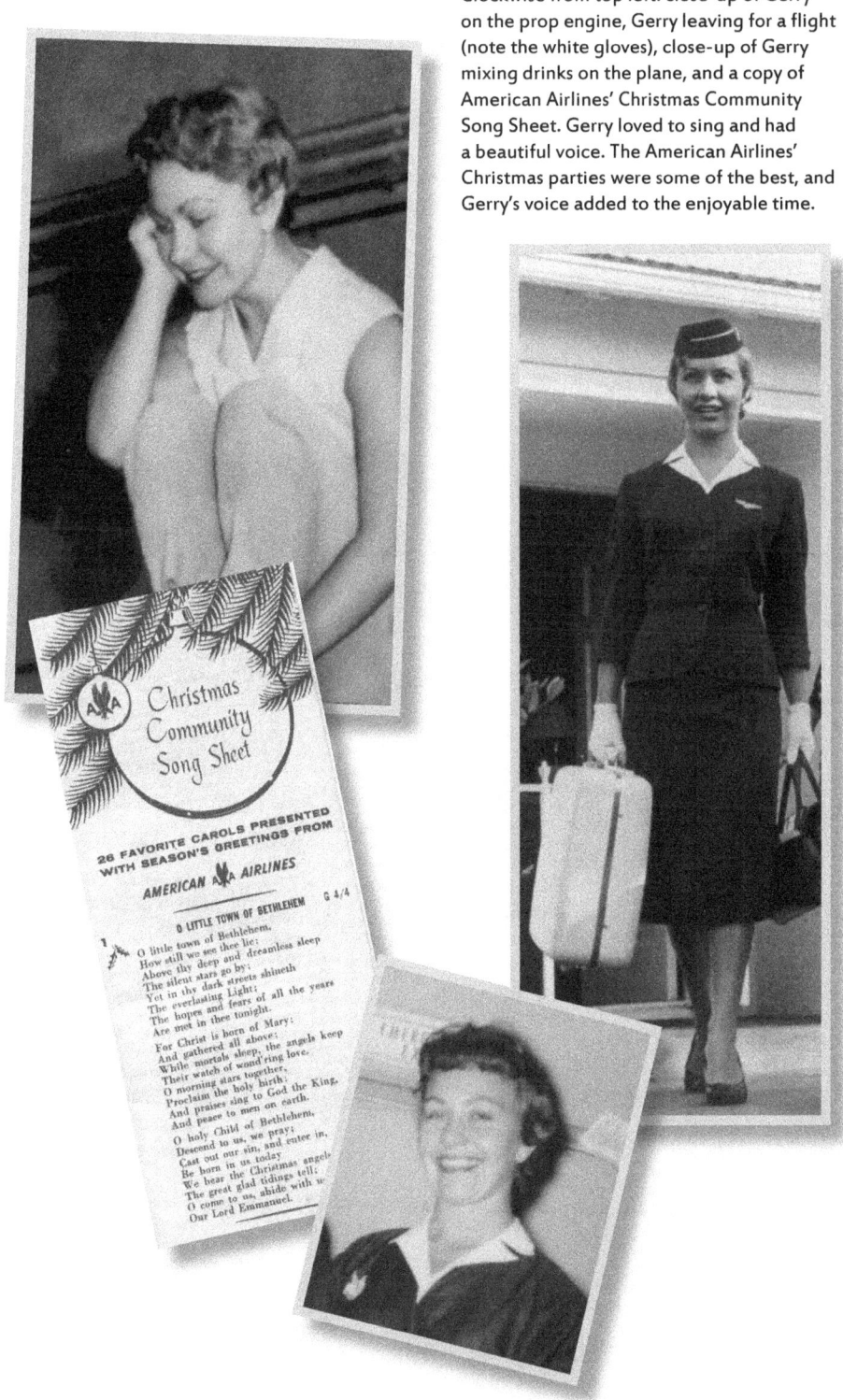

Clockwise from top left: close-up of Gerry on the prop engine, Gerry leaving for a flight (note the white gloves), close-up of Gerry mixing drinks on the plane, and a copy of American Airlines' Christmas Community Song Sheet. Gerry loved to sing and had a beautiful voice. The American Airlines' Christmas parties were some of the best, and Gerry's voice added to the enjoyable time.

Polly boarding one of her first flights as stewardess.

Right: a local newspaper clipping announcing Polly's graduation. It reads:

WINS WINGS

Pauline Hope Harlan, daughter of Mrs. Wm. G. Harlan, 2524 N. Linden, is now a stewardess for American Airlines and is currently assigned to flight duty out of the company's crew base at Midway airport. Miss Harlan graduated from Holy Family High School and then attended Wright Jr. College before winning her wings.

Below: Polly

Polly Harlan Viertel

AMERICAN AIRLINES STEWARDESS, 1957–1958

The following peek into the world of flying comes from my dear friend and former American Airlines stewardess school classmate. We hit it off right away in the windy city of Chicago as we packed ourselves into the hangar at the ever so cold Midway International Airport in April 1957.

For me, it did not come easy. It began when I was reading the want ads at home in Chicago. The following day was to be the last day for American Airlines stewardess interviews in the Chicago area.

At the time I worked in downtown Chicago at Continental Bank in the Trust Department as the secretary to three lawyers. I worked until five p.m. As it happened, it was a heavy work load day, and I was unable to leave early to get to Michigan Avenue for the interview. At day's end I raced out the enormous Continental doors, in my three inch heels that were killing me, into the wind that was blowing viciously off of Lake Michigan. My long hair was flying behind me, my nose running almost as fast as my tired feet. I knew I was late as I approached the building where the interviews were being held. I worried about the tardiness, but don't interview sessions run overtime, especially in a city as large as Chicago?

I was breathless and in total disarray and was greeted by a crabby receptionist who, annoyed at my lateness said, "Interviews are over, and besides, you aren't the type." I explained how important this was to me, to no avail. About that time a man came out of the inner office and asked, "What's going on?" Before the receptionist could answer, I explained why I was late. I apologized and asked if he'd take a few more minutes to interview me. Somewhat reluctantly he obliged.

We went back to his office where things got off to a slow start, picking up a little when I mentioned all the civic activities, clubs, and volunteer work I was involved in. Then he tried to put me on the spot with what I call a "Miss America" type question, "a make you squirm" type thing, at least it felt like that. "How would you initiate a conversation with a passenger?" As he and I had been talking, I observed his colloquial accent was from the East. He sounded like my boyfriend of three years. Eric was from Brooklyn, New York, and I had met him at U. S. O. where I volunteered. So, I decided to give it my best shot and asked him if he was from New York. Bingo! "Maybe, Brooklyn?" Bingo, again! So I suggested we could talk about New York: Flatbush, the Dodgers, the famous bridge, or the Brooklyn Botanical Gardens. He asked if I had ever been to New York, and I had to admit I hadn't, but I'd read up on it. I told him, "Someday I hope to travel and New York will be my first destination." "You have long hair, and it would have to be cut," he said. I assured him that was okay. "Well, you'll be notified by telegram whether you're accepted or not." I told him that my job required I give two weeks notice, time to retrain someone to replace me, so I needed to know. I also said that he already knew so could he please tell me. Almost in exasperation he said, "OKAY, you made it! You'll be in the April class,"

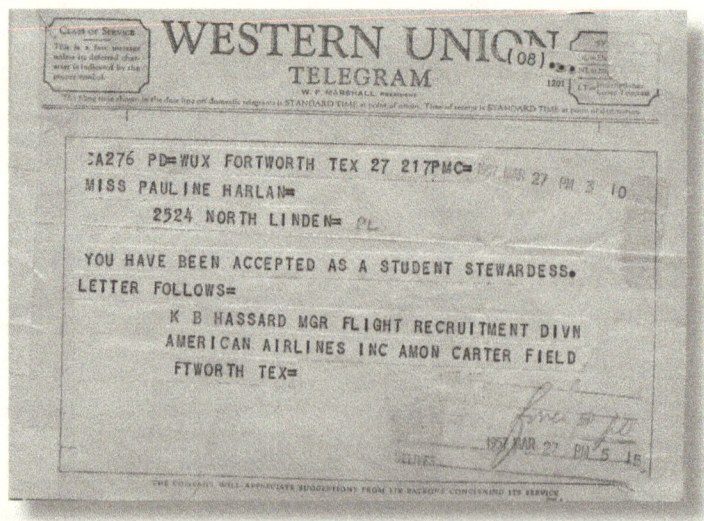

The telegram came anyway.

The entire interview had taken more than 45 minutes, so it was after six p.m. and beginning to darken outside. We walked out of the building together, he congratulated me, and I was walking on air. "Thank you Mr. Sadler for this golden opportunity." It really was a rare opportunity. For the year I went to stewardess school, 28,000 girls were interviewed, and only 640 were selected for training and notified by telegram. The staggering statistic is that only one out of every 60 girls interviewed actually graduated from the training program. In 1957 there were 1300 stewardesses flying with American Airlines.

Next I had to get a physical. I had thought that taking the three buses from the north side of Chicago to Midway Airport on the south side (the site where the physical was to take place) would be the difficult part. Wrong! When I arrived at the doctor's office for my physical he was out, and only the nurse was there. She routinely checked me. Then came the eye chart examination. I read the chart as far as I could, but it wasn't enough to meet standards. The nurse asked if I wore glasses. I never had and told her so. "I'm sorry, but I cannot pass you," she said. "You need glasses and glasses are not allowed." I went to the reception area stunned! I hadn't known I was near-sighted. I thought everybody saw as I did. I was very upset.

A man walked in from the hallway and seeing my distress asked if he could help in any way. I explained how I thought I'd been hired by American and had already given my notice at Continental Bank. Now, I had just failed the eye examination. So, on my bank lunch hour I ran over to Michigan Avenue to an optical place where they sold eye charts. They had four different charts, and I bought one of each. When I got home I memorized them all. Fairly confident, I went back to Midway Airport for another examination. The one on this wall was an old chart. So I read aloud all the letters I could and as before could go no further. Then I explained to the doctor what I had done. He laughed and said "Well, you did just fine, you passed." He congratulated me, as Mr. Sadler had and we shook hands. So kind. Sometimes things just seem to work themselves out if you do your best and try your hardest. And a little luck, determination, and faith all help too.

Polly's dormmates in stewardess school. Back: Marilyn DeHaan, Joann Pinkston Front: unknown, Mabel Harrison, Carol Blessington, Jane Grubb, unknown

Below: Jane Grubb, Carol Blessington, Marilyn DeHaan, and Polly Harlan

Studies had been strenuous but a pre-graduation program lightened things up. We presented it with the entire 57-6 class participating. The theme was Harry Belafonte, who was the rage at the time. We performed songs he made popular, such as, "Daylight Come and I Wanna Go Home."

Left: Picture of class time.

Right: Picture of the talent show put on by Polly's class.

Clockwise from top left: Polly's graduation certificate; Mildred Jackson pinning on Polly's wings; Maureen Comensky, Marilyn DeHaan, and Polly Harlan on graduation day; Marilyn DeHaan, Polly Harlan Carol Blessington, and Jane Grubb; Polly and her mother celebrating Polly's graduation.

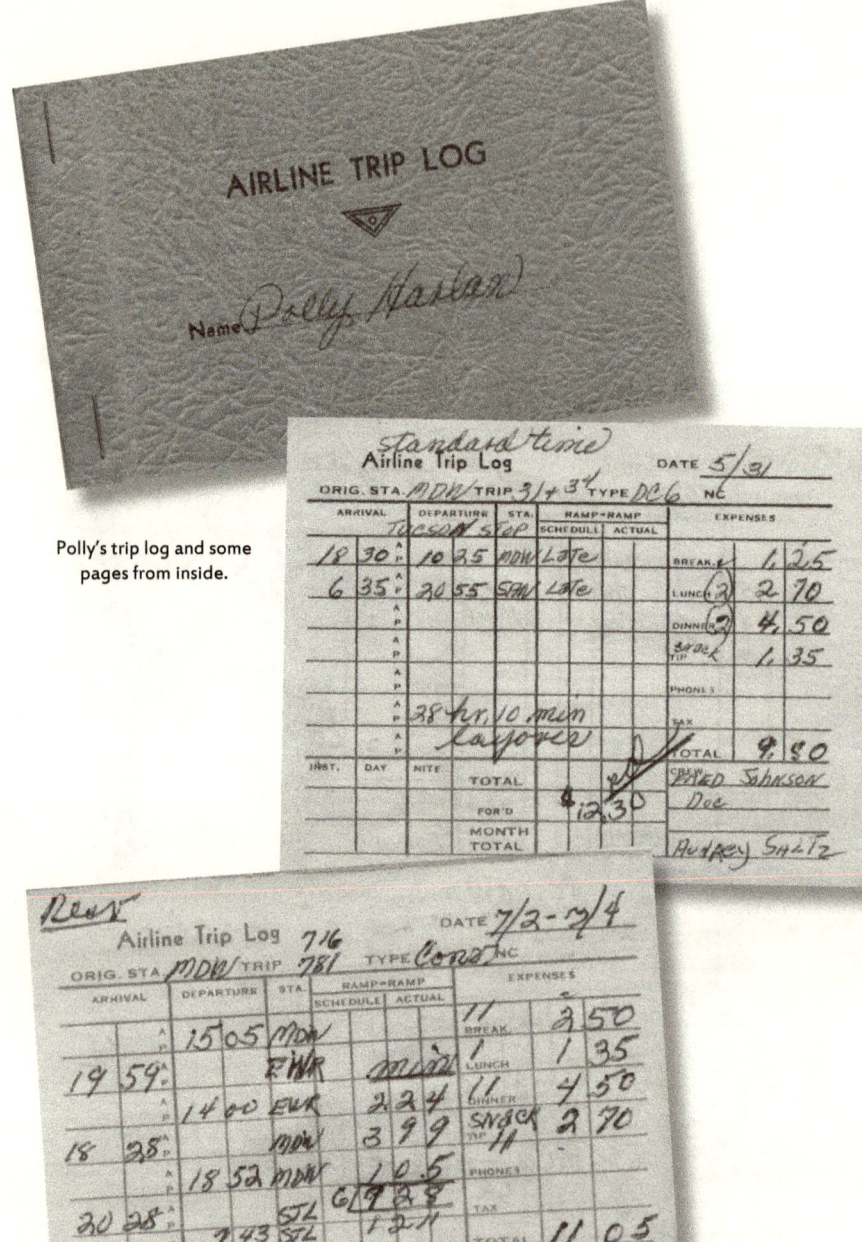

Polly's trip log and some pages from inside.

The crew and Polly on some of her first flights.

My fourth trip as a stewardess for American was on the Convair. The other previous flights had been on the DC-6 or DC-7, which both required more than one stewardess. This fourth trip had me really nervous. It was on June 4, 1957, a trip to Cincinnati. The crew included Captain Walt Lux and First Officer Don Froehicker. On the Convair you work alone, serving 40 passengers.

Not only that, but the stairway had to be operated manually by the stewardess. There were three different levers to accomplish this. When there is a chance you could quite possibly destroy the entry into the aircraft by performing an incorrect sequence, well, it made my heart beat fast. All went well retracting the stairs for takeoff. Also the meal service went fine. Then, time to lower the stairway in Cincinnati. Again, just fine. I bid farewell to appreciative passengers, and the crew came out of the cockpit. I mentioned my relief at not having had a problem with the stairs routine. Captain Lux looked at me plain faced and said "Yes, you lowered them just fine. Too bad you hit the ramp agent." I was horrified. A split second later though, he and the copilot laughed and said, "Just kidding."

This was our monthly earnings record from American Airlines. $375.96

I worked many non-stop flights, but I'd often work "milk runs." A milk run is a flight that has many "legs." That is, it goes to more than one city on one trip. At each city, passengers disembark and new ones board. The newly boarded are offered a meal. This particular flight had five or six cities to go to before we reached our final destination. Very tiring. As we approached the end of this rather tedious trip, I thought the flight seemed to be going well. I made the arrival announcement, passed out coats, checked seat belts and made sure all trays and refuse were gathered up. Then I seated myself at the back, exhausted, and belted myself. We touched down, the props reversed, the brakes applied. All of the sudden I heard a succession of loud bangs. Then, rolling down the aisle came dishes, utensils, trays, peas—everything having to do with the meal service. I had forgotten to lock up the buffet where trays are stored. It was messy, loud, and awful. The aisle passengers left the plane, many expressed feelings that ranged from how bad they felt for me, to what a memorable trip it had been. I guess I've never forgotten that trip either.

Periodically, all stewardesses had to have a flight check by a supervisor. It was necessary to assess the progress of the stewardess, as well as to be sure company standards were being followed. My flight checkride was out of Chicago on a Convair. I had been warned by the crew that my checkrider was Hazel White, chief supervisor, in charge of all stewardesses and flight checkers. So, I tried extra hard to do everything by the book, perfectly, the way we were taught. I did the pre-check list, and made sure the meal service was correct in count, ovens on, etc. I passed out magazines, pillows, blankets, memorized names, trying to address each passenger by his or her name. Once airborne, I served the meals, including to the crew. The Convair held 40 passengers, and it was completely full. All seemed to go well, I thought to myself, as I gathered up the trays. As I neared the last seat where Hazel sat, I was surprised to see she was busy writing and no tray in sight. Assuming she must have put her own tray in the buffet, I headed there. Surprise again, perplexed, I sneaked a peek to see if the missing tray was under her seat. No tray. So, totally confused I asked her timidly, "Your tray?" Her reply, "Polly, you didn't serve me a meal." "Don't worry. I'm not hungry, but in the future be certain that you serve everybody." I had forgotten to serve the chief supervisor, my check rider, and to this day I do not know how it happened.

We served with style and our passengers were guests in a fine home. We served meals with a buttoned-on napkin that would stay put, instead of almost immediately falling to the floor. The napkin was large enough to protect a small child's lap as well as his shirtfront. Adult passengers enjoyed a meal without a spill on their fine clothing.

I worked another memorable flight out of Dallas as a "reserve" stewardess to Los Angeles. It was a night flight, and these flights were always extraordinary because of the city lights. The senior stewardess gave me the assignment of gathering passenger names. One of the men smiled kindly as he gave his name as C. R. Smith. Since he was with a group of four or five others, all of whom were chatting together and having a good time, I thought he was joking. Feeling clever I said, "Oh, well Mr. Smith, I am Miss Taylor, Liz Taylor," even though my wings clearly said Miss P. Harlan. He didn't say anything but looked a little puzzled. After the flight was over I found out it really was C. R. Smith, President of American Airlines. For days I worried I'd get reprimanded for being such a smart aleck, but nothing happened.

Checkrides were always somewhat frightening to me. I wanted to be perfect as a stewardess for American yet did not always feel all that confident when being checked. I just did not want to mess up. As I boarded the Convair aircraft for this ride check I saw the supervisor right away. Since I was the only stewardess, I knew she was there to check me. I mentioned this to my crew, one of whom was Dick Utz, who was my downstairs neighbor at the

Raleigh Apartment in Dallas. A lot of girls liked Dick, and I think he knew it. Anyway, he came up with an idea. That's all he said. I didn't see all that much of the checkrider, other than during takeoff and landing. Of course she gave me the pre-flight check and emergency procedure check, but Dick kept her occupied with chit-chat in the cockpit for the most part. I had a good checkride, free of nerves.

I was raised in Chicago, where I was originally based, so, when I transferred to Dallas, I made certain to bid flight schedules home when I could. Crews stayed at the Palmer House in the Loop (downtown) but I'd take the elevated train to Logan Square where my mother and brother lived. One trip was almost my doom. We forgot to set the alarm clock, and I woke up at the exact time I figured the crew was about to board the limo to the airport. Hurriedly I phoned the Palmer House and asked for the captain. Fortunately he was still there. I explained what happened and that there was no way I'd be able to get to the airport in time. The captain calmly asked where I lived, and he and the rest of the crew picked me up in the square. I made the trip back to Dallas with them. Pink slip avoided! I've forgotten the captain's name, but not the kindness.

One day in Dallas I hung my laundry out to dry. Among it were my airline blouses, all I owned at the time. Crew Schedule called me for a reserve trip, so I went to retrieve the blouses and found a space where five blouses had hung. I panicked! Cheerfully my roommates, Dana Rawding, Joann Hansen, Claire Hurlebaus, and Jeannette Fredette, each gave me a blouse for my four day trip. Whew!

My favorite sport was figure skating. It still is. My friend from stewardess school Argie Hoskins was in town, having flown in from L. A. I seldom saw Argie since my transfer out of Chicago/Midway and hers to L. A. I decided to call in ill so I'd not be called out on a reserve flight. We outfitted Argie with a pair of my slacks, a sweater, and off we went to the arena. We were having a wonderful reunion when a tap on my shoulder caught my attention. I almost fainted when I saw who the tapper was. It was my Dallas American Airlines supervisor, Dottie! I could not believe it—what are the odds? With the promise I'd never pull that stunt again, she let me off the hook. Thank you, Dottie! Whoever heard of an ice-skating supervisor?

Argie out skating with Polly. Polly was a gifted skater.

Prior to flying for American, I'd been a member of the Chicago Figure Skating Club. Everyone knew Sandy Culbertsen as the best skater at the club. She won many competitions, so I was not surprised when I saw a huge poster advertising the Ice Capades with Sandy as the star. I was mentioning this to Argie and a man overheard the conversation. He came over and introduced himself as the owner of the Ice Capades, John Harris. He invited Argie and me to be his guests at the next performance, which we happily accepted. We sat in the front row and had the best time. On January 25, 1959, American had its Inaugural 707 jet flight, and Argie was given the honor of being part of the crew for this historical event. Aboard the Flagship California was John Harris, along with a ship-load of dignitaries. Unfortunately a reunion wasn't possible because Argie was kept so busy.

There were five of us living in the little apartment in Dallas. In February of 1958, Jeannette Fredette was the first of us to be married. Dana Rawding, Claire Hurlebaus, Joann Hansen, and I were to be the bridesmaids. We were all fitted. The gowns were pale blue and the ceremony was to be at Perrin

AFB in Dennison, Texas, 60 miles or so from Dallas. Everything was all set, and though I was on reserve I was certain I'd be okay. Wrong! Two days before the wedding, crew schedule called me for a trip. No excuses when on reserve, so off I went. I returned to Dallas the day of the wedding. The apartment was empty, and all the pilots from across the hall and throughout our apartment complex were gone to Perrin for the wedding. I missed everything. I think Jeannette's cousin ended up wearing the dress I would have worn.

Jeannette's wedding.

A month later, I was alone in the apartment yet again. We always let the door remain open so the pilots from across the hall could use our telephone. A pilot strolled in and seeing me boxing up clothing, asked if he could help. He held his finger in the center of the string as I knotted it. Then he asked how come I was sending my clothes home, "Are you transferring?" I told him they were out-of-season clothes, and our closets didn't have room for them. Then he offered me a ride to the post. I told him I would take the bus. "But my car is right downstairs, let me drive you." He did. He then took me to breakfast, lunch and dinner. Three days later, I received a proposal of marriage to which I remember saying, without hesitation, "Sure." When my roomies had all returned from their trips, we ate on the bed. They hadn't known I was dating him—well, I hadn't for very long—and they were surprised and excited by my news. I found out that Lee had been in Jeannette's wedding party, and we would have met sooner had I not been called for that reserve flight.

Lee's graduation and the end of his hitch as a jet pilot for the Air Force took place in May, so we wanted to marry then. Mother said, "No. If it's true love then you can wait until fall." So we waited, only seeing each other for one week at my home in Chicago the month of July. Then two weeks before the wedding, I flew to Salt Lake, and we were married September 6, 1958. Argie and my roommates were bridesmaids.

Polly and Lee's bridal party at the reception.

Left: Argie Hoskins, Claire Hurlebaus, Lee Viertel, Polly Harlan, Billy Rae Chidester, and Dana Rawding

Below: Lee Viertel

Until the sixties, a stewardess' career ended when she married. So my career with American was over when I wed my husband, Lee Viertel. It had been a decision I didn't take lightly. I had felt so blessed to have been chosen in the first place. But it was a decision I'd do all over again. After my resignation and marriage, my mother was hired by American Airlines as a reservationist. She was among the first to learn the Sabre computer, the computer American Airlines used for reservations. As an employee she received the Flagship News and in it read about the Kiwi Club for former American Airlines stewardesses. By now my husband Lee had been hired as a pilot for Northwest Orient Airlines, as it was called then, so we lived in Minneapolis, Minnesota. The first meeting I attended at the Kiwi Club I was introduced by Grace Nyrop, a former American Airlines stewardess whose husband, Donald Nyrop, was president of Northwest, the company for which my husband flew. By the 1980s Lee became Chief Pilot, and so occasionally he and I were seated with the Nyrops at special dinners. Grace and I enjoyed recalling our careers with American. It was fun to compare aircraft we'd flown, places we had gone, and experiences we remembered. It's a small world sometimes.

In 1984 my daughter Linda became a flight attendant for American, and I, as her mother, was given the privilege of pinning on her wings.

MISS P. HARLAN

Left: Flight Attendant Linda Viertel, Polly's daughter

Below: Linda's Class of 1984–2

Stewardess Joan Scofield Sheldon

A Boeing 707. Joan was on the inaugural flight from Los Angeles to Philadelphia.

Joan Scofield Sheldon

AMERICAN AIRLINES STEWARDESS, 1959–1961

Joan and I were based in Los Angeles at the same time. I saw her name on the bid sheet. I don't remember if we ever flew together, but time has brought the crossing of our paths, if not in the air, then certainly by mail. My friend Joan is terrific. Time and space are intriguing and both have the power to change the wind, rain, and friendships.

Firsts are always fun stories to tell and to remember for a long time. The day American Airlines inaugurated its first flight of a 707 jet aircraft from Los Angeles to Philadelphia in the fall of 1959, I was one of the stewardesses on board. It was an exciting event for the public as well as for the passengers and flight crew. I felt honored to be one of only eight stewardesses who were awarded the schedule that included that flight.

Having flown for only a few months, I did not have enough seniority to serve up front, so I wouldn't see any of the first class passengers during the flight. My only chance to see if any celebrities might be on board was to enter the plane through the passenger gate. The rest of the crew, as usual, avoided the passenger entrance, or "holding tank" as we called it, and went to the ramp directly from the crew lounge. This day, however, I headed for the passenger gate to see what kind of people would be flying on this big jet. I also liked the idea of being the first person they would let on board.

The crowded gate area was tingling with excitement. Two or three reporters were interviewing passengers. Important faces stood out in the crowd. One could sense the overabundance of standbys. One particularly dark, handsome teenage boy, about 16, pressed the ticket taker for any news of no-shows.

His foreign-accented grandmother hung onto him, looked out at the plane, and worriedly said, "But d'are are no propellers." He glanced at me (enviously, I thought) and, seeing me in uniform, knew I would be getting on board while he and his grandmother might not. I sadly looked back at those who would perhaps not make it.

Soon we were on our way to the East Coast in less than four hours. We were met at our destination by yet another crowd which included the mayor of Philadelphia who gave each person, as they deplaned, a souvenir to remember their first jet flight, a small copper replica of the Liberty Bell.

The replica of the Liberty Bell

Twenty years later, that bell "tolled" a remarkable story. I met my dark, handsome husband, Ron Grubman, on a skiing trip in Switzerland. He lived in San Francisco and I in Southern California. In 1979, after a year of 400-mile courting, I moved to the Bay Area. As he helped me unpack, in my new house, he noticed the bell, and asked me where it came from. When I told him, his eyes lit up in amazement as he replied, "You were on that flight, twenty years ago? Unbelievable! I tried to get on that same plane for two weeks."

Then he told me that his Russian-born grandmother and he were at the airport, in Los Angeles, that day, trying to fly standby to their home in Philadelphia. They made it on the next day's flight. Is there yet another story here, one I don't know how to tell? Is there a strange link, perhaps, between the envious glance of a sixteen-year-old boy at a twenty-two-year-old stewardess who is headed for a jet-ride he wants to be on, and an unconscious remembrance that attracts him to her twenty years later? Now, when anyone asks us how we know we were meant for each other, we answer: "Oh, it was jet fate."

Left: Joan sitting in the cockpit of a plane.

Right: Joan in front of some flowers in full uniform.

Margaret Bassetti

Margaret Bassetti

PASSENGER ON THE FIRST TRANSCONTINENTAL JET FLIGHT

As a passenger on the American Airlines 707 Inaugural flight from Los Angeles International to the New York Idlewild Airport on the 25th of January, 1959, Margaret Bassetti was fulfilling a dream. I admire Margaret for her adventurous life—then and now as she continues to look forward toward the future.

This memoir takes the form of an interview between Margaret and her great niece Lorraine Walston. The interview took place on September 2, 2013.

In an effort to document a piece of history, I, Lorraine Walston, interviewed Margaret Bassetti. At age 96, she remembers a great deal about the inaugural flight day, and in having this chat with her, she provided me with some interesting, new details I hadn't heard before.

How did you hear about the flight?

> There was an article in the paper. I read it, and was interested to go. I worked at Harts Department store in Downtown San Jose, California. Any time I wanted to go somewhere, I went to Val Handle at the local travel agency. He was just a couple blocks from where I worked, and I could get there easily and quickly, even during a lunch break. I guess you could say I saw the news in the paper, I wanted to go, I booked the ticket through Val, and away I went!

How much did the ticket cost? Do you remember?

Yes, it was $265 round trip. Not too expensive!

Did anyone go with you?

No! It was just me. I went to the San Jose Airport which at the time was being run from a trailer in the parking lot. I drove right up to the trailer, parked in front of the door, got out of my car, and boarded my plane to Los Angeles where the historic flight was leaving from. When I came back, my car was still there at the front door!! That seems kind of funny now!

So you flew to Los Angeles, right?

Yes. I had driven before, but this time I flew. I stayed overnight in a hotel near the airport. My car was in San Jose, so without transportation to really get around, I just ate a sandwich for dinner. I was traveling alone and I was too excited to eat much else anyway. In the morning, I got up, went to the airport, and got ready for the flight to New York.

How much stuff did you take with you? What did you pack?

Oh, I packed a coat for sure. It was going to be cold in New York. I took just a small "travel case" which held just my nightgown, some toiletries, and basic clothing. I wasn't going to be gone too long!

The big flight left from Los Angeles. You were in town the night before. How did you get to the airport?

I just got a cab from the hotel to the airport. Not a big deal.

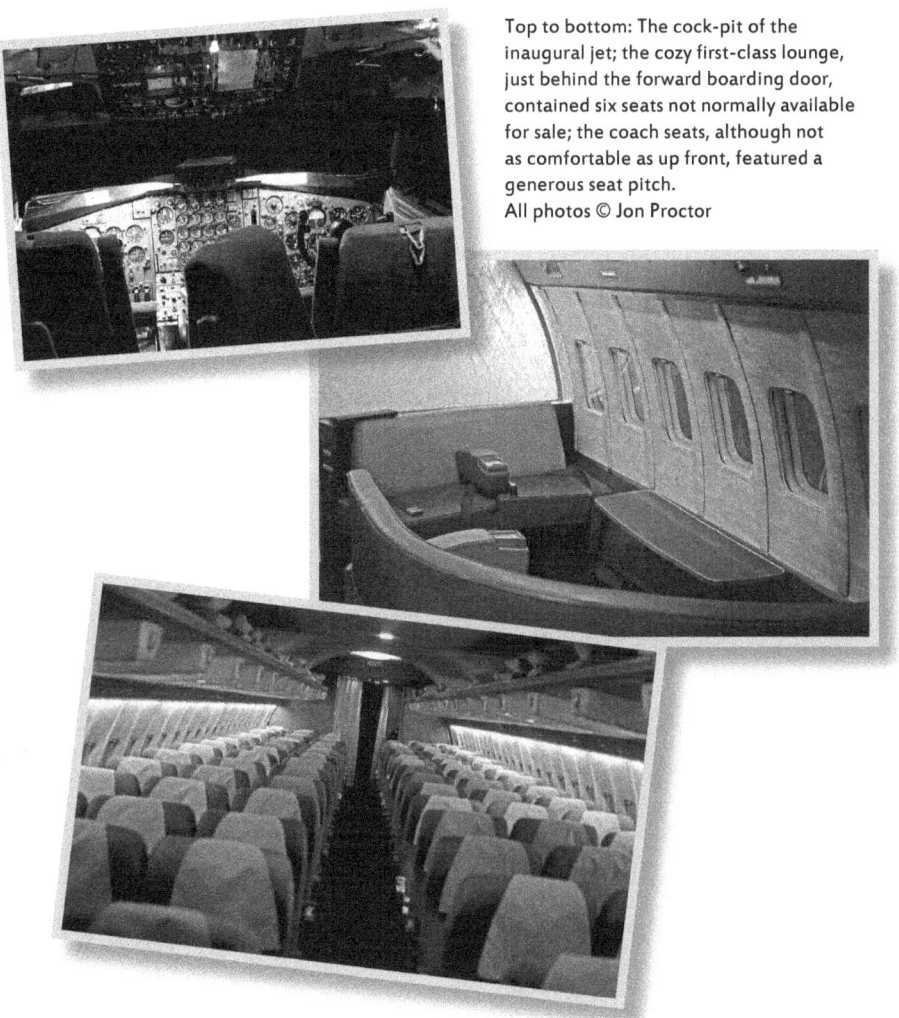

Top to bottom: The cock-pit of the inaugural jet; the cozy first-class lounge, just behind the forward boarding door, contained six seats not normally available for sale; the coach seats, although not as comfortable as up front, featured a generous seat pitch.
All photos © Jon Proctor

What special things did American Airlines do before you got on the plane? Did you have a special waiting area? Did they have a reception for the passengers?

>Governor Brown was there. Not the current Governor Brown, but his father! I don't remember any receptions, or speeches, or anything like that. It seemed like a regular flight. I know when we were waiting to board, everyone had someone to talk to, except me. So Governor Brown and his wife came and talked to me for a while. That was nice!

When did you get the medal? At the end of the flight?

> No, I think we got it in the middle of the flight.

So what happened when the plane landed? Was there a band? Balloons? A speech? How did they celebrate the milestone?

> I know it was cold, and it had snowed but the ground was shoveled. I don't remember a band or balloons, but there were reporters. I think being cold and dark, we just got off the plane and went on our way.

So New York, in January, is cold and snowy. Were you excited to be there?

> Of course for the history, yes, we were all excited. But it was my first time in New York, and that was fun. My hotel was near the airport, and I caught a cab to get there. The hotel cost me $5 for the night! It was called the Vine Hotel, or the Pine Hotel, or a name like that. The cab driver wanted to pick me up in the morning to take me back to the airport for the return trip home. I thought he was getting a little too friendly, so I said, "No, thank you," and just called the cab company in the morning when I needed to go.

So the passengers were talking about the history? What did they say?

> They were all excited while they were on the flight, but when it landed, I think most people just wanted to get off. I was curious what others were saying, so I read about it in the papers at all the airports on my way home. I picked up a paper from each city I stopped in. I visited friends in a couple cities, so I went through five cities all together—Chicago, Denver, Phoenix, Las Vegas, and San Jose. I didn't get the direct route home!

The front and back of the commemorative medal, courtesy John Dean. These "Jet Dollars" were commissioned privately by American Airlines. They were designed by Joseph di Lorenzo and were printed by the Medallic Art Co.

Below, clockwise from top left: photos of Margaret with her mother, in her home, and at a birthday party.

Do you still have the ticket?

> I am not sure. I had it until my last move. I think it's packed in an envelope, but I don't know where.

What do you remember about the flight?

> I sat in the middle of the plane. I asked Val, the travel agent, for an aisle seat, but I ended up between two men. One was the Mayor of Oxnard, California. I also remember Jane Wyman, Ronald Reagan's wife, was an honorary stewardess. She came by a lot. I had her sign my menu/program. It's in the envelope with my ticket. I also remember all the men were wearing suits, and long winter coats. There wasn't enough room to hang all the coats, so some were thrown on the floor. I remember thinking I was taking a nap. It was the first time during takeoff that I thought the plane was going right to the sun. Take off was so steep it was like we were laying down. I could have taken a nap but I might have missed something!

I have a menu from that day that I found on the computer. What do you remember eating on the flight?

> I'm not sure. I do know I ate a cherry tomato for the first time in my life. I didn't know what it was, so I bit into it. Seeds squirted out of my mouth, and some landed on both of the men I was sitting next to! That was funny for sure! I think I had champagne to drink.

What do you remember about the stewardesses or the pilots?

> I remember Jane Wyman. I enjoyed meeting her. I also remember that the pilots must have done a GREAT job—the flight seemed so short!

Fifty-four years later, what thoughts do you have about the flight now?

> I'm very happy I did it. I enjoyed the adventure, and being a part of history! Given the chance even today, I'd do it again!

What other adventures would you like to go on? Are there other pieces of history you are hoping to be a part of?

> Yes! I am on the list to go to the moon. I'm excited to go there. I read an article in the paper that they are working on that again. I can't wait. Maybe I'll get to go on my 100th birthday!

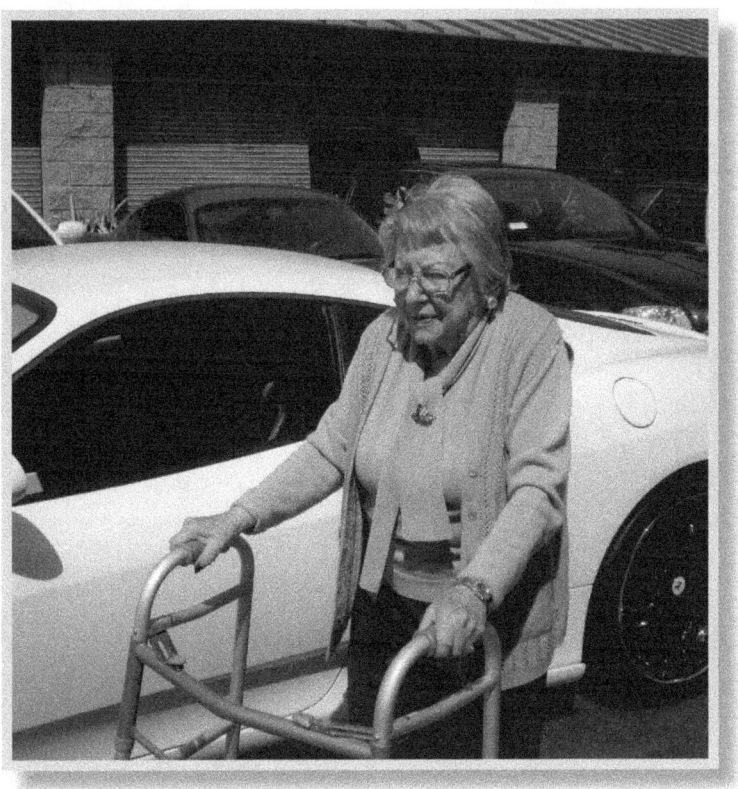

Margaret Bassetti, Lifelong Adventurer

Bob Cawley at microphone.

Robert Cawley

AMERICAN AIRLINES PASSENGER DURING THE GOLDEN AGE OF FLYING

Robert Cawley is a diversified production executive, creator, writer, producer, and director whose TV productions have won a total of 20 Emmy Awards.

Major hits include, The Juliet Prowse Spectacular *for 20th Century-Fox;* Peter Marshall, One More Time, My Little Corner Of The World, *winner of the American Family Heritage and Freedom's Foundation Awards, and* How To Change Your Life, *winner of the coveted Angel Award. His documentary,* AIDS: The Global Explosion *was nominated for a Prime Time Emmy. Motion pictures include,* Treasure Of Tayopa, Glory Road, *and* Butterfly, *which was nominated for three Golden Globe Awards including best picture. This was the first movie to go platinum with three million copies sold in home video release.*

As a composer, Cawley wrote "Raindrops On My Window, Teardrops In My Heart" for Marty Robbins and "The Witchcraft Of Love" which was the theme of the TV special, Sinatra In Paradise. *He also wrote the score for the TV series,* Danger, Wild Cargo.

Cawley is a member of the Greenbrier Military Jr. College Hall of Fame and is a member of the Columbus Musicians Hall Of Fame. He is the author of three books. Treasure of La Dura, Components of Murder, *and* Target Tayopa. *He is currently writing,* Wheezer, *a memoir.*

Cawley has served as consultant for motion picture and TV production to the College of the Arts at Ohio State University. He has taught at the University of Southern California and Columbia College of Los Angeles. He currently teaches at the College of Southern Nevada. He and his wife make their home in Las Vegas (see also page 180).

It was in the mid-fifties, and I was a director with NBC in Hollywood. My show, *Curt Massey Time* with Curt, Liltin' Martha Tilton plus Country Washburn (composer of the hit "One Dozen Roses") and his orchestra, was on the way to winning three Emmy Awards. We worked four days a week, with Friday's show being videotaped on Wednesday. I was contacted by Producer Lee Worman regarding directing and writing the musical score for a syndicated TV series, *Danger, Wild Cargo*, starring Jack Adam as "Jungle Jack" and Bob Corrigan as the man filming his capture of wild animals for several circuses around the world. "Miss Canada," Vel Ritche, played Corrigan's love interest. The series would film Friday, Saturday, and a half-day Sunday on location eighty miles north east of Phoenix, Arizona. Looking forward to moving from TV into movies, I jumped at the chance.

The first weekend of filming I was booked on a TWA flight. Everything was calm and collected until we were near the San Bernardino mountains. Looking out the window, I saw the right engine on fire and flames whipping over the wing. At that moment, the pilot announced we were turning back to Los Angeles and would be booked on a later flight. Transferred to another flight, we were on our way to Phoenix. We had just crossed the San Bernardino mountains, when looking out the window, I saw the right engine was on fire. Come on, twice in one day? The fire was extinguished, and the pilot assured us we would make it to Phoenix, and we did, but I made up my mind I would give American Airlines a chance to transport me back and forth for the duration of this assignment.

I love to fly and had traveled many miles by air in and out of the USA, but I was thinking maybe the jinx was on this entire venture. We had encountered problems the first weekend of filming with wild animals, and my thought that this has carried over to my flying was a little too much.

The following Friday morning I was aboard the American Airlines flight that would take me to Phoenix. It must have been pretty obvious to the stewardess that I was in a crisis condition. Seated in the tail section, I was already a white-knuckled passenger before the plane started to roll. A beautiful stewardess, whose name was Argie Hoskins, asked me if I was okay. I don't know what I mumbled, but when the plane started to roll forward to take off, she sat down beside me, smiled, and one of her soft hands covered my gripping knuckles, and we were off and flying.

Since that time, I have flown thousands of miles on American Airlines and have had my crews and talent booked with American Airlines as well. The attention and assistance of the stewardesses was perfect. The flight crew always made it a happy experience. Did Ms. Hoskins make a difference? I would think so. When I wrote the score for Danger, Wild Cargo, which enjoyed years of international play, the song written for the love scenes was entitled "Argie's Theme."

An NBC camera pendant and a model airplane.

Top: Stewardess Diane Miller

Middle: Diane

Bottom: Diane and Shirley preparing food on the plane

Diane Miller Engelskirger

AMERICAN AIRLINES STEWARDESS, 1961–1966

At the 31st Biennial Kiwi Club Convention, which was hosted by the Las Vegas Chapter, Diane and I sat by each other at the opening luncheon on May 7, 2014. We had never met before, but it didn't take long before we were swapping stories of flying days. It is so fun to make new friends! And to think she almost cancelled her trip!

Name: Mr. Hirtzel
Destination: BUF

That was what was written on the seating chart.

It was our last trip for the day, and we were heading to Buffalo, New York, and that would be our last trip for the next two days. Our crew was based out of Buffalo, and it was home for the other stewardess on our flight, my friend Shirley Daigler. From Buffalo, I would be heading towards Erie where my parents lived.

This trip began differently than most, in that we checked the passengers tickets. You see, we had one too many passengers for the number of tickets that were pulled at the gate in New York. We started checking from the middle of the plane. I worked toward the front, and Shirley worked toward the back. As I was just finishing, Shirley walked up to me and said there was a gentleman in the back going on to Erie after we landed in Buffalo. I told her to tell him I would give him a ride to Erie and save him the money for the airfare. After I finished checking tickets I walked back to the gentlemen, introduced myself, and told him I would meet him inside by the gate. After we finished deplaning I thought to myself, "Did I do the right thing?" He was dressed well but not classy and carried an old leather grip.

When I finished my duties I went to the gate where Mr. Hirtzel was waiting for me. I told him that I needed to stop by my apartment to change and pick up a few things. He said that would be fine. I drove to my apartment, and when I returned to the car I told him I would need to get gas for the trip to Erie. Mr. Hirtzel offered to pay for the gas, but I refused his offer and said that it was okay because I was driving to Erie anyway. When we arrived at a toll booth he again offered to pay the $1.05 fee. I said, "No, I'll pay. I was driving to Erie anyway." To tell you the truth, I kind a felt sorry for him just due to what he was wearing and the bag he was carrying, and then when I asked him where he wanted me to take him in Erie, he said, "Just drop me off at the park in North East, and I will walk the rest of the way home." My thought was he didn't have much money and didn't want me to see where he lived.

The park in North East

I do not remember the conversation, but I must have talked about my family because a couple of years ago I found a letter that Mr. Hirtzel had sent to my parents telling them how he had met me, and he knew I had come from good stock. He had a way with words.

I continued on to my parents' home, and I then told my father what I had done. On my next trip to Erie, my father asked me if I would like to know who I had driven. Well, I found out I did not need to feel sorry for Mr. Hirtzel at all! My father told me that Mr. Hirtzel was on the Board of Directors of Hamot Hospital, the Board of Directors of St. Vincent's Hospital, the Board of Directors of North East National Bank, owned his own company, and was a multi-millionaire. He lived in a beautiful white house just across from the park where I had dropped him off.

After that encounter, my family and Mr. and Mrs. Hirtzel became very good friends. So much so, that we enjoyed vacationing in Canada at his fishing lodge that could house 10 to 16 people. My father was a family physician, and Mr. Hirtzel wanted him to open an office in North East. But Hamot Hospital requested my father to open the residency program for family physicians.

Mr. Hirtzel had a little black book with a lot of stewardess/flight attendants' names. He referred to them as his "pigeons." No matter what city he was in, he would call five to eight of them and ask them out to dinner. He also had a special gift for them when they married—a spatula with a set of his favorite recipes! He also gave a lot of other gifts to his "pigeons."

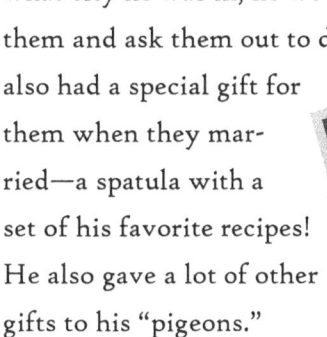

The spatula given to Diane from Mr. Hirtzel as a wedding gift—the gift he gave to all his "pigeons."

Mr. Hirtzel was a philanthropist who helped many students go to college and earn their degrees. I know two girls that he helped become airline stewardesses in the mid-sixties.

Well, Mr. Hirtzel and my father remained friends up until the early eighties when Mr. Hirtzel's age and memory started to deteriorate. In 1991, Mr. Hirtzel passed away at the age of 87, and Mrs. Hirtzel passed away four years later. They were both good people who did not have any children to carry on their legacy.

I thought this story would not be complete without his picture, so I made it a mission to locate one. I drove to North East, which is about ten miles from my home, to locate the company that Mr. Hirtzel owned. I drove around and around and just as I was about to give up, right there it was in front me: Electric Materials Co. I drove in and stopped at the security office. I told the officer what I was looking for, and he said, "I might be able to help you." He made two phone calls, and success was made. But I needed to return in one hour. An hour passed, and then I met a woman by the name of Ann. She at one time was Mr. Hirtzel's secretary and was gathering material for the 100th anniversary of the Electric Materials Co. She told me of the books of all of the stewardesses' names. I said that they were most likely his "pigeons," and told her my story along with the fact that my father was a doctor whom Mr. Hirtzel wanted to move to North East to open up an office. Ann asked me, "What was your father's name?" I responded, "Dr. Roland Miller." She looked at me and said, "Oh, my gosh! Your father was our family doctor when I was growing up, and he is the doctor that brought me into this world!" I wonder what Mr. Hirtzel would have thought of that coincidence.

My friend Shirley and I continued to work together for several years in BUF. Then we transferred to DAL. From there Shirley moved to LGA, and I went back to BUF to finish my career as a stewardess.

Mr. Philip D. Hirtzel
Photo courtesy of Electric Materials Company

Stewardess Judi Stilwell Martino

Judi Stilwell Martino

AMERICAN AIRLINES STEWARDESS, 1963–1968

Judi played an important role at American Airlines from the modeling end of things. We connected after our careers at American Airlines were over. She is very nice, a modest lady, kind, and always appropriate.

I was recruited on my college campus, Miami University, Oxford, Ohio, in the spring of 1963, and that began my five-year flying career with American Airlines. I looked at that recruitment book and saw cities that I would love to see: New York, Boston, Los Angeles, San Francisco, etc. (American did not fly international in those years.)

I went to Stewardess School in Fort Worth, Texas, that summer, and then after six weeks of training was assigned to be based in Chicago. I roomed with four other stewardesses. They were all college graduates and wonderful girls. The rules were quite different then, and we could not be married, so one by one I kept losing roommates, as the average time for a stewardess to fly was eighteen months. We also had a rule that we would have to quit at age thirty-two, but when you are twenty that seems far off! Of course all that has since changed, but that is what we signed up for!

I had only been flying for about a month and was "on reserve" when I got a call from crew schedule telling me I would be deadheading to Washington, D. C., and flying on a White House charter press plane for President Kennedy from Washington to Hyannis Port, Massachusetts. I could not believe my good fortune! What a way to start my career!

Unfortunately, Mrs. Kennedy had just lost their baby, and President Kennedy was flying to Hyannis Port to be with her. Our press plane landed first, and then what a thrill to see Air Force One land and be so close to it and then to see the President himself! John-John and Carolyn greeted President Kennedy when he came down the stairs. It was such an exciting day!

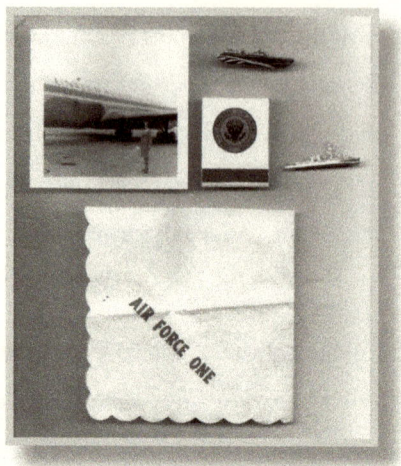

Memorabilia from Air Force One.

The Captain of Air Force One invited us to go on board and gave us mementoes that I treasure and still have today: a gold PT109 pin, Air Force One napkins, matchbooks, and a book that Jackie Kennedy had written about the White House. Sadly, President Kennedy was shot three months later in Dallas and was flown back to Washington, D. C., on the plane I had been so thrilled to see.

I loved the five years that I flew and am forever grateful for those days. I was fortunate to also do many "special assignments" during those five years and felt very honored to be chosen to model for American Airlines' recruitment book in 1968. I also toured many cities to introduce a whole new look in uniforms. We went from the traditional look to a much more modern uniform. We even had white go-go boots! All the while, I thought, "How ironic that I was this small town girl from Ohio who had looked at a recruitment book and dreamed of visiting those far away cities, now to be featured in this book."

American Airlines' stewardess advertisement featuring Judi.

The other highlight was a flight that changed my life; it was a very short flight from Cincinnati to Louisville, Kentucky, in December of 1964, when, unknown to me at the time, my future husband would be boarding my plane! We used to get "fact forms" telling us if we had any VIPs coming aboard, and this particular flight listed singer Al Martino. I picked him out immediately as he came up the stairs and briefly spoke to him as I greeted the passengers. Once in flight, I thanked him for a Christmas album that he had asked the other stewardess to give me, as I was in the back cabin. I went up to thank him, and he invited the other stewardess and me to a party Capital Records was hosting in his honor to celebrate his new album. Al and I married four years later and often recounted that day we met; that it was "Love at First Flight."

I had many highlights during my five-year career, but meeting President Kennedy and then my husband are hard to top! I felt fortunate to see so many wonderful places and to meet so many great and interesting people. I am forever grateful that I stopped in that recruitment office and made the decision that changed my life. Thank you American Airlines!

Stewardess Judi Stilwell

From Flight Engineer to Captain, Tony moved on to become Line Captain on the A300 and Boeing 767/757, primarily flying international routes ranging throughout Europe, the Caribbean, South America, and the Pacific. Tony retired from American in 2008.

Tony Vallillo

AMERICAN AIRLINES CAPTAIN, 1977–2008

Lt. Colonel Tony Vallillo began flying with the United States Air Force in 1971 as a student flying T-41, T-37, and, T-38 trainers. He spent much of his military career as Pilot and Commander of the Lockheed C-141A Starlifter and C-5 Galaxy with Worldwide Airlift Operations for Military Airlift Command. Tony has extensive military flying experience in Europe, the Pacific, South America, Africa, and the Middle East, including active duty in Operations Desert Shield and Desert Storm.

Captain Tony Vallillo spent his entire 31 year commercial career with American Airlines, starting out as Flight Engineer on the B-707 and B-727 and quickly advancing to First Officer and Captain. Tony then became Chief Pilot for the JFK Base where he was in charge of over 600 flight crew members and was also Flight Manager of the American Terminal and Ramp. While at JFK he planned and participated in the design and construction of the new flight operations complex. Tony moved on to become Line Captain on the A-300 and B-767/757 primarily flying international routes ranging throughout Europe, the Caribbean, South America, and the Pacific. Captain Vallillo retired from American in 2008.

Around noon on a bright but cool mid-February day, I strode across the ramp at Palm Springs International Airport in California (PSP) headed for the airplane that would carry us to Dallas/Fort Worth (DFW) via Phoenix. Our crew was in the middle of a three day trip, and we had flown out yesterday from New York via Baltimore and Los Angeles. The Captain and the First Officer (FO) had enjoyed a round of golf in Palm Springs while I, not a golfer, explored the mountains west of the Springs in a rented car with one of the flight attendants. Today we would go as far as DFW and enjoy another layover and, most likely, a good Tex-Mex dinner. Then on to Newark Liberty International (EWR) on the third and final day, all to put a total of 14 hours or so in both my logbook and my bank account.

We were flying a series of Boeing 707s on this trip, and I was the flight engineer. The flight engineer, or FE as he or she is known in the trade, is the third crew member up front, responsible for the tending of the fires and the watering of the horses, so to speak. Actually, the FE tends the engines and the airplane's systems—electrical, hydraulic, air conditioning, and so on. Today, of course, the FE has followed the Navigator into the mists of aeronautical history. But in those days, 1978 to be specific, the FE position was the entry level for new pilots at just about every airline. And I, as a new pilot at American Airlines (AA), started my career sitting sideways right behind the Captain and FO, just as every new pilot did.

It was not to be expected, however, that a pilot with but a single year of seniority (I was hired just over a year earlier) could fly the 707. In the airline industry of that day, pilot pay was determined principally by the weight and speed of the airplane he flew. The 707, while at the lower end of the spectrum at AA (we flew the 747, DC-10, 707 and 727 when I came aboard) nevertheless paid more than the 727, the junior airplane in our fleet. I was incredulous when, after a mere three months on the line and still very much on probation, crew qualifications called me to pass on the news that I had been selected for 707 training. After feeling a brief thrill that perhaps this promotion was based upon merit, I discovered that, to the contrary, no one senior to me had bid for this transition when it had appeared on last month's bid sheet. If no one rose to the occasion, then the occasion fell to the most junior person at the base, which at that moment was my humble self!

Off I went to our centralized Flight Academy hard by the DFW airport, to immerse myself for a month and a half in the intricacies of the 707. This was something of a good deal, not least in that it took me away from New York in a very blustery March, and plunked me down in the relatively balmy climes of central Texas. The school itself was outstanding, as were all of AA's schools—our line had the best training in the industry, then as now. I wound up training in the very simulator in which I had, six months or so previously, taken and passed the evaluation that was part of the interview process at AA.

Early days of flying with Tony getting into an Air Force T-Bird.

In any event, with over five years of big four-engine jet cargo experience in the Air Force, I had no problems taking in all of the details of 707 operations. By the time I approached the airplane on the ramp at Palm Springs, I had 11 months of experience on the 707 (and also the 727, on which I remained qualified).

One preflight, engine start, and takeoff later, I was filling out the "pay sheet" in the airplane log as we climbed to our cruising altitude for the short hop over to Phoenix, when I took more careful note of the airplane number of our steed-for-the-day. It was N7501A. This was the lowest tail number I had yet seen on the fleet, and I inquired of the Captain whether it was the first one we flew. It was, he told me, the first one Boeing built for us, although it was not the first one flown on a revenue trip. And thereby, as things so often happen, hung a tale.

If you ask several people the question, "When did the jet age begin?" you will probably get a variety of answers. Some will say WWII, when the Germans fielded the ME-262 jet interceptor. Others, thinking more along the lines of airline flying, might speak of the British Comet jet, which first carried passengers in scheduled operations in May 1952. My vote, though, would go to August 7, 1955. It was on that day that famed Boeing test pilot "Tex" Johnston flew the 707 prototype through not one but two barrel roll maneuvers in the sky above Seattle's Lake Washington, and not coincidentally above the heads of just about every airline president in America.

The Comet had suffered from a major structural defect that resulted in several spectacular crashes in the early 1950's, and the entire fleet was grounded until the cause was eventually found to be metal fatigue, resulting in a complete redesign. There was a lingering lack of confidence among airline people in the structural integrity of jet airplanes, until that moment when Tex flew the 707 upside down past the likes of C. R. Smith, Pat Patterson, Juan Trippe, Eddie Rickenbacker, and the rest of the airline brass that Boeing had assembled. Although Boeing's president, Bill Allen, nearly had a heart attack on the spot, being uninformed beforehand of Tex's intentions, the visiting brass were left in no doubt as to the sturdiness of the Boeing design. The jet age (in its passenger incarnation at least) was born on that day, and the rest is history.

Actually, the fact that Boeing had a 707 prototype at all was the result of a gamble on their part. Starting in the late 1940s, Boeing had become the free world's biggest manufacturer of large jet airplanes, selling scores of fast, high-flying jet bombers to the US Air Force. These bombers were refueled in the air by piston powered tanker planes, which could only "keep up" with the bombers at full speed, while the jets limped along at their slowest possible speed trying to remain hooked up on the refueling boom. Boeing decided that what the Air Force needed was a fast, high-flying jet tanker plane to go with its fleet of bombers, even though the Air Force had yet to come to that conclusion. So they took a big gamble and designed and built a prototype of that tanker plane, thinking that they just might also be able to sell it to the airlines. Both ends of the plan worked superbly—the tanker, known as the KC-135, serves the Air Force to this day. The passenger jet, the 707, which ended up being around 20 percent larger than the Air Force tanker, was an even bigger success, far outselling the eventual offerings from Douglas and Convair, with just over 1000 units delivered in a production run that didn't end until 1994.

The Boeing 707 wrought a quantum change in world transportation, literally creating the "Jet Age" and the "Jet Set." It carried twice as many passengers as the Douglas DC-7s and Lockheed Constellations that it replaced, and it cruised at nearly twice the speed. Flying times were cut in half; and, thanks to the incredible foresight of the early pilot union negotiators, the weight/speed formula used to compute hourly pay in the pilot union contracts cranked out an increase of more than 100 percent! Small wonder that the most senior pilots eagerly bid the training for the new airplanes, which the poets in the American Airlines marketing department soon christened "Astro-jets" (after a brief flirtation with the more evolutionary "Jet Flagship").

Everybody went back to school for the 707. Pilots and flight engineers, of course, but also stewardesses (as they were known then) and mechanics, baggage handlers, fuelers, and the passenger service agents in the terminal, to say nothing of the catering staff! In those days, the pilot school was a much longer affair than it was when I got to it in 1977. Prior to the early 1970s, aeronautical pedagogy involved learning every nut and bolt on the airplane, as well as the procedures and limitations for operating it. Although this sort of in-depth knowledge would be expected for mechanics, the pilots had to ingest most of it as well. This was not always an easy task for an older pilot, and all of the Captains who were in line for these bids were indeed old. In a curious and roundabout way, the collision of age and a new and much faster airplane was a factor in the adoption of what came to be known as the Age 60 rule. C. R. Smith, in particular, was not eager to populate the left seats of his new Jet Flagships with geriatric pilots who started their careers in the open cockpit airmail, and he was one of the strongest supporters of FAA Chief Quesada's dictum that no one could fly as a pilot in airline service upon reaching his 60th birthday.

There were no real flight simulators in those Pleistocene days, so all of the flight training for the new jet was done in the airplane. Much of this involved the dreaded V1 cut—the deliberate throttling back to idle of an engine (invariably an outboard engine) just as the airplane's nose was lifted for takeoff. This would result in a not inconsiderable swerve toward the "dead" engine, and instant application of a boot full of rudder control (the pedals on the floor at the pilot's feet) was required to keep the airplane under control. In addition, full stall demonstrations were also performed, which involved slowing the airplane to a speed below that required for the wings to generate enough lift to keep it airborne, and then performing the required recovery. Maneuvers such as these are quite dangerous if not performed perfectly, and since even the instructors were new to the jets it was not long before the ravens came home to roost. The first crash of a 707 occurred within the first year of operations, on an AA training flight. In the first four years of operations, AA suffered three 707 crashes, with two of these occurring on training flights. These grim statistics provided the final impetus for the implementation of simulator training, a concept that AA pioneered in the airline industry.

By today's standards, the 707 was not a particularly nice handling airplane. The early ones were underpowered for their weight, and takeoff rolls were "long and distinguished," to quote the character Goose from *Top Gun*. So long, in fact, that runways had to be extended all over the world to accommodate them. At New York's Idlewild Airport (which is now called JFK) Runway 31 Left was extended to an incredible 14,511 feet, which was the longest civilian runway in the world at the time. The international flights used up just about all of that length on takeoff.

Landings were challenging as well. The approach speed of the 707 at typical landing weights was 30 or so knots faster than the older prop planes, and the early jet engines were incapable of quick bursts of power—it often took up to eight seconds for the thrust to increase to full after the throttles were shoved from idle to maximum. That, and the fact that jet engines do not blow air across the wing like a propeller does (creating instant lift) meant that approach path and speed had to be managed much more carefully than on a DC-7 or a Constellation. The 707s, and indeed all jets, could not be flown so much by the "seat of the pants."

The 707's flight controls lacked hydraulic boost on the ailerons and elevators (this did not make an appearance until the Boeing 727), having only a single hydraulic booster unit for the rudder. This meant that roll control (which controls the airplane's bank attitude or tilt and is achieved by turning the yoke left or right like a car steering wheel) was a direct cable hookup from the pilot's yoke all the way to the trailing edge of the wings, a cable run of nearly 100 feet. There was quite a bit of friction in a linkage that long, and the effort required to turn the airplane was greater than in modern designs.

At that time, to be sure, these characteristics were really no different from those of the prop planes that preceded the 707. All of the large piston powered planes were equally underpowered, and flew like trucks, so the pilots of the 707 were certainly no worse off in those respects. And the big bucks they would earn would pay for plenty of Charles Atlas courses to develop any strength that might be required to fly the bird. The biggest problem many of them encountered in training and on the line was the need to rev up their thought processes to stay mentally ahead of (or at least up with) an airplane going twice as fast as any of them had ever gone before. This was not always possible for the older men, and a few of them wound up going back to the DC-7 to finish their now age 60 limited careers.

When all of the training, checking, and proving runs were complete, it was time to start scheduled service. Pan American had already inaugurated the Jet Age on October 28, 1958. American was on track to be the first domestic operator in January 1959; but to the enormous chagrin of C. R. Smith, the airline found itself pipped at the post by the crafty Ted Baker, president of National Airlines, who leased a pair of 707s from Juan Trippe of Pan Am and started service from Miami to Idlewild in December of 1958. American, like baseball slugger Roger Maris a few years later, had to settle for an asterisk—first domestic service by an airline *using its own equipment.*

It was on January 25, 1959, that American launched its jet service. Captain Charlie Macatee and a crew of seven (including the author of this book) took N7503A, the Flagship California, operating as American flight 2, from Los Angeles to Idlewild in a then-record time of four hours and three minutes. Flight times in that era were significantly shorter than those you will see in today's schedules. Until the early 1960s there was no 250 knot speed limit below 10,000 feet like there is today, and the low cost of kerosene back then (10 to 20 cents per gallon) made reduced speeds for fuel conservation meaningless. Indeed, the entire point of the jets was high speed; and so immediately after takeoff the gear and flaps were retracted and the speed was allowed to increase right to the "red-line" limit, which for the 707 was close to 0.9 Mach (90% of the speed of sound, close to 600 miles per hour). This speed was maintained with full power from the engines, in a continuous gradual climb all the way across the country until it was time to descend for landing.

Today, of course, we are limited to 250 knots at altitudes below 10,000 feet, and we climb, cruise, and descend at speeds calculated for best fuel economy rather than highest speed. This has added between 30 minutes and an hour to transcontinental schedules over the years, but no one seems to mind. Most passengers are no longer interested in speed, but rather in the cheapest possible ticket, so modern jets plod along at around 75–80% of the speed of sound instead of 90%.

Meanwhile N7501, our steed on this PHX-DFW trip and the first AA 707 off the Boeing assembly line, was otherwise engaged at the time of the transcontinental inaugural, probably still involved in the flight test and training program up in Seattle. When it eventually made it to the line, 7501 garnered the name Flagship Michigan, which it held until the Astrojet era a short time later, when the city and state names were dropped. She got a facelift in the early 1960s with four of the newer fanjet engines, becoming as a result a 707-123"B". She got yet another facelift around 1969 when the orange lightning bolt paint job, which descended directly from the DC-3s, was replaced with the red white and blue stripe livery. In that garb she traversed the American skies for nearly another decade, including this trip with yours truly. After we parted company at DFW later that morning, N7501 and I would meet but once more in our careers, two months later in early April of 1978. On that day I was called at home by crew schedule to get over to Newark Airport (EWR) and fill in for a sick engineer on a hop from EWR to Chicago ORD. The flight, of course, was uneventful, as were all of my AA trips.

When I parted company with N7501 at ORD I had no idea that she was already on the block, but she must have been, for by all accounts she was sold nine days later to an outfit called Tiger Air. Tiger apparently didn't hang onto her for long, because she appeared on the roster of Cypress Airways in early 1979. At that point she was very close to the end of her days, because she was written off in August 1979 after some kind of landing accident at Bahrain. When I first encountered her we were both fairly young (20 years is by no means old for an airliner—some of our 727s ended up flying for nearly 40 years), but she was at the end of her career, while I was just starting mine. The erstwhile Flagship California, N7503A, went into the sunset even earlier, being grounded early in 1977 just weeks after I was hired, and scrapped later that year.

The Inaugural Flagship California on its way to being scrapped.
Photo © Brian Lockett, Air-and-Space.com.

They and all of their sisters of the venerable Boeing 707 lineage were put out to pasture not because they were worn out (she probably had around 50,000 hours in her log when I flew her, which is midlife for an airliner; a few of our high time 727s retired with around 90,000 hours logged) but because the astronomical increase in the price of fuel doomed them all. The last few 707s in airline service as of early 2013 were in Iran; where fuel, at least, is presumably cheaper.

The Air Force kept their KC-135 tankers, albeit with modifications to newer more powerful and much more fuel-efficient engines in recent years. That fleet, numbering over 400 at this point, is over 50 years old, but due to the relatively little flying time the Air Force put on them over the years, they can serve longer, albeit with increased maintenance costs.

The Air Force also uses actual 707 airframes as AWACS airplanes, as well as a few other airborne radar surveillance platforms (such as the JSTAR), and these also soldier on.

American retired all of their 707s by around 1983, with most of the JT-3 fan engines going to the Air Force for the first re-engine mod on the KC-135s. The 707s were replaced by several different airplane types over the years, specifically the Boeing 757 and 767 and also the Airbus A-300-600R. I flew all three of these types extensively during my career, and I made my last flight for American on the 767-323, the intercontinental version of the 767. Notwithstanding that and all of the other flying I have done in a long career, the logbook entries I am most proud to have recorded are those three involving N7501A. I had the privilege of flying a piece of history.

707–323 on the hangar line at JFK. Photo by Tony Vallillo.

Contributors

JON PROCTOR
Son of a pioneer American Airlines Pilot,
Heath Proctor
27 years TWA
Author, photographer, and historian

CURT JACOBSON
Son of an American Airlines Mechanic and
Flight Engineer, Roy G. Jacobson
Contributed photos of his father

MARYLOU PARKES WHIPPLE
American Airlines Stewardess
Secretary, teacher, traveler
Mother of Thayne Whipple

AUDREY RADZIWON MCGINTY
American Airlines Stewardess, Class 57–6
Wife, Mother
"Once a stewardess, always a stewardess"

GERRY MCMASTERS LOCKHART
American Airlines Stewardess
Wife, Mother
"Once a stewardess, always a stewardess"

PAULINE "POLLY" HARLAN VIERTEL
American Airlines Stewardess, Class 57–6
Wife, Mother
"Once a stewardess, always a stewardess"

JOAN SCOFIELD SHELDON
American Airlines Stewardess
Wife, Mother
Homebuilder, traveler & published author

MARGARET BASSETTI
Passenger on American Airlines'
707 Inaugural Flight 2
Passenger list for the moon

LORRAINE WALSTON
Great niece of Margaret Bassetti
Admirer of the piece of family history

ROBERT CAWLEY
Passenger on American Airlines
Production executive creator, writer, producer, director, and 20 Emmy Awards-TV

DIANE MILLER ENGELSKIRGER
American Airlines Stewardess, Class 61–4
Wife, mother, traveler
"Once a stewardess, always a stewardess"

JUDI STILWELL MARTINO
American Airlines Stewardess
Wife, Mother
"Once a stewardess, always a stewardess"

TONY VALLILLO
Military flying experience
American Airlines Captain
Civil Air Patrol Command Pilot
Writer and interested in flight simulators

BOB PROCTOR
Son of a pioneer American Airlines Pilot,
Heath Proctor
Former American Airlines Dispatch Clerk
Photographer

BILL PROCTOR
Son of a pioneer American Airlines Pilot,
Heath Proctor
Former TWA Pilot and photographer

BRIAN LOCKETT
Creator of Air-and-Space.com
Historian and photographer

PATRICK "PAT" BUKIRI
Midway Airport Photo Galleries Member
Historian and photographer

JIM WISSEMES
Southwest Airlines Mechanic
Photographer

BOB GARRARD
American Airlines employee, retired
Photographer

BETH MACATEE SNYDER
Daughter of Captain Macatee
Contributed photos from her father

MARTHA MASON
Niece of Mildred Jackson
Contributed photos from her aunt

LAUREN MAZIE BANGERTER WILDE
Full-time wife, mother, and homemaker
Nap-time editor and designer

Argie's Challenges for Success

As I became a talented American Airlines stewardess, they had no awareness of the challenges I had experienced all my life with cognitive processing. They knew that I was bright, attractive, and had a warm and giving personality.

But my brain held a secret monster and a beautiful gift—dyslexia. With today's understanding of dyslexia, or specific language disability, I know my challenge exceeds the popular notion of what dyslexia is as it pertains to both receptive and expressive language processing. For me, the fear of demand language and the reward of spontaneous language was a puzzlement. If you ask me a specific question, I can't think of the answer, but if you give me the subject I can talk all day about it. I never fear being asked to speak at public meetings until question and answer time. To top it off, I have a massive sequencing challenge. It has been a nightmare. Sequencing challenges emerge everywhere from little, daily tasks—"Turn the other way. Which is the left or right? Say it again. Do it again still another way"— to big life decisions—"What next in a relationship?"

It has been difficult to understand my intelligence, confused in some areas and obviously high in others. My years with American Airlines proved I am okay and that I'm not dumb. They gave me the opportunity to prove myself in complex and sequential behaviors which also required personal and social skills.

With my sequencing challenge, I learned to *stop* my brain, *look* at what I was doing, and *listen* to my thoughts and words before taking the next step. The next step says, "Now you are ready." Compensating for a weakness is a studied intervention which serves to change a given behavior. Placing non-sequenced thoughts into an order for a given action is the template for a desired behavioral outcome. I learned how to do new tasks because I understood the process of cognitive awareness. While flying, I intuitively came to understand my brain and how it functions. After becoming a special education teacher with additional training in brain functioning, I learned to understand my own brain.

As a special education teacher with twenty-five years of teaching experience, I have tested many students and identified their learning styles and their challenges. I designed interventions for remediation, followed by focused instruction and student discipline.

Those who have some awareness of dyslexia and the impact it has on the learning process may not be aware of dyslexia's upside and some of the wonderful gifts it brings. Here, I am referring to gifts such as intuitively seeing a picture or a concept immediately as a whole before examining its parts to see how it is put together; the ability to connect dots rapidly. Gifts such as being more curious than average, thinking in pictures instead of words or thinking in words instead of pictures, being intuitive and insightful, and having more than the average awareness of environment, have been both thwarting and endowing. I see the dust on the furniture and the grains of sand on the beach. My vivid imagination enables thinking outside the box. I can utilize my brain's ability to alter and create perceptions. I think and perceive multi-dimensionally as I am considering the task. I can experience thought with such detail that it is viewed as reality as the details become the whole. And there are others!

I am currently writing another book entitled *Don't Call Me Dumb!* This book addresses the intellectually high functioning adult with cognitive challenges, who, after not understanding their beautiful gift, can become friends with their brain.

I did it!

www.ingramcontent.com/pod-product-compliance
Lightning Source LLC
Chambersburg PA
CBHW031942080426
42735CB00007B/233